Tobacco, Pipes, and Race in Colonial Virginia

For Harold,
Of course.

Tobacco, Pipes, and Race in Colonial Virginia

Little Tubes of Mighty Power

Anna S. Agbe-Davies

Walnut Creek, California

LEFT COAST PRESS, INC.
1630 North Main Street, #400
Walnut Creek, CA 94596
www.LCoastPress.com

ISBN 978-1-61132-395-5 hardback
ISBN 978-1-61132-396-2 paperback
ISBN 978-1-61132-397-9 institutional eBook
ISBN 978-1-61132-743-4 consumer eBook

Library of Congress Cataloging-in-Publication Data on file.

Printed in the United States of America

♾™ The paper used in this publication meets the minimum requirements of American
National Standard for Information Sciences—Permanence of Paper for Printed Library
Materials, ANSI/NISO Z39.48–1992.

Contents

Little Tube of mighty Pow'r
Charmer of an idle Hour,
Object of my warm Desire,
Lip of Wax, and Eye of Fire:
And thy snowy taper Waist,
With my Finger gently brac'd;
And thy swelling ashey Crest,
With my little Stopper prest;
And the sweetest Bliss of Blisses,
Breathing from thy balmy Kisses.
Who when agen the Night returns,
When agen the Taper burns;
When agen the Cricket's gay,
(Little Cricket, full of Play)
Can afford his Tube to feed
With the fragrant Indian Weed:
Pleasure for a Nose divine,
Incense of the God of Wine.
Happy thrice, and thrice agen,
Happiest he of happy Men.

Isaac Hawkins Browne,
"A Pipe of Tobacco: Imitation II," 1744

Illustrations

Figures

Tables

Acknowledgments

This work would not have been possible without the people and institutions who gave access to and, more importantly, context for collections from some of the most compelling archaeological sites Virginia has to offer. My former colleagues in the Colonial Williamsburg Department of Archaeological Research—Marley Brown, Andy Edwards, Kelly Ladd-Kostro, Dave Muraca, and Bill Pittman in particular—were unfailingly generous with their time and expertise and facilitated my use of the collections from the Page site, Port Anne, and Rich Neck. Alain Outlaw and Merry Outlaw of the Wheatland Foundation, Inc., shared their findings from the Drummond site with me, and Tom Davidson of the Jamestown-Yorktown Foundation provided access to those pipes. I was able to include Jamestown's Structure 144 thanks to the generosity of Bill Kelso, Jamie May, and Bly Straube, who shared artifacts and data from the recent Jamestown Rediscovery excavation as well as the pipes curated from earlier explorations of that structure. The pipes from the remaining Jamestown structures, as well as Green Spring, appear here thanks to the curatorial staff at Colonial National Historical Park, William Cahoon, Jackie Holt, and David Riggs. Linda Rowe of the Colonial Williamsburg Foundation's Department of Historical Research helped me to work with the transcriptions of deeds, orders, and wills from the York County Records Project on which the final chapter of this book, in particular, relies. Records research and data collection was funded by the National Endowment for the Humanities under grants RS-0033-80-1604 and RO-20869-85.

The initial artifact study on which this book is based received funding from the Ford Foundation's Diversity Fellowships Program, a Jamestown Scholarship from the National Park Service and the Organization of American Historians, and institutional support from the Colonial Williamsburg Foundation. My mentors Robert Schuyler and Marley

Brown were instrumental in shaping that research. Follow-up analysis was supported by a post-doctoral fellowship from the Ford Foundation's Diversity Fellowships Program and from the University Research Council at the University of North Carolina: a Research and Study Leave, a University Research Grant, and a Junior Faculty Development Grant.

Throughout, I've had productive discussions about pipes with a range of scholars, including Beth Bollwerk, Matthew Emerson, David Gadsby, David Givens, Jillian Galle, Julie King, Taft Kiser, Al Luckenbach, Seth Mallios, Cameron Monroe, Fraser Neiman, and Katie Sikes. I hope that the research presented here advances our conversation.

The careful critique and deep specialist knowledge of four anonymous reviewers have made this book far better than it would have been otherwise. I am also grateful to all of the people who have read bits of the manuscript (sometimes totally out of context!) and offered suggestions, feedback, and support. Thank you, Glaire Anderson, Lorraine Aragon, Jocelyn Chua, Jean Dennison, Tori Ekstrand, Marisa Escolar, Michael Gutierrez, Jennifer Larson, Towns Middleton, Tim McMillan, Amanda Thompson, Silvia Tomášková, Margaret Weiner, and Ellen Welch.

I'm excited to be taking elements of this work in still new directions. Alex Bauer, Craig Cipolla, Zoe Crossland, Carol McDavid, Bob Preucel, and Steve Mrozowski have all contributed to my expanded understanding of Peirce, pragmatism, and semiotics in archaeology.

Finally, I would be remiss if I did not acknowledge those who helped me go the last mile with this manuscript. Mitch Allen has been unwavering in his support for this project, for which I am very grateful. I am also indebted to Left Coast Press's production manager Ryan Harris, as well as book designer Hannah Jennings and copy editor Michael Jennings, who helped transform a lot of words into a proper book. Thank you to indexer Michele Hughes for showing me how that exercise can advance a book's argument and agenda. I must also mention the crew of writers (you know who you are) whose camaraderie and good cheer propelled me through the final weeks of revisions. And last, but far from least, my husband Eric Deetz not only brilliantly executed some of the illustrations—on quite short notice—but has been throughout the best sounding board and champion one could hope for.

Introduction
Chapter 1

"Now look at *that*. You can't tell me that's not an Indian pipe." David gestured towards a display case out of which peered a small face (Figure 1.1). It embellished the bowl of a clay tobacco pipe that had lain buried for many years before archaeologists recovered it from the seventeenth-century site of Pope's Fort and set it upon a tiny pedestal.

Figure 1.1 Why feature an artifact from Maryland in a book about pipes in colonial Virginia? This pipe belongs to the same local pipe tradition, and the response that its decoration evokes captures the "problem" of local pipes in a nutshell. *Photograph courtesy of Historic St. Mary's City.*

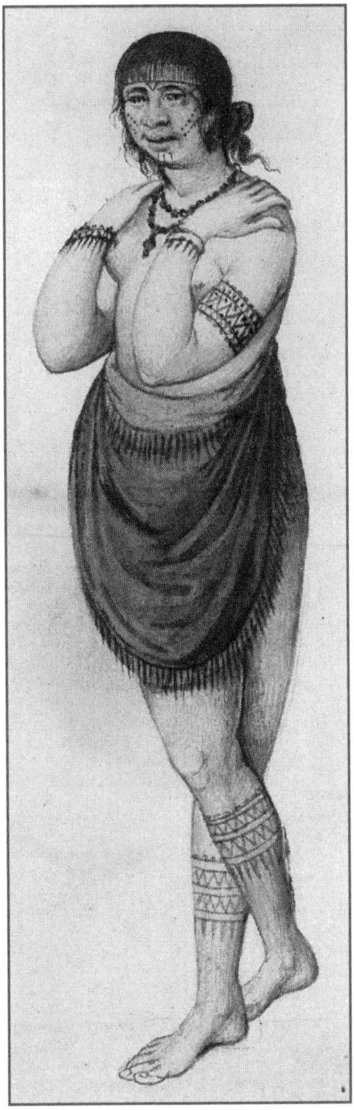

Figure 1.2 John White's likeness of "One of the wyves of Wyngyno" and these nineteenth century portraits of men and women from what is now Nigeria and Chad show but two of the many worldwide examples of facial decoration similar to that which inspired the maker of the St. Mary's City pipe. (Left, © *Trustees of the British Museum. Right, People of Northern Nigeria and Chad, 1820s; Image Reference 054, as shown on Hitchcock.itc.virginia.edu, compiled by Jerome Handler and Michael Tuite, and sponsored by the Virginia Foundation for the Humanities and the University of Virginia Library. Courtesy of Special Collections, University of Virginia, Charlottesville.*)

He looked at the pipe and saw it in light of images like John White's portraits of Pomeiock and Secotan villagers in sixteenth-century "Virginia," now North Carolina. One woman gazes directly at the viewer, her face adorned with geometric designs (Figure 1.2a). My thoughts, on the other hand, turned toward a fellow student I had met while excavating at a site in the Republic of Benin. I don't remember asking Didier about the lines of scarification that radiated out from the center of his face, but they highlighted its planes and angles much like the lines on the little face in the case. Where David saw links to a Native American artistic tradition, I saw connections to an African past (Figure 1.2b).

My friend and I had no hope of reconciling our two points of view on a busy field trip, with so much else to see. But I kept turning our conversation over in my mind. Why did we think that the association with one group or another mattered? I wasn't even firmly committed to my interpretation; I

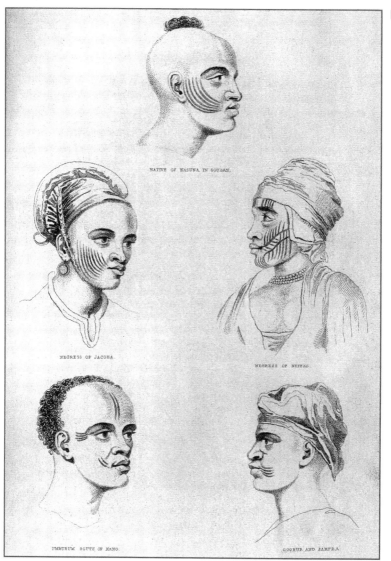

b

NATIVE OF KASUNA IN SOUDAN.

NEGRESS OF JACOBA.

NEGRESS OF NIFFEE.

IMBURUM SOUTH OF KANO.

GOOBUR AND ZAMFRA.

simply thought it was as likely as his. How did our respective standpoints shape what we thought about life in colonial St. Mary's City and the further meanings of the pipe? Because surely there was more to the pipe's meaning than this question of attribution and identity. And yet it seemed as if our dilemma—who made this pipe—were the most natural thing in the world.

But, of course, it wasn't natural. Our quandary was an artifact of our training as archaeologists and our enculturation as members of contemporary American society. If that pipe was a product of social transformations initiated in the seventeenth-century Chesapeake Bay colonies, then so, too, were our ideas. My interest in clay pipes like the one in the case originated with analyses proposing African antecedents, and then the subsequent backlash (for example, Emerson 1999 and Mouer et al. 1999). However, my focus quickly shifted to the foundations on which both positions rested. There was also a related problem having to do with the social context(s) in which inhabitants of the early colonial Chesapeake produced and distributed pipes. Therefore, I am concerned in this book with comparisons among pipes within particular contexts (that is, archaeological sites) and between the pipe assemblages that come from these contexts, not necessarily with the local pipe tradition in the abstract, divorced from time and place.

Pipes mass-produced in England and the Netherlands betray their origins in the clay and stone versions made and used by the people whose land they settled, and who had first taught them to "drink" (as early English descriptions termed it) tobacco smoke. The white, brittle pipes were soon found throughout Europe and virtually everywhere Europeans colonized or traded with tobacco smoking populations. However, smokers in England's Chesapeake Bay colonies had another option. Clay pipes were also pro-

duced locally (Figure 1.3). These local pipes can be distinguished from their imported European counterparts by a number of characteristics, including clay color (shades of reddish and yellowish brown instead of white) and composition,

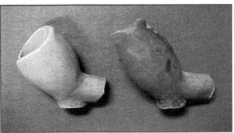

Figure 1.3 Local pipes are sometimes decorated, as with the two bowl fragments from Port Anne (*top*). Others, like the two pipe bowls from the Drummond plantation site (*bottom*), are very plain and closely resemble imported pipes.

shape, manufacturing techniques (sometimes handmade instead of molded), and decorative style (often much more elaborate, but with less reliance on intricate stamps or molded decoration).[1] Interestingly enough, these distinguishing features do not always coincide, so that archaeologists encounter pipes that resemble European imports in every other way but are deep red in color, or are handmade and sumptuously decorated with motifs that predate the arrival of Europeans in Virginia but also include letters from the Roman alphabet.

The imported pipes feature prominently in the archaeology of sites that post-date the arrival of Europeans in the Americas. By the 1620s, tobacco had become an export staple for England's Virginia. But tobacco *consumption* was

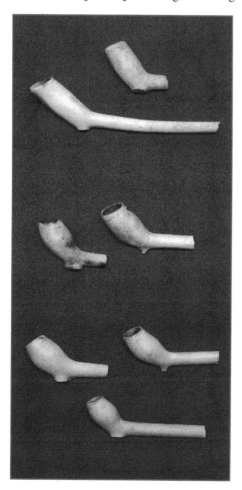

also an important part of life in the colony. At that time there was no consensus about the relative health merits or demerits of smoking, and there do not seem to have been strong social prohibitions limiting consumption by anyone because of either age or sex.[2] Sites are commonly littered with pipe fragments—they were widely used, break easily, and do not decay once buried. Rapid but subtle changes in their size and shape allow archaeologists to date them with some precision (Figure 1.4).

Figure 1.4 These imported pipes are typical of the wares produced in English workshops during the seventeenth century. Note the different bowl styles. The lower register contains examples ca. 1610–1640. The two pipes in the middle date to ca. 1620–1660. The pipes at the top are typical of the years 1650–1680.

J. C. Harrington, one of the first archaeologists to excavate U.S. sites associated with colonists as well as Native Americans, was also an early innovator in the study of clay tobacco pipes. Historical archaeologists still use—and tweak—his mid-twentieth-century techniques for dating assemblages of pipes. Harrington's discussion of local pipes in "Tobacco Pipes from Jamestown" is worth quoting at length, particularly because of the way in which his remarks foreshadow the work that was to come.

> In addition to these white clays [the imported pipes], there are a great many pipes of similar shape, also made in a mold, but of yellow clay.... It has usually been assumed that these "yellow bowls" were made in Virginia, or at least in the American colonies; and this conclusion is supported by the absence of such pipes in collections in Great Britain.... This...also suggests that the colonists made them for their own use and not as an export item....
>
> One of the most intriguing problems is that of the hand-molded pipes.... Many are obviously of Indian manufacture, but some may have been made by the settlers following Indian styles and techniques. To further complicate the problem, some of these pipes which are most Indianlike in character have well-formed English initials incorporated in the bowl decoration. Is this a case of the Indian copying an European idea; was the maker an "educated" Indian; or did a white man make an "Indian" pipe and put his initials on it? Detailed comparisons with pipes from Indian sites of the region would be an essential part of such a study. (1951:n.p.)

In a few short paragraphs, Harrington set the stage for decades of research on locally made pipes in the Chesapeake.

In the years that followed, archaeologists spent a great deal of time and effort trying to align the pipes with any number of parent traditions. Such arguments often, though not always, proceed as though pipe makers and pipe users belonged to a single group—but what if they didn't? When material culture becomes an object of trade, the pathways of dissemination (exchange) no longer *necessarily* match those of replication (social learning; that is, culture) (Costin 1998; Urban 2001:47). Can we assume that pipe-makers and pipe smokers were the same people?[3] I'm not sure that we can. The pipes represent not only ideas, passed from one generation to another, but interactions and relationships. This book considers the possibility that pipemaking was a specialized activity, with people using pipes that they had not made. If that were the case, we would next want to examine the nature of the relationships between user and maker. These questions are interesting for their own sake; the answers shed light on the workings of the seventeenth-century colony, especially its economy. The answers furthermore provide a new angle from which to consider what the pipes may have meant for members of that society (Bauer and Agbe-Davies 2010).

To take the problem even further: What do the pipes mean for archaeologists? And what does the study of them teach us about the discipline? The remainder of this chapter sets the scene. After an overview describing the place of tobacco, smoking, and pipes in the seventeenth century, I review the literature on local pipes and connect it to the methodological and theoretical underpinnings of the book, including the importance of a critical approach to classification. Chapter 2 expands on the concept of classification, arguing that the prevailing analytical methods constrain our interpretations of local pipes. I then turn to a description of the pipes analyzed in this study, with an emphasis on the technologies employed in their production, rather than on their decoration. The chapter concludes with a discussion of the parallels between the classification of artifacts and the classification of people.

Chapters 3 and 4 introduce the sites from which the pipes in this study came. Chapter 3 addresses the five plantation sites and considers the question of standardization and specialization. Analysis of the individual assemblages contradicts long-held ideas about how "local" these local pipes are. Chapter 4 focuses on Virginia's capital city at Jamestown and the six structures there that contributed pipes to this study. The town sites and the plantation sites then come together in comparisons that demonstrate the distinctive characteristics of each assemblage, confirming distributed, rather than centralized, production. In Chapter 5, I consider power, its deployment in the colony, and the role of elite power and elite social networks in the production and distribution of the pipes. Chapter 6 returns to classification, this time from a seventeenth-century perspective. I use court records (land certificates, orders, and wills) to show how residents of the early Virginia colony engaged in the piecemeal construction of the racial and ethnic categories that continue to shape modern life, including archaeological practice.

The Task at Hand/The Rules of Engagement

An attempt to understand the labor relationships that produced pipes and put them in the hands of smokers in this small corner of the Atlantic World, this book also explores alternatives to the prevailing focus on decoration and identity, what that focus indicates about the practice of archaeology, and how it shapes disciplinary discussions and substantive contributions to the field. In this way, the book intervenes and neutralizes the problem that David and I shared. It disrupts the argument at several levels—archaeological technique, method, and theory are all implicated in reworking our approach to these pipes, and by extension our practice. The technical challenges are perhaps the most obvious: these artifacts have so far defied attempts to develop a standard nomenclature. When basing categories on decorative attributes, we privilege a narrow range of the characteristics that might be used to understand how people used pipes in the Virginia colony. Such a technique eliminates a majority of the pipe fragments actually found because they are undecorated, too fragmentary, or simply too idiosyncratic (we end up with as many "types" as pipes). In this book, I outline a strategy that incorporates all fragments into the analysis and shifts the unit of meaning from the artifact to the attribute. These techniques also expand the range of significant attributes to include those related to manufacturing style, capturing additional ways in which culture shapes material.

My move requires a shift in method as well. More than sixty years after Harrington's initial ruminations on the pipes from Jamestown, archaeologists are no nearer to agreeing whether we should credit his "white man," or any other exemplar, with the pipes. Culturally bound creatures that we are, archaeologists default to "incomplete" analogies, as David and I did. We saw a similarity between the characteristics of the object we faced and other phenomena familiar to us and concluded that the similarity represented a real relationship. Wylie (2002a:149–151) explains that "strong" analogies also take into account the number of similarities, their relationship to observable differences, their persistence across multiple examples and a range of settings, and the extent to which the similarities are "modest relative to the breadth and specificity of those cited."[4] With the pipes, big claims about attribution are found to rest on a very complex and ambiguous dataset. Our methodological training teaches us to see certain things as data (such as decorative style), to see certain questions as important (such as cultural affiliation). The deep-seated ideologies that guided the earliest scientific archaeologists continue to influence practice today. Standard operating procedure in archaeology reinforces a stubborn tendency to proceed as if a real one-to-one correlation exists between the decorative repertoire of an artifact tradition and the ethnic designation of the people making and using the artifacts.

The frustrating thing is that we know better. Archaeology, for the most part, gets it: ethnic groups and races are socially constructed categories. They are dynamic and relational, rather than static and essential (Battle-Baptiste 2011; Epperson 2001; Mullins 1999; Orser 2004; Voss 2008; Wilkie 2000). We have established the theoretical argument that "pots" do not equal "people." Yet these insights do not appear to have changed the way archaeologists analyze these pipes, or colonoware,[5] or any number of other artifact classes that have emerged as "markers" for a group of people. I have argued recently that the deficit is more methodological and technical than theoretical (Agbe-Davies under review a). Underlying all of these challenges—technical, methodological, and perhaps (still) theoretical—is the problem of unit creation, of classification. We need an attitude toward technique and method that is as critical as our theory.

In historical archaeology, classification is often routinized and to all appearances conceived of as a pre-analytical step. Perhaps this is because we often consult the written record for information about what our artifacts "are." I call my study an exercise in *critical systematics* (for more on systematics generally, see Dunnell 1971b; O'Brien and Lyman 2003; Read 2007). As many have argued, classification is neither an automatic nor ideology-free enterprise. It is in fact fundamental to subsequent analysis, structuring our capacity for understanding phenomena, whether they be objects or people. Critical method, like critical theory, turns our focus explicitly to the research process and the means by which we produce knowledge. So, by critical systematics I mean that instead of solving old problems that are (implicitly) organized around essentialist notions of group identity and static concepts of material culture, we might self-reflexively examine the culture (that is, social learning) of our discipline. Where do our foundational concepts about human social organization and the qualities of objects come from, and what limitations do they place on our research? With this particular study, the artifacts themselves lead to a critique of those concepts and of taxonomic classification specifically. A critical approach to systematics is not an indictment of previous classifications as such, but of analyses restricted to a narrow sense of where meaning lies and intent on making meaning fit into predetermined schema. A critical systematics entails selecting a technique because it suits the problem, not because it's the next step in a well-established routine. The techniques respond to the object of study, or the sample, and the research question at hand. A critical stance also means that one thinks through the consequences of the classification: its research implications and its implications for the wider world.

My term "critical systematics" also points to *critical race theory* (see for example, Bell 1987; and contributions to Crenshaw et al. 1995; Delgado 1995). This body of scholarship aims to demonstrate the constructed nature of racial categories and the structural elements of racial hierarchy.[6] So to understand this book, it is important to understand what the word "race" means in this context. Race is constructed, but it is also very real.

Anthropologists of the twentieth and twenty-first centuries strive to unlearn the lessons passed down from, among other sources, seventeenth-century Virginia. Anthropologists, and others, have also shown that the key hypotheses underpinning the *biological* reality of races do not hold up to scrutiny. Humans vary physically, certainly. Many of these variations are inherited. Many inherited variations cluster in populations. However, early ethnographers were quick to discover that behavior and personality were not linked to what they often called "physical type." Even more damning, many of the variations used by previous generations of researchers to distinguish one "race" from another are actually quite malleable. Furthermore, variations—both macroscopic and microscopic—cross-cut these groups, these so-called "races." There is more genetic variability within these groups than between them (for more information, see American Anthropological Association 2011; Boas 1912; Brace 2005; Marks 2002; Montagu 1997; Smedley 1993). Despite tremendous effort to find the right characteristics to use, scientific methods are unable to define clearly the categories we *know* exist. This "knowing" is the key. Race, rather than being a classification of physical types, is a system of beliefs about human difference. Races are categories that have *social* meaning, regardless of their biological inadequacy. Which brings us back to the construction of race.

That construction process is particularly visible in the development of race-based slavery in early Virginia (Chapter 6). Critical race theorists examine how social structures, especially the law, are used to create and renew racial categories and racial inequality. They, along with mainstream historians, often point to colonial Virginia as an example of how race was made (Billings 1991; Coombs 2011; Haney López 1995; Parent 2003), but laws alone cannot change a society. Daily social interactions and material culture also contribute to the "structuring structures" that enable such cultural shifts. The concepts and logics developed in seventeenth-century Virginia—and elsewhere in the early Atlantic World—laid the foundation for subsequent notions about the relationship between biological inheritance and social identity, ideas that continue to shape modern life, including archaeological practice. Archaeology, like all sciences, is yet another realm in which we produce and enact the ideas of society. So it really shouldn't be so surprising that an uncritical and historically constituted approach to classification (of people as well as things) has allowed the study of local pipes to revolve inconclusively around the question of whether their designs indicate production by Native American, European, or African makers. Using a critical focus on classification, this project problematizes the relationship between material culture and race.

Which makes this as good a time as any to briefly explain some of my decisions about language. In this book, I refer, for example, to "Native" or "African" Virginians. These anachronistic terms crowd out the many other, more specific, terms I could use: Algonquin; Pamunkey; Edo; Bantu (Gleach 1997; Kulikoff 1986; Rountree and Turner 2002; Thornton and Heywood 2007; Walsh 1997). There are points where more specific names enter the narrative, but for the most part I rely on these presentist labels, and do so for several reasons. First, they are no less "real" or natural than the names that people of the period may have recognized and claimed. Yet, using such obviously generic language eliminates, I hope, the temptation to believe in the essentialist categories they represent. Second, the process of *ethnogenesis*—the development of social categories such as "Native" (or "Indian") and "African" (or "Negro")—demands that we consider who, or what, these Doeg and Kongo people were becoming (for more on ethnogenesis, see Fennell 2007; Voss 2008). Similarly, I find it helpful to distinguish my voice from the language that I encounter—whether in the scholarly literature, "the past," or "the real world"—and that I use specifically to capture the nuances of meaning *in context*.

I also refer throughout to "bound" or "bonded" laborers. Such bondage may have been temporary, or permanent and hereditary. However, our terms "indentured servant" and "slave" bring with them all kinds of associated meanings that were *in the process of being established* in early colonial Virginia. In fact, as we shall see in subsequent chapters, these categories underwent considerable transformations over the course of the seventeenth century. And in fact, the terminology of the period was very different from our own. For the purposes of this book, it is frequently the *fact* of a person's bondage (not the duration) that is most salient, so that is what I choose to reference. As will become clear, the available archaeological and archival record offers only glimpses of these people. In many cases it seems we will never know regarding the residents of a given plantation—housed

in miserable conditions, doing backbreaking work, with no legal authority over their own lives or bodies—what was undoubtedly to them the
most crucial fact: whether they eventually moved on or were trapped for
generations. When I can be specific, I am, but I prefer to avoid the (sometimes) false precision and over-determination of our more-familiar terms.
But however we choose to refer to these people in the past, whatever their
origins or legal status, young or old, lowly or elite, the life of each one was
directly or indirectly touched by Virginia's "fragrant *Indian* Weed."

Pipes and Smoking in the Atlantic World

Tobacco cultivation, of multiple species, was widespread in the Americas.
Ethnohistoric and ethnographic accounts generally agree that the plants had
sacred as well as secular and recreational uses. Iroquoian and Algonquian
people in what became Virginia used pipes and smoking to solemnize political encounters, to accompany and encourage exchange, to please or appease
deities, and to facilitate social relations generally (Bollwerk 2012; Hall 1977;
Linton 1924; Mann 2004; Nassaney 2004). Some have even argued that
tobacco and smoking became increasingly important to Native people as
they attempted to strengthen their societies against the immigrants who
streamed across the Atlantic into their world (Turnbaugh 1975).

For North America's first inhabitants, tobacco was a man's crop
and a man's product (Bollwerk 2012; Hall 1977; Linton 1924; Rountree
1989; von Gernet 1995:70). Likewise, many early European consumers
were male adventurers, sailors, and soldiers who found this substance
calmed, "fed," and emboldened them, with the added benefit of allevi-
ating boredom. Native Americans and Europeans both used tobacco to
smooth social relations, within and across ethnic boundaries, a concept
that survives in American popular culture as the idea of the "peace pipe"
(Hall 1977; Rountree 1989:125). Though Europeans often associated
tobacco with scenes of adult male conviviality, such as the tavern or the
coffeehouse, women and children smoked, too—despite the warnings of
some medical experts who observed that since children were already hot
and dry, too much tobacco might unbalance their humors (Courtwright
2001:70, 101; Goodman 1995:52, 132).

American Indians consumed tobacco in a variety of ways, including
chewing, drinking, inhaling it as snuff, taking enemas, and smoking—
smoking being the most common (Goodman 1993:33–34). When the
English established their settlements in the New World, the people they
encountered were pipe smokers. As the English and other northwestern

Europeans adopted tobacco into their medicinal and recreational repertoires, they became pipe smokers as well. Europeans began making and using tobacco pipes in earnest in the 1580s and 1590s (Walker 1977:30–32, 244), with a formal manufacturer's organization and charter established in England in 1619 (Oswald 1975:4–7). The clay pipes made in Europe resembled American prototypes, and there was a considerable degree of technological and stylistic sharing between the two traditions. It wasn't long before colonists were trading tobacco as well as products of the London pipe industry to Native American recipients who, accounts claimed, valued the pipes for their "strength, handsomenesse, and coolnesse" (Goodman 1993:167).

Tobacco was the source of the Virginia colonists' individual and collective livelihoods. It was the single most valuable export of the region. Said Benedict Leonard Calvert as late as 1729, "Tobacco, as our staple, is our all, and Indeed leaves no room for anything else" (in Walsh 1993:170). It served as the local currency. It was often Virginians' drug of choice. A late seventeenth-century European visitor to Virginia reported:

> Everyone smokes while working and idling. I sometimes went to hear the sermon; their churches are in the woods, & when everyone has arrived the minister & all the others smoke before going in. The preaching over, they do the same thing before parting. They have seats for that purpose. It was there that I saw that everybody smokes, men, women, girls and boys from the age of seven years. (Chinard 1934:118)

By 1670 consumption of tobacco in England was one pound per capita per year. Based on the available records, that year saw enough tobacco imported into England that 25 percent of the population could have indulged in a daily pipe-full (Courtwright 2001:15; Goodman 1993:59). Voyages of conquest and trade spread tobacco throughout the Old World during the seventeenth century, to Europe's rivals in the Ottoman Empire; to China, a valued trading partner; and to Africa, where tobacco was introduced in the 1630s (Baram 1999; Courtwright 2001:16; Goodman 1993:52; Price 1995:170–171), not long before Europeans began enslaving Africans in earnest.

So Africans' acquaintance with tobacco and pipe smoking was almost as long as that of Europeans (Shaw 1960). Much of their tobacco was consumed using pipes imported from Europe. Account books from English firms engaged in the slave trade record the purchase of pipes for exchange on the continent (Walker 1977:415). Pipes made of European "ball" clays are regularly found in African contexts (for example, Kelly 1997; Schrire et al. 1990). Walker (1975:166) reports that some slave traders purchased pipes specifically for the use of captives during the middle passage.

The physiological effects of tobacco consumption are well documented today and similar effects were acknowledged in much of the contemporary literature produced following tobacco's introduction to Europe. Sixteenth- and seventeenth-century writers recognized that tobacco eases hunger and thirst and that it is a stimulant with some calming properties. Medical experts incorporated tobacco into their humoral theory of medicine and determined that the heating and drying effects of tobacco (when smoked) had many medical applications. Tobacco even came to be accepted as a "panacea," or cure-all, in certain circles (Courtwright 2001:57,70; Goodman 1993:38–42; Goodman 1995; von Gernet 1995:76–77). The plant was a good fit with Europe's medical concepts and needs at that time.

Tobacco is a mild hallucinogen, one of the properties that may have led to its nearly universal spread throughout the Americas. It is among the more predictable and less poisonous substances that can be used to stimulate visions and facilitate communion with supernatural powers (Goodman 1993:20–25; von Gernet 1995). Indeed, some have argued that tobacco's hallucinogenic properties were also vital to its acceptance in post-medieval Europe (Goodman 1995). Courtwright (2001:59) explains the modern importance of stimulants and intoxicants, what he calls the "psychoactive revolution," in this way:

> It is probably no coincidence that the rapid growth of European distilling, and the explosive growth of tobacco imports, took place during what historians call "the general crisis of the seventeenth century." Those born in 1590 who managed to survive until 1660 (as most Europeans assuredly did not) lived through a period of inflation, unemployment, pestilence, frigid weather, crop failures, riots, massacres, and warfare without parallel since the grimmest days of the fourteenth century. Plainly, these were people who could use a smoke and a drink.

Virginians needed the relief that tobacco could provide as much as, if not more than, their peers across the Atlantic, and became consumers for many of the same reasons.

Meanwhile, an English merchant describing the smoking habits of Sierra Leoneans in the early seventeenth century noted that it "seems to be half their food." A later traveler commented, "They are always smoking Tobacco, which serves to amuse them, and deaden the Appetite" (Walsh 1997:61). In this sense, tobacco resembles a later colonial export staple: sugar. Both served as food substitutes and drugs, binding consumers and producers into tighter and tighter relations, while at the same time offering some distraction for the laborers on whom the whole system depended (Mintz 1985; Wallerstein 1980:164). Locally made and consumed pipes are one avenue for exploring the self-medication and addiction of the very people who produced tobacco for the rest of the world-economy, linking their production and consumption back to the system of which they were an integral part.

Archaeologies of Local Pipes

Despite this evidence for the ubiquity of pipes and the multivalence of smoking in the seventeenth century, in the years immediately following Harrington's analysis archaeologists were sure about "who" had made the pipes they found. Some held that colonists had made the "yellow bowls" at Jamestown for trade to nearby Algonquians. Others asserted equally forcefully that the association of local pipes with Native American artifacts indicated Indian makers, regardless of a site's date or the additional presence of European manufactures (MacCord 1969; Winfree 1969). Contrarians claimed that settlers were manufacturing pipes for use among themselves. Stewart (1954) granted that the Jamestown pipes were "obviously the product of white men," but said that those from his site were not.[7] Sure, yes, but in agreement, no.

Through the years, archaeologists have used a variety of names for the pipes. In keeping with my approach to classifying people and social roles, I've chosen the more generic "local" in place of the currently common "Chesapeake" or "colono." This is in part because, as explained earlier in this chapter, such terms are more than simple labels; they pack a host of meanings and implications that this book is meant to examine critically. I need a word to designate pipes made in Virginia during the colonial period, in contrast to pipes made abroad. "Local" fills the bill.

Eventually, archaeologists' attention turned to describing specific collections of pipes. Several, following Harrington's lead, separated "handmade" from "mold-made" pipes or created categories based on decoration. For example, analysis of an assemblage known as the Knowles Collection, a large and unfortunately unprovenienced group of pipes, included categories for local mold-made copies of European pipes, local handmade copies of European pipes, and Indian pipes (Pawson 1969).[8] The archaeological site of Camden yielded pipes grouped as follows: thick, crude elbow pipes decorated without the use of metal tools; pipes with smoother and harder clay bodies, decorated with a metal tool; and pipes of darker clays, having squared-off lips and more richly decorated with metal tools (Heite 1972). At the late seventeenth-century colonial site of Nominy Hall, the analyst categorized local pipes as handmade and decorated, handmade and undecorated, and mold-made (Mitchell 1976; 1983). In each case, the goals were primarily descriptive, and focus limited to a single site, usually interpreted as being left behind by Indian occupants. Analysts explicitly understood the differences between types to be measures of the pipes' (and by extension, the peoples') relative Indian-ness or European-ness. Analysts treated pipes with non-Native decorations or made in molds as evidence of acculturation to European lifeways.

With pipes excavated from European settlements, where archaeologists' primary orientation was towards historical archaeology, rather than the pre-contact period, researchers based the categories of the mold-made local pipes on identification and dating keys established for imported pipes (such as Atkinson and Oswald 1969; Oswald 1975). Nevertheless, at Pope's Fort, Miller (1991) found that over 70 percent of fragments came from local pipes, much like the one described at the opening of this chapter, rather than imported pipes—and the majority of those local pipes were not mold-made, and thus did not conform to keys developed for imported pipes. A study of the pipes from Green Spring plantation is typical in describing the local pipes using a range of attributes emphasizing shape, augmented by decoration, color, and bore diameter (Crass 1981; 1988). In the most systematic and broad-ranging of these studies, Henry (1976; 1979) described forming techniques, bowl shape, and decoration, finding correlations among the variables, such as the fact that decorations occurring on handmade bowls of a certain shape were absent from mold-made bowls. Again, the primary purpose of many publications was descriptive, to provide information about finds to other archaeologists (for another example, see Noël Hume 1979; I. Noël Hume and A. Noël Hume 2001). The articles include extensive verbal descriptions and ample illustrations of the forms and decorative techniques used at a given site. Although authors sometimes identified what they called "types" in their respective collections, there was no generally accepted classification scheme for use across sites, as with the "type-variety" system (Gifford 1960; Sabloff and Smith 1969), on which several efforts were clearly based. In the early stages of my own research, I thought that its contribution would be to finally develop a standard nomenclature and classification. As subsequent chapters demonstrate, I have become skeptical of that project.

Some of these later studies went beyond description and sought to understand the social significance of the local pipe tradition. For example, they explored whether limited access to imported pipes motivated local pipe manufacture. Archival evidence shows that the tobacco economy of the colonial Chesapeake experienced a boom-and-bust cycle—with increasing emphasis on the "bust" as time went on. Henry (1979) linked this cycle with local pipe production, reasoning that residents of the Chesapeake colonies would be unable to afford imported pipes when the tobacco market was bad. Miller (1991) noted that at Pope's Fort local pipes often occurred in deposits with Dutch, rather than English, pipes; perhaps the Dutch and local varieties indicate periods of economic isolation during the English Civil War. These archaeologists linked the production and use of tobacco pipes to economic and social processes and structures on a scale larger than the individual or a sub-group within the colony, as do I.

In the final decades of the twentieth century, the pendulum swung back to the question of identity with a major study arguing that many locally made pipes were the handiwork of the growing African population in the seventeenth-century Chesapeake (Emerson 1988; 1994; 1999). Emerson's project was the first to analyze collections from more than one site in detail, drawing from sites dating ca. 1620 to 1740 from throughout Tidewater Virginia and Maryland. To support his thesis, Emerson analyzed the decorative characters (individual design elements), decorative motifs (specific shapes), and decorative schemes (organizational patterns) found on what he called "Chesapeake" pipes. He then identified analogues to these characters, motifs, and schemes in pipes and other decorative arts dating from the seventeenth to the twentieth centuries in West Africa, concluding that for pipes, these associations were stronger than those with Native American and European decorative traditions. While these ideas gained acceptance with a number of scholars, the argument remains controversial.[9]

One line of criticism rejects Emerson's association of certain traits with West African decorative traditions and notes equivalent similarities between pipes from pre-contact Native American sites and those from colonial-period sites. Another cites the archival record which refers to Native

Americans making pipes after colonization, but does not mention people of African descent doing the same (Magoon 1999; Mouer 1993; Mouer et al. 1999). The controversy shows no signs of satisfactory resolution, and indeed, has been characterized as "a debate headed nowhere" (Singleton and Bograd 1995:26), not for lack of evidence, but for the principles on which it is based. My project's critical approach to systematics allows a renewed focus on related questions of production and distribution, without eliding the central importance of racial categories in seventeenth-century Virginia.

Recently, archaeologists have begun to raise new questions about locally made pipes, rather than working to identify their Native American, European, or African precedents. For example, Neiman and King (1999) examined the distribution of local and imported pipes within three early colonial sites. They found at these sites from Tidewater Virginia and Maryland notable differences between the distribution of local and imported pipes. Furthermore, the locally made pipes clustered near the living- and work-spaces used by bound laborers, as opposed to planters' families. Rather than asking who made the pipes, they addressed the (as they noted) logically independent problem of who *used* the pipes. In a different vein, archaeological chemistry has verified the material similarities between the "yellow bowls" from Virginia sites and available clay deposits, demonstrating once and for all that such pipes *were* made of local materials (Bollwerk 2012; Key and Jones 2000; Moore 1996) and that similar pipes found in New England are not Virginian in origin (Capone and Downs 2004). Clear evidence of pipe-manufacturing, including kiln furniture and prepared—but unused—clay, sheds light on specific stages of the manufacturing process (Luckenbach and Cox 2002; Luckenbach and Kiser 2006). A recent reanalysis of pipes from Jamestown adapts Harrington's dating technique for the local pipes (Monroe and Mallios 2004).[10] At the same time, attempts to understand the pipe decoration in terms of cultural affiliation have grown more nuanced. Building on Emerson's work, Monroe (2002) has delved deeper into the social function of decorated pipes among African Virginians, interpreting changes in the decorative repertoire as a response to increasing racial hierarchy and a move toward in-group solidarity. Another study treats one motif, the star, as a sign that communicated across ethnic boundaries (Sikes 2008).

My work belongs to this last set, with researchers delving into new questions, paying close attention to archaeological context, the processes by which the pipes came to be, and the idea that the pipes can indicate social *relationships* as well as social identities. Of course, the problem of "who" made the pipes is important, and of course race is important. I chose not to look at these problems directly, in part because I hope to catch them out of the corner of my eye. This refusal can be, and has been, variously interpreted: that I am saying that race is imaginary—it is not; or that pipes were made by unmarked (and therefore English) hands—I believe no such thing. I remain (temporarily) agnostic on this point because I believe in thinking about one thing at a time. This sequential and iterative approach manifests in the analytical techniques and methods that are explained in Chapter 2 and applied in Chapters 3, 4, and 5. It is also congruent with my growing interest in *pragmatism* as a framework for archaeological research (Agbe-Davies 2011; under review a and b).

Pragmatism

Archaeologists invoke pragmatism as a framework for critical reflection on archaeology's impact on living people, and for fostering collaboration with archaeology's publics (Jeppson 2001; McDavid 2002; Mrozowski 2012; Saitta 2007). Another major strand employs semiotic theory in interpretation (Preucel 2006; Preucel and Bauer 2001). I am especially interested in pragmatism's take on science and its methods: fallibilism as opposed to foundationalism;[11] the importance of methodological plural-ism; and the concept of science as an ongoing conversation (Baert 2005b; Reid and Whittlesey 1998). So by way of conclusion, I connect the present effort with some of pragmatism's key concepts, to demonstrate the broader implications for archaeology as a scientific enterprise, and for knowledge production more generally.

William James, an early proponent, christened "pragmatism" in the late nineteenth century, giving this name to the ideas expressed by his col-league Charles Sanders Peirce (James 1907; Peirce 1994c). How far back (and how far out) to trace the genealogy is a matter of some discussion. Ralph Waldo Emerson may have a place in the canon, as might late colo-nial thinkers and their Native American interlocutors (Pratt 2002; West 1989).[12] James and Peirce, as well as later scholars like John Dewey and W. E. B. DuBois, saw pragmatism as a way to understand what truth is, and how to pursue it. How should we believe?

There is some overlap between the colloquial sense of "pragmatic" (practical, non-dogmatic) and the habits of mind encouraged by guid-ing principles such as Peirce's "pragmatic maxim," which maintains that we know things via the effects that they have.[13] Another similarity is the aim to deal with particulars rather than abstractions (James 1907). I liken this emphasis to the archaeological concern for context (Agbe-Davies under review a). Context is intimately connected to the discipline's way of thinking about time and place, as well as our emphasis on the associations among materials. Accordingly, I chose pipes for this study not for their individual characteristics, but for the archaeological contexts (sites, deposits, phases) from which they came.

Every collection would ideally yield at least 100 locally made pipe fragments; some had many more.[14] I was especially interested in sites with clear archaeological evidence of ceramic manufacture—a majority of those selected. In several cases individual features related to ceramic production, such as kilns or borrow pits, provided the pipe fragments for study. Mine being an argument about simultaneously circulating pipes, I needed to control for time. I selected a limited span in the second half of the seventeenth century (mostly 1660s–1690s).[15] The late seventeenth century represents the beginning of the end for this pipe tradition. It was also a time of profound social upheaval and change in the Virginia colony, as the General Assembly crafted a series of laws solidifying a system of perpetual slavery based on race and the populace endured a series of events now known as Bacon's Rebellion.

The armed struggle, even if defined broadly, lasted only a couple of years, but was the product of long-simmering tensions within the colony itself and beyond its borders. The internecine conflict was in some sense sparked by antagonisms between European and Native combatants. The protracted race war between settler and colonized ultimately provided a blueprint for the racial domination of an ever-increasing number of people with origins in Africa. Not coincidentally, the rebels included freemen and a substantial number of indentured servants and slaves, as well as elites excluded from then-governor William Berkeley's inner circle. Written sources document alliances and fault lines among the land- and labor-owners who monopolized colonial power in multiple forms (political, economic, and social). Information about these planters and their relationships is the basis for an inquiry into the factors that shaped pipe distribution patterns among their plantations and town lots. While there has been a great deal of attention to the differences among pipe styles, here I intend to understand them *in context*, as part of a system of production and consumption relating plantations and people to one another.

The pragmatist focus on *relationships* rather than *entities* manifests explicitly in Peirce's writing about signs. His conception of the sign is of a triadic relationship including not only the *signifier* ("ground") and the *signified* ("object"), but also the "interpretant"—that which the sign evokes (Peirce 1994a). This evocation includes, at some level, the agent for whom the sign means. While we cannot ignore the past actor-as-agent (maker, smoker, observer), the contemporary analyst-as-agent matters, too. The pipes continue to be signs, even into our own time. This is the essence of a critical systematics.

Another important inspiration from Peirce, perhaps the first to influence my way of thinking about the pipes, is his idea of the *index* (Agbe-Davies 2004b; 2010). According to his second trichotomy of signs, a sign may be an "icon," an "index," or a "symbol." An *icon* resembles its object. For example, many have argued that the pipe decoration shown in Figure 1.5a is a representation of a deer—it means "deer" because it resembles one. A *symbol's* relationship to its object is one of convention or law. Emerson's study of pipe decorations revealed an uncanny parallel between the pipe motif shown in Figure 1.5b and a symbol found on beer vessels made by contemporary Ga̧'anda people in Nigeria (Emerson 1994:43). There is no resemblance between the appearance of the decoration and

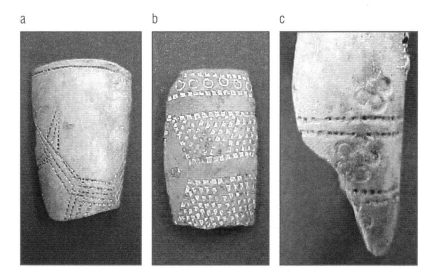

Figure 1.5 The pipe fragment on the left (from Jamestown Structure 100) is decorated with an icon signifying a four legged animal—likely a deer. Among modern Ga'anda people, the decorative motif on the middle pipe fragment (from Rich Neck) is a symbol of the transition to adulthood. The floral decoration on the pipe stem on the right (from Green Spring) is an index of the pipe maker's tool kit.

the idea of the transition between youth and adulthood; nevertheless, that is what the decoration means in that context. The connection between the motif and the idea is entirely conventional.

An *index* is another matter altogether. It is "a sign which refers to the Object that it denotes by virtue of being really affected by that Object" (Peirce 1994a:248). The flower-shaped impressions on the pipe fragment in Figure 1.5c are a kind of sign, too. They signify that someone making pipes had access to a wide range of specialized tools just for creating decorations on crafted objects. This pipe fragment was "really affected by" that long-gone craftsperson and tool kit. Likewise, the archaeological record as a whole refers to past actions by virtue of being traces of those past actions (for a fuller exposition, see Preucel 2006; Preucel and Bauer 2001). In fact, this kind of interpretation is our greatest disciplinary strength. While the symbolic content of the pipe decoration is an important aspect of pipes-as-signs, it is not the only aspect, nor, perhaps, the one most amenable to archaeological inquiry (Agbe-Davies under review a).

❍

Like the semiotic approach to language, this study aims to understand actual instances of sign-making (the manufacture of individual pipes, the formation of pipe assemblages), but not to produce an ideal descriptive model of a sign system. The pipe fragments are here analyzed in a manner that is both empirical and inductive,[16] proceeding not from foundational principles, but fallible premises, each conclusion serving as the premise for the next problem. If pipes were produced casually, for on-site use, we would expect assemblages to have hyper-local characteristics (Chapter 3). If production were centralized, we would expect the variation among sites to be random (Chapter 4). If elite social networks shaped the paths along which pipes moved, we would expect the distribution of pipe styles to reflect the relationships of the owning class (Chapter 5). This is part of what I mean by thinking about one thing at a time.

Accept an idea as true and see where it leads. Watch how relationships unfold in a particular context and evaluate their implications for the next round. Consider how the terms of analysis structure the conclusions. Think about how our research reverberates in the wider world, and how our work emerges from that same world. This pragmatism is the opposite of the value-free opportunism caricatured by the term's colloquial usage. Pragmatism is about consequences, and so is this book.

Classification, or, This Is Not a Pipe
Chapter 2

I have a terrible confession to make: I'm not really very interested in pipes.

Partway through the research that led to this book, a mentor of mine, Marley Brown, recalled to me the warning he had gotten from *his* advisor: research topics have a way of taking over one's scholarly persona. If he wasn't careful, he would become forever Pipe Man. He turned to me, "How about you; do you want to be Pipe Woman?" Frankly, the thought filled me with dread. I had come to the pipes because of my interest in that interpretive stalemate: the problem of Indian or African origins. Initially, I thought that our typologies needed refinement or revision to allow a definitive answer. I gradually came to think that the problem was not technical (a flawed typology) but methodological (a narrow concept of classification) and theoretical (asking the wrong questions). Our difficulties with technique, method, and theory are linked.

Pipes, like all artifacts, don't speak for themselves. Archaeologists, like all people, have to produce meaning for and from them. One of the tools for doing so is a *classification*. For our purposes, "classification" refers to a set of categories used to make distinctions among a collection of artifacts. As such, a classification is a system of abstractions (the categories) that derive from entities (for example, pipes).[1] The fact that these categories exist *in relation to* one another is crucial (W. Adams and E. Adams 1991; Dunnell 1971b). A classification, then, is a tool, devised by the researcher, used for organizing archaeological data into analyzable units (Brew 1971 [1946]). It underlies any scientific understanding of archaeological materials, but is not an end to itself.

Classifications are powerful when they serve some purpose. Their quality is evaluated not by some measure of completeness or symmetry, but from their fit with an application. There is no right or wrong way to classify locally made tobacco pipes, only a right way to classify them given a particular set of questions. The distinguishing variables and the significance attributed to them, the manner of identifying them, and so forth all depend on what we want to know. For example, one purpose of this book is to determine how people moved local pipes around the colony, to ascertain whether archaeological assemblages suggest intra-household production and consumption of pipes, or specialized production with exchange from producers to consumers. If we do see specialization, then what social relationships characterize that industry? This particular set of problems requires classificatory and grouping strategies that take into account the nature of the material, the manner of manufacture, the location of the finds, and so forth. As I will show, the methods selected must also be able to recognize variation in a broader range of specimens than are commonly used in the study of local pipes.

Certain classificatory strategies (taxonomic typology) and attributes (decoration) tend to dominate archaeological practice. This chapter opens with a brief review of how archaeologists have tackled the task of classifying artifacts, with an emphasis on alternatives (namely, modal analysis and technological style) to these dominant strategies. This overview informs a discussion of the classificatory strategies deployed in this study. I also connect the various forms of "style" to what period texts and artifacts reveal about how people made clay pipes like the ones archaeologists find strewn across colonial era Virginia. The non-hierarchical and iterative process of modal analysis contrasts with the static results of other systems modeled on the classic example of a typology: Linnaean taxonomy. The final section, on Linnaeus's influence and scientific classification more generally, links the problem of how to classify the pipes to the problem of how to classify people, demonstrating the parallels between these problems and connecting both to developments in colonial Virginia. Throughout the chapter, examples will offer glimpses of the collection of pipes included in this study. They feature even more prominently in Chapters 3–5, in which I employ the methods explained and discussed here.

Classification, Typology, and Style

The divisions that we humans use to organize and make sense of reality are often arbitrary. The line that separates "blue" from "green" varies from one society and one language to the next. Indeed, they may not even exist as "two" colors. No matter how much sense they make, no matter how natural or real they may seem, the divisions we use to comprehend and contemplate our world are not necessarily inherent in phenomena we seek to understand. Over the years, archaeology has witnessed a number of debates concerning the nature of our "types" and their appropriate use (for a synopsis, see Wylie 2002b). Should types be universal or problem- and collection-specific? Do typologies exist to group similar units (lumping) or separate dissimilar units (splitting) (Hayden 1984; Hill and Evans 1972:233; Read and Russell 1996; Taylor 1983 [1948]:127)? What is the "reality" of the types the archaeologist observes versus the types used by people in the past (Brew 1971 [1946]:77; Ford 1954:42; Spaulding 1953)? Any classification of the locally made pipes has to confront such questions.

Brew's stance was a pragmatic one at heart. He asserted:

[W]e need more rather than fewer classifications, different classifications, always new classifications, to meet new needs. We must not be satisfied with a single classification of a group of artifacts or of a cultural development, for that way lies dogma and defeat. We are, or should be, in search of all of the evidence our material holds. Even in simple things no single analysis will bring out all that evidence.

We must continually analyze not only our material but also our methods.... We need have no fear of changing established systems or of designing new ones, for it is only by such means that we can progress. At the same time we must not present our new system or systems as a standard to be used and adopted by everyone and forevermore. (1971 [1946]:105)

Brew's exhortation applies not only to the particular classifications archaeologists devise, but the classificatory project itself. His call echoes through the typological discussions that characterized archaeological writing in the second half of the twentieth century. Classificatory strategies should suit the specific data and specific problems (for example, O'Brien and Lyman 2003:23; Rouse 1971 [1960]; Sabloff and Smith 1969:279; Sackett 1990:41). "Problems" include succinctly describing the variability present in an assemblage, inferring social organization from the distribution of class-members within or among sites, developing a regional chronology, and so forth (W. Adams and E. Adams 1991:157–168). In the end, classification systems enable verifiable statements about which entities are "the same" *for the purposes at hand*.

Early archaeological classifications were often meant to provide standardized names for finds and to facilitate communication among archaeologists. Most of the terms applied to intuitively grouped sets of artifacts in which divisions were made along lines that seemed significant to the originator, but could not necessarily be replicated through the application of a set procedure or strategy (Dunnell 1986:159,165; Read 1989:164). Yet many of these intuitive classification systems were quite effective for the purposes of chronology and other historical questions that dominated the period (Adams 1988:41).

As archaeologists turned their attention to questions of artifact function and cultural significance, a series of disputes about the meaning and purpose of classifications emerged. Some, feeling that the purpose of a classification was to identify categories meaningful within the society represented by the archaeological record, felt that classes had (or should have) a meaning and existence independent of the analysts' concerns, one that potentially could be discovered (for example, Krieger 1944:272; Spaulding 1953). Some carried this argument to its logical conclusion, that one classification would be the "right" one—the one that correlated with past social meanings. This outlook prompted attempts to create universal, or complete, classification systems.

Other archaeologists started with the idea that classifications existed primarily in the mind of the analyst, for analytical purposes (Ford 1954), and could therefore be multiple (see especially Brew 1971 [1946]; Rouse 1971 [1960]). The rallying cry of these, and later archaeologists, was that classification systems must have a clearly defined purpose if they are to be any use at all and that the measure of any classification is its ability to answer the analyst's questions about the material at hand (W. Adams and E. Adams 1991; Dunnell 1971b; Hill and Evans 1972:253). This is not to say that the data are infinitely malleable and any classification is "right." Rather, there are as many potential "right" classifications as there are problems to be solved with the data. This orientation toward the relationship between reality and knowledge calls to mind Peirce's pragmatic maxim, that "our idea of anything *is* our idea of its sensible effects" (Peirce 1994c:401). What, then, are the applications (and effects) of a classification?

Archaeology has progressed beyond assuming neat one-to-one correlations between artifacts and social groups. It is passé to accept uncritically specific artifacts or artifact styles as "markers" of certain social groups or as having a single coherent meaning. Observation teaches us that people, whether they are producers or consumers, are not automatons mindlessly replicating patterns from one generation to the next. And in fact, the coming discussion of decorative and technological style shows that decorative variables in particular respond to social learning in ways that do not always reflect production groups (see also, Lathrap 1983). Nevertheless, observation also teaches us that disjunctures in style may still follow social disjunctures; the trick is to determine which ones and under what circumstances.

There are several paths to follow. For one thing, archaeologists have turned their gaze to smaller areas and groups, comparing families, households, and other units *within* societies or regions rather than the societies or regions themselves. That strategy has been taken to its logical conclusion with the study of the patterns that individual producers introduce into material culture (Eerkens 2000; Hill and Gunn 1977). Such efforts have inspired researchers to recognize increasingly precise classificatory groups and give greater attention to context and to associations among classes and attributes.

Archaeologists have also rebelled against the notion that *style* applies, by definition, only to those aspects of culture that served no selective value: style as the antithesis of function (Dunnell 1978:199). Far from being epiphenomenal, style has very important functions. We think of style as those aspects of material culture that convey information, having meaning in terms of their (communicative) function (Wobst 1977:320).

Most exciting has been the application of the style concept to technological as well as decorative aspects of material culture. In this sense style refers simply to the choices made among equivalent options: stylistic meaning resides not only in decoration, but in all aspects of artifact

Figure 2.1 The form of this pipe bowl from the Page site (*left*) represents one kind of style—decorative. The traces left by carving out the bowl with a bladed tool (*right*) represent another kind of style—technological.

variation. Decoration is style-rich, but so too are the technical choices made by artisans. Essentially, "style is more often built in, rather than added on, to objects" (Sackett 1990:42). This project examines decorative style alongside—rather than instead of—what has been called the "style of technology" or "iscochrestic variation" (Lechtman 1977; Sackett 1990). For example, the analyses that follow consider the methods used to form a pipe bowl as well as the shape of the bowl itself (Figure 2.1). With a new sense of "style," the standardization that is the hallmark of specialized production can be measured by material and metric—not only decorative—attributes (Blackman et al. 1993:61). One of the unintended consequences of the recent turn to "technological style" has been a new attention to the relationship between social behavior and artifact variation (Conkey 1990; Dietler and Herbich 1998) and renewed attention to the attributes used to group and classify artifacts (Hegmon 1992:530).

Classification and Pipes, Imported and Local

Wrangling over classification fosters gaps in our understanding of many artifact forms (see discussions in Dunnell 1971b; Shepard 1956:307). This certainly has been true of the local pipes of the seventeenth-century Chesapeake. Local and imported pipes are often found side-by-side on seventeenth-century sites in Virginia. Early studies of local pipes relied on identification keys developed for pipes mass-produced in England. However, many local pipes do not fit easily into these categories. Furthermore, the local pipe "typologies"—as they are often called—did little more than place the pipes into groups. Even then, some of the new identification keys had nearly as many categories as artifacts.

Imported pipes are ubiquitous in historical archaeology. Examine virtually any archaeological site where the occupants participated in the modern world-economy between 1600 and 1900, and chances are you'll find it littered with the shattered fragments of clay tobacco pipes. Noël Hume writes that the English tobacco pipe in particular is "possibly the most valuable clue yet available to the student of historical sites, for it is an item which was manufactured, imported, smoked, and thrown away, all within a matter of a year or two" (1969:296). A complimentary reason for archaeologists' interest in ball clay pipes is their variability—within limits. There was a certain degree of regional variation, but most important distinctions among pipe styles have to do with changes in the tradition *over time*. Identification keys for the shape of pipe bowls help archaeologists to date pipe assemblages or, some might argue, even single specimens.

Another technique devised for dating pipe fragments uses the diameter of the stem bore—the hole through which smoke passes between the pipe bowl and the smoker's lips. Harrington (1954) was the first archaeologist to systematically measure the bore diameters of pipe stems after he noticed that the bores of older pipes (as identified by bowl form) were larger than those of later pipes. He then found that the assemblages within certain date ranges would be dominated by stem bores of a particular size (see Figure 2.2). With a large enough sample, following his procedure can give a reasonably accurate date range for a sample of pipe stems (Noël Hume 1991:297–302; Schrire et al. 1990). A few years later, Binford (1961) converted the data in Harrington's histograms into a formula, which he used to calculate a single year (a "mean date" of occupation). These pipe stem methods are attractive[2] because pipe bowls do not always remain intact enough to identify specific shapes. Attempts to apply

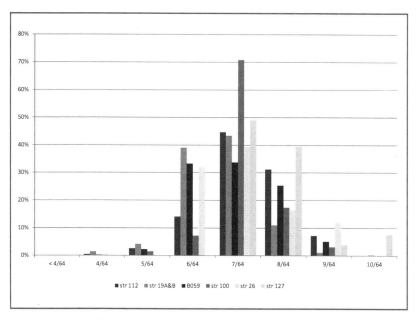

Figure 2.2 This "Harrington histogram" of the bore diameters of *imported* pipes excavated from selected contexts at Jamestown indicates that each structure's assemblage falls within the 1650–1680 timeframe, though the use of Structure 127 may have begun somewhat earlier than the others. "B059" is Block 59, which includes Structure 27. The pipe quantities are from the database of Jamestown artifacts as of 2001.

bowl form and stem bore dating techniques to local pipes have not gained much ground. In part this is because the stem bores of locally made pipes are usually larger than those of the imported pipes from the same deposit. Monroe and Mallios (2004) offer a formula for using the measurements of bores to produce a mean date of deposition using only local pipe stems, but generally archaeologists have been more interested in the communicative power of local pipes than using them to establish site dates.

The characteristics that distinguish locally made pipes from their imported cousins include their reddish- and yellowish-brown clays, a variety of mold-made and handmade shapes, elaborate decorative motifs, and limited geographical and temporal boundaries. As detailed in Chapter 1, these differences have prompted researchers to consider the different meanings the two varieties may have had in the past. Could local pipes have been a substitute when smokers could not obtain imported ones

(Miller 1991)? Could the pipes be signatures of different groups of smokers (Neiman and King 1999)? What are the temporal and spatial limitations of local production (Capone and Downs 2004; Magoon 1999)? Finally, and most prolifically, archaeologists have attempted to understand the meaning of the decorations found on these pipes: What did these decorations signify and for whom were these messages intended? Interest in this question has led to an emphasis on decorative technique and motif in the literature on Chesapeake-made pipes (for example, Bollwerk 2012; Emerson 1988; Monroe 2002; Mouer et al. 1999; Sikes 2008).

In some sense, the imported pipes serve as a foil for the local pipes, but rather than ask why people chose one or the other, or what these two alternatives mean relative to each other, I am interested in what different local pipes mean in a modern context. Referring back to Peirce's triadic relation among signifier, signified, and interpretant, the interpretant in this case is the meaning that the signifier evokes for modern archaeologists. Specifically, I want to know what meaning does any one of the attributes, of any assemblage, evoke? A pragmatist like James would say that it depends on what you want to know. Using the pipes as indices of past actions, I'm interested in understanding how they differ from each other and what those differences can tell us about how many people participated in production and how production and distribution may have been organized.

Many classifications of locally made pipes take the form of a *taxonomic typology*, meaning that the attributes of pipes are ranked hierarchically, and individual types are defined by a series of branching divisions. One familiar taxonomy is the Linnean system of scientific classification for living species, discussed at the conclusion of this chapter. The potential challenges for an archaeological taxonomy lie in the fact that intuition and tradition often drive the selection of defining characteristics and their placement within the hierarchy of divisions (as discussed in Dunnell 1971b:73). One often assumes that the relationships among the criteria are natural; for example, that bowl shape is a more fundamental distinction—and therefore hierarchically "higher"—than decorative motif or the use of particular clays. In Figure 2.3, the presence or absence of "Indian influences" marks a more fundamental difference than the use of agatized versus single-colored clays.

A few researchers have used an alternative method, *paradigmatic classification*. In contrast to a taxonomy, where classes are produced by a serial ordering of oppositions, indicating the relationships among the types, in a paradigmatic classification, classes are produced by the intersection of two or more dimensions of variation (Dunnell 1971b:71–83).

Motif location	Mold-made shape	Handmade shape
beneath bowl	—	3
bowl back	6	41
bowl front	4	24
bowl indeterminate	—	8
bowl left	—	6
bowl right	—	7
circum bowl, other	8	97
circum lip	45	55
circum stem	1	12
entire surface	—	2
heel	16	1
juncture stem and bowl	19	40

Table 2.1 This contingency table also represents one of many possible paradigmatic classifications of local pipes. Here, classes are created at the intersection of motif location and pipe-shaping method.

These classes can be represented in the form of a contingency table. See, for example, Table 2.1, which contrasts the location of decorative motifs on mold-made pipes versus pipes made with hand tools.

Years ago, Irving Rouse described yet a third way, which he called "analytical" classification (he also used the phrase *modal analysis*). Here, entities are grouped according to their attributes into a *series* of successive categories or "modes" (Rouse 1939; 1971 [1960]). Refer to Figure 2.3. Modal analysis would first compare all of the pipes with agatized clays against those with pink or buff clays, then re-sort the entire assemblage to divide fragments with heels from fragments of pipes made without heels, and finally sort them again according to the origin of the pipes' influences. In modal analysis, the constituent attributes of an artifact are the units of analysis, rather than the artifacts themselves, still less their categories. Modal analysis is also particularly useful for looking at fragments, and for answering questions about technology and manufacture—objects and themes that until recently have been missing from studies of Chesapeake-made pipes. So what modal analysis enables is a focus not on kinds of things, but on distributions of attributes. As we will see in the conclusion of this chapter, there are parallel arguments in biological anthropology for how we think about physical variation in humans.

Rouse himself emphasized the suitability of modal analysis for studies dealing with fragments, technology, and exchange, all of which are crucial here. And as Deetz and Dethlefsen (1972) have noted, the emergence of attribute analysis, as opposed to typological analysis, has proceeded largely due to the availability of technology for recording and processing the large quantities of data that it generates. Rather than continue to identify classes paradigmatically, the modal strategy that I use here takes advantage of that computing technology and uses distinctions at the attribute level, rather than the object level, to discover which sites might have been drawing on similar sources for pipes.

Critical attention to the many forms of classification (and non-classificatory grouping) allows archaeologists to select methods and procedures best suited to their purpose(s). But it seems that despite the variety of questions we might ask and the nuances of the different assemblages we work with, archaeologists have come up with a very limited range of strategies for dealing with locally made pipes.

Troublesome Types

The literature on classification is often written in terms of "types" and "typologies." And yet, "type" has a very narrow meaning in archaeology. Some of the entities and concepts identified as "types" in local pipe studies are a different kind of thing entirely: descriptions; analytical groupings; naming systems; or identification keys (Dunnell 1971b). A "typology" is in fact a particular kind of classification system, one made "specifically for the purpose of sorting entities into mutually exclusive categories [the types]" (Adams 1988:43; W. Adams and E. Adams 1991:91; see also Hill and Evans 1972:233). All typologies are classifications, but not all classifications are typologies.

Many analyses of local pipes use an approach similar to the type-variety method (see Sabloff and Smith 1969), using bowl shape as the principal organizing attribute, followed by decoration. For example, Figure 2.3 separates pipes first by clay color, then shape, surface treatment and decorative motif (Pawson 1969). Choosing to emphasize resemblance to standard English bowl forms as opposed to clay working techniques

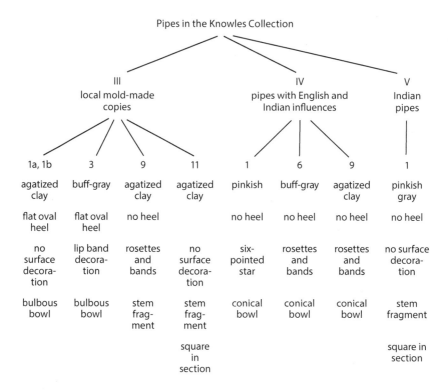

Figure 2.3 This taxonomy of some of the pipes in the Knowles collection is derived from the text of a report describing the pipes (Pawson 1969).

doesn't change the number of groups at the lowest level (Figure 2.4), so the two taxonomies result in the same taxa. However, they have very different implications for the relationships *among* the taxa, because of the order in which the variables are considered. This is what is meant by "hierarchy" in taxonomies. Pawson's original system (Figure 2.3) assumes that bowl shape matters more. The alternate system (Figure 2.4) treats clay as more important. Neither places much stock in the use of identical decorating stamps in complicated patterns (grouping III 9, IV 6, and IV 9) or the unusual presence of square stems (groups III 11 and V 1). How can we know which set of assumptions is correct? We can't. Not unless the groups are *for* some specific purpose or problem. If the problem is identifying manufacturing groups among artifacts recovered

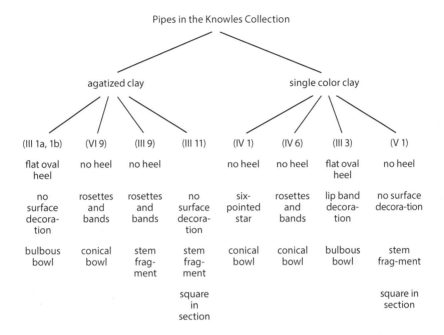

Figure 2.4 This alternative taxonomy of the same pipes in the Knowles collection makes different assumptions about the relative importance of raw materials and form in classifying these artifacts.

from use sites, then which attributes should the analyst choose? The leading candidates for the top spot in the hierarchy are form or shape, decoration, and technique of manufacture.

The Argument for Form

One could argue that, for the pipes, bowl shape should be used as a primary attribute, given how informative form has been in the study of imported pipes. However, the inclusion of hand-built specimens in the local tradition introduces a variability not seen among the imported (mostly mold-made) pipes, which have been so exhaustively studied. Attempts (for example, Heite 1972; Pawson 1969) to adapt English pipe form categories (for example, Atkinson and Oswald 1969; Oswald 1975) soon revealed that many locally made pipes do not conform to this limited range of shapes. Consequently, archaeologists have added a number of forms more typical of the Chesapeake tradition (for example, Emerson 1988; Henry 1979).

Even so, pipe fragments are seldom complete enough to compare with archetypes. Taxonomic frameworks, which followed the type-variety method in using form as a foundational variable, have led local pipe researchers to select against highly fragmented and undecorated specimens, the result being that analyses are based on samples that are a tiny, non-representative fraction of the original assemblage. So while such samples are useful for other projects—such as studying stylistic change over time, or characterizing regional traditions—they are not useful proxies for living "populations" of pipes. Specimens that are complete enough to identify using traditional taxonomic criteria are not necessarily representative of the assemblages from which they are drawn (Agbe-Davies 2004a).

The Argument for Decoration

Analysts also use surface decoration as a primary characteristic to distinguish one class from another. Decoration has been useful in identifying social relationships among artisans (see Deetz 1965; Lathrap 1983). However, decoration is not necessarily the most, or the only, feature of an artifact to be shaped by social learning (culture). And furthermore, like the case for completely fragmented specimens just discussed, when decorated and undecorated pipes are compared, it is apparent that the decorated specimens are not representative of the entire population, either. For example, out of all the fragments with bore diameters—the most commonly occurring measurable dimension—approximately one fifth exhibit decoration. The bores of decorated fragments are slightly, but significantly, smaller (Agbe-Davies 2006).[3] The subset of decorated pipes does resemble the overall assemblage in terms of some of the technological features described later in this chapter, for example bowl forming techniques and the presence of multiple bores. But for other technological attributes, such as the configuration of the firing core, or surface treatment, decorated pipes are not representative of the variation present in the greater assemblage.[4] Analyses relying primarily on decorative aspects and/or complete specimens may exaggerate the importance of rare variants, mask the presence of other variants, and misunderstand relations among them.

Form and surface decoration also intersect in problematic ways because completeness biases samples of pipes. It is true that bowls and bowl fragments are the most likely elements of a pipe to exhibit decoration and easily differentiated formal variation (that is, bowl shape). However, the tools used most commonly to decorate complete bowl fragments

Figure 2.5 These two pipe stems, both from Port Anne, show the use of two distinct tools to create a dentate decoration. On the left is a design created using tool 1; on the right, a design created using tool 4.

are not the same as those for all decorated pipe fragments, nor do they occur in similar proportions. For example, a comparison of two plantations included in this study (Page and Green Spring) shows that twenty-five of the twenty-six individually identifiable tools used to create decorations were observed on the partial fragments, but only nine of the twenty-six were observed in the much smaller sample of fragments counted as "complete" bowls. More damningly, the individual decorative tools occur in different ratios than among more complete specimens. So, of the two most common tools (1 and 4),[5] tool 1 dominates the Page assemblage, and tool 4 is most common among the population from Green Spring (Figure 2.5). When fragmented specimens are omitted, the pattern is reversed—1 is more

Tool ID number	Proportion of complete decorated pipes	Tool ID number	Proportion of all decorated fragments
3	25%	3	15%
20	25%	13	14%
13	17%	7	11%
		14	11%

Table 2.2 The prevalence of individual tools used to decorate pipes changes depending on whether one is examining only complete pipes (*left*) or all decorated pipe fragments (*right*).

common than 4 at Green Spring, and 4 is more common than 1 at Page. The difference between the bowls and the fragments is even more striking when one examines the remaining decorative repertoire that remains after the dentate-imparting tools are excluded (see Table 2.2). Artifacts that are complete enough to be identified by form do not adequately represent the range or frequency of other attributes, calling into question any typology using only fragments for which form can be determined.

The Argument for Technology

We cannot assume that decorative attributes will be the only ones that will distinguish one group from another or one person from another. In fact, a number of studies suggest otherwise (for example, Stark 1999 and contributions to Hill and Gunn 1977). The proverbial "ways to skin a cat" are often socially learned, engendering similarity in the efforts of members of a social group. Other nuances in the manner of skinning cats can be learned through experience or creatively developed and may distinguish individuals from one another. Turning away from cats, there is more than one way to make a pipe, which goes part way to explaining why even simplistic associations between social groups and artifact styles sometimes hold up (Sackett 1990:33). However, we might argue that technological style is more often a product of distinctive motor habits, specialization, routinization, and individual quirks than generic forms (which are inherently limited) and decoration (which, while infinitely variable, is easily imitated).

So styles of *form*, *decoration*, and *technology* may be useful for identifying the influence of particular pipemaking traditions. The presence or absence of particular styles may indicate influences shaping the pipemakers' repertoires. However, none of these styles on its own is entirely without problems if the aim is to describe assemblages of actual pipe fragments. Furthermore, none seems to recommend itself as having hierarchical priority over the others. Paradigmatic classification does not require such a determination.

Shifting to Paradigms

A paradigmatic classification has no ordering of divisions from greater to lesser, as a taxonomic typology does. In a paradigmatic classification, each attribute included is of the same order of magnitude. It eliminates the ambiguity found in taxonomies in which decisions about which attributes out-rank others pre-determine the relationships among the different taxa. Still, the method is less commonly applied to locally made pipes than a taxonomic approach. Paradigmatic classifications allow the researcher to experiment with interesting combinations of form, decoration, and technology.

Form + Technology

Henry used a paradigmatic strategy in her landmark study of locally made pipes from the St. John's site in Maryland. She found, among other discoveries, that the shape of a pipe bowl coincides with the basic manufacturing technique: whether a pipe had been made in a mold or shaped by hand (Henry 1976:33–34; 1979:20). Similarly, the pipes I studied showed mold scars to be significantly and strongly associated with certain bowl shapes.[6] Because paradigmatic analysis associates modes with other modes, rather than sorting fragments into types, the characteristics of the incomplete bowls could be associated with mold manufacture. For example, among the pipe fragments I studied, certain bowl base forms (square heel, "pseudospur") tended to occur with either mold-made or free-form bowl shapes.[7] As with the bowl shapes, bowl base variants were significantly associated with the presence of mold scars.[8] The concordance between bowl base, bowl form, and manufacturing technique supports the argument that these individual characteristics reflect important differences among pipes that can be traced across and through assemblages, not so incidentally underwriting the turn to modal analyses in the coming chapters.

Form + Decoration

Another paradigmatic association that Henry observed in the St. John's collection was between decoration and bowl shape: the decorations that appeared on mold-made shapes did not occur on "handmade" shapes and vice versa (Henry 1976:41–43; 1979:20,31:Table 2). Subsequent research has confirmed this tendency (for example, Emerson 1988; Monroe 2002). Paradigmatic analysis of the pipes from in and around Jamestown confirms the association between specific bowl profile shapes and decorative motifs (Henry 1979; Monroe 2002). In other words, it revealed classes defined by adjunct style. In fact, it is possible to recognize associations between a specific decorative tool or motif and one particular bowl form. However, although form and technology go together, and form and decoration go together, form, decoration, and technology do not predict for each other. For example, the association between decoration using dentate lines or bands at the juncture between the stem and bowl and "molded" rather than "handmade" bowl shapes can be recognized simply by casual review of the collection, but the association is not exclusive; the motif is just as likely to be found on either kind of bowl.[9] Fortunately, decoration is not the only kind of style at our disposal.

The *location* of decoration, on the other hand, is closely associated with distinctions between mold-made and handmade shapes. "Molded" shapes are likely to be decorated at the lip, possibly at the juncture with the stem, or on the heel. The handmade bowls can have decoration at the lip, but also encircling, or on the sides, front, or back of the bowl, and very seldom show decoration on the heel, even on the rare occasions that heels occur on handmade shapes (refer back to Table 2.1).[10] Of the ten most common motifs, the handmade shapes are more likely to have triangles rendered in dentate

a

b

c

Figure 2.6 On this pipe bowl from Rich Neck (*a*), the running stamp is used around the lip of the bowl instead of a dentate tool. A more typical use is encircling the stem, as with this fragment from Green Spring (*b*). On the left (*c*) is another stem from Green Spring, clearly an imitation of the decorative motif on the other Green Spring stem, but using very different tools.

lines, or multiple repeating stamps, whereas pipes with molded shapes are associated with a range of what I have termed "running stamps" (Figure 2.6).[11] These are variants on what Luckenbach and Kiser (2006) call the "Bookbinder" technique. Finally, among the fragments studied here, the complete *lack* of decoration occurs with greater frequency for some bowl shapes than others, although the distinction seems to have little to do with the difference between being made in a mold or by hand.

Technological + Decorative "Style"

A technological mindset can be brought to the study of decoration also. For example, there is a significant and strong association between molded or handmade shapes and *the kind of tool* used to render those linear decorations at the juncture between the stem and the bowl (see Figure 2.7 for the parts of a pipe). Likewise, there is a significant and strong association between the type of tool used and whether the pipe has a round heel or none at all (see Tables 2.3a and b). These paradigmatic tendencies anticipate the modal analyses in which characteristics such as bowl shape and tool type and round heel presence/absence are used *separately* and sequentially. This attribute—rather than object-centered process—allows more fragments to be included in the site-to-site comparison. If the attributes are redundant, as the paradigmatic classification suggests, modal analysis will capture the variation that statistical comparisons of paradigmatic classes cannot always verify.

Such analyses can be extended beyond just one "type" of pipe (as defined by the distinctive placement of dentate decoration). I found that, more generally, the particular dentate tool used is associated with other pipe making decisions. So as much as the decorative motif itself,

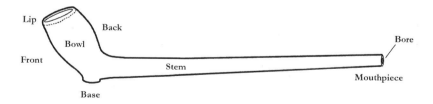

Figure 2.7 None of the artifacts included in this study is as complete as the pipe shown here. The labeled parts correspond to the terms used throughout the text. *Illustration by J. Eric Deetz.*

a

Tool	Round/indeterminate heel	None
1	10	71
4	80	41
14	3	6

b

Tool	Handmade	Mold-made
1	17	1
4	12	16
14	2	1

Table 2.3 Some decorative attributes are strongly associated with one another. For example, pipe makers used several different kinds of tools to create dentate decoration. Looking at pipes decorated like the ones shown in Figure 2.5, marks from any given tool are associated with the kind of base the pipemaker chose and how the pipe itself was formed. The statistical significance of these associations was tested using the chi-square technique ($x^2 = 57.4$, df = 2, p <0.001 and $x^2 = 12.6$, df = 2, p =0.002).

the specific tool used to impart the characteristic dotted lines of a dentate design can reveal manufacturing styles. In one case, the tool used co-varied not with bowl form, but with surface treatment techniques. Pipe fragments on which the dentate tool left regularly spaced, relatively large (1–1.5 mm), square impressions (tool 4) tended to be smoothed, whereas decorations that had been executed with an implement with smaller (< 1 mm) and more rounded and irregular teeth (tool 1) tended to be burnished. The different dentate tools are also associated with other specific forming and finishing technologies (see Tables 2.4a, b, and c), demonstrating connections among the various modes.

Technology + Technology

Among the more interesting classes based on technological attributes are those that speak to specialized production. For example, I wanted to know if there were any relationships between modes representing firing conditions and mold manufacture. Fabric color, firing clouds, and the

a

Mold scar	1	4	14
absent	465	204	39
present	20	82	4

b

Bowl group	1	4	14
handmade	40	22	3
mold-made	9	23	1

c

Striation type	1	4
burnishing facets	179	123
smoothed particles	15	22

Table 2.4 Different dentate tools are also associated with specific technological styles, even on pipes with different motifs (and therefore, according to some other analyses, different "types"). Again, the significance of the association can be demonstrated using the chi-square technique.

appearance of a fragment's core can all speak to firing conditions; these can be compared against each other and against the presence or absence of mold scars to suggest that some, but not all, Virginian pipemakers used specialized equipment such as kilns, kiln furniture, and molds.

Clay color offers information about firing. Examining the eight most common colors,[12] fragments with higher values (that is, lighter colors) are more likely to have mold scars.[13] However, other characteristics that may be influenced by firing conditions, such as chroma (that is, strength of color) and firing clouds, have no significant association with mold scars. So it seems that pipemakers who used molds may not necessarily have used different firing technologies than those who made pipes without molds.

Interestingly, firing clouds are correlated with certain core configurations, but not with surface color. One possible reason is that color is due to factors besides firing conditions. Another reason is that color correlates with site of excavation. In fact, color is one of the few categories for which grouping sites by neighborhood improves the strength of association between variates and their groups (as discussed in greater detail in Chapter 5).

⋮

In sum, taxonomic and paradigmatic analyses have their place in the study of the early Virginia's clay pipes. But critical examination reveals that associations among attributes, even when statistically significant, do not produce mutually exclusive categories or "types." Furthermore, sites seldom yield sufficient artifacts to analyze for intersite comparison, once sorted into such classes. Finally, though this is not a necessary characteristic of the techniques, previous analyses have often relied on form and decorative style, to the exclusion of technological style. Other studies have made assumptions about which sets of variables should be treated as most fundamental.

None of these approaches is incorrect, but they suit neither my questions nor the data at hand. In fact, although associations among attributes are not mutually exclusive—and thus the different attributes and variables cannot be used as proxies for one another—taxonomic and paradigmatic analyses have nevertheless demonstrated that the distribution of modes across objects is not random. And so the preceding forays into other analytical strategies have been essential for laying the foundation for the modal analyses that follow.

Modal analysis is necessary because it is only when the modes are decoupled from each other and examined individually that the variables occur in sufficient numbers to be considered statistically. It is the redundant patterning of the different attributes considered as *modes*, rather than characteristics of *types* or *paradigmatic classes*, that reveals the similarities crossing assemblages and could indicate production and exchange relationships.

Modes and Modal Analyses

The end result of modal analysis is not a single typology. And modal analysis need not replace paradigmatic or taxonomic classification (Read and Russell 1996; Rouse 1971 [1960]). In his discussion of the forms of classification to apply to different archaeological problems, Rouse suggests that "modes are the best unit to use in studying cultural distributions. One may trace their persistence and their relative popularity through time... *or their diffusion from area to area*" (1971 [1960]:119, emphasis added), which is the essence of the present project. Of course, analyses of artifacts alone will not really tell where a ceramic object was made. Many ceramic studies do not link products to an actual source of raw materials, but rather show relationships among artifacts stemming from the production process, so-called "workshop sourcing" (Orton et al. 1993:145). Workshop sourcing works because ceramic objects can be grouped not only based on their source in a common clay bed, but also on the similar processes used by their maker(s) to procure, prepare, and manipulate those raw materials (Chilton 1999; Neff 1993:33; Stark 1999). The goal here is to determine if sets of locally made pipes were made using the same techniques (both technological and decorative), suggesting that the pipes come from a common (group of) producer(s).

Pipes decorated with distinctive tools that I have termed "running stamps" have proved especially useful for understanding the relationships among pipe modes and how these relate to conventional "types." Running stamps appeared in a variety of forms (Figure 2.6a), and the variants can be distinguished easily from each other (unlike some of the more generic tool imprints, such as dentate lines). One of the most common of these stamps has radial motifs alternating with square or lattice-like shapes. This "x&grid" running stamp often occurs in conjunction with other stamped motifs, most notably a floral stamp and a dentate design with elongated "teeth" (Figure 2.6b). The decoration for these pipes extends even to the clay itself. For the pipes with the more delicately crafted x&grid tools, aga-tized clays are significantly and strongly associated with the assorted variants,[14] even though the motifs occur nearly as frequently on non-agatized clay. When x&grid decoration occurs on non-agatized pipe fragments, they are less likely than the agatized fragments to also have the associated floral stamps and less likely to show the decoration anywhere other than the lip of the pipe bowl. There is also very little overlap between the specific x&grid tools used on agate bodied fragments and those used on pipes made from a single color of clay.

These pipes illustrate several key points about the methods used in this study. First, they allow us to demonstrate that even a distinctive combination of decorative variables is no guarantee of production by the same maker(s). Fragments with this decorative suite of motifs—the aforementioned "Bookbinder" type (Luckenbach and Kiser 2006)—demonstrate quite clearly that pipe makers could and would imitate designs, even without access to their means of replication.[15] Several pipe fragments—all from the site at Green Spring—bear a version of this combination of motifs, but using a completely different tool kit and without the distinctive agate clays (compare Figure 2.6b and c). Second, although the compound motif *seems* to correspond to a specific bowl shape, by requiring the intersection of multiple modes to identify the category we so reduce the number of examples that we cannot attempt a systematic or statistical comparison with other "types." Finally, these pipes confront us with a conundrum similar to the one presented to students of human biology by the idea of "race." The distinctive stamps that characterize the "type" are actually found more frequently on fragments of other "types." We will see at the end of this chapter the solution that biological anthropologists have developed to address their problem. If we seek an archaeological method that will allow us to use fragments, that doesn't require the intersection of traits, and that will not force us to rely on decoration, but that permits the assessment of technological style as well, we need look no further than modal analysis.

As already noted, modal analysis allows data to be collected on the entire excavated sample, rather than focusing on decorated and more complete specimens. Modal analysis does not require intact objects to establish groups since each mode deals with a single attribute and does not require the co-presence of multiple attributes to create a class. Attributes such as firing cores, fabric composition, and construction techniques are more readily observed from fragments, another reason that modal analysis is well adapted to include technological and manufacturing attributes in addition to form and decoration (Rouse 1939:26, 139–140; 1971 [1960]). The variables included in this study include commonly used characteristics—such as bowl shape—but also the techniques and tools used to form, hollow, and finish said shapes.

This critical systematics requires a recording system in which one may sort the material by one mode and then another. The classes must be defined so that no one attribute implies any other, and there is no judgment about the relationships among objects because of shared characteristics. It is especially important that no shared characteristic be deemed more significant than any other in assessing how similar objects are to one another (Agbe-Davies 2004b).[16] The overarching principle at work may be thought of as a kind of modular coding of pipe variables, keeping different variables as separate as possible. This design is a function of the research questions, the quantity of material sampled, and the method of analysis.

Characteristics of Local Pipes: A Range of Nominal Variability

For this study, I collected information on a wide range of variables (Agbe-Davies 2004b), but here the emphasis is on variables that help to indicate production or technological style. The attributes and variables described in this section follow the progression suggested by Rouse (1971 [1960]): materials; techniques of manufacture; shape; decoration; and use.[17] This progression organizes an overview of the characteristics observed in the nearly 5000 pipe fragments examined for this study juxtaposed with first-hand accounts of pipemaking during that era. Together, they establish the modes analyzed in Chapters 3–5 and the pipemaking actions that each mode represents. This chapter focuses on the tasks; Chapter 5 delves more deeply into the social organization of labor. The descriptions are almost exclusively from European sources. Pipemaking makes very little mark in the written record of the colonies. Likewise, pipemaking continued among the Native people of Virginia (Bollwerk 2012), but without much impact on the archival record (for exceptions, see Mouer et al. 1999).

Materials

Only recently have archaeologists started studying the material properties of locally made pipes, after long maintaining that the homogeneity of the region's clays or modern chemical contamination would mask distinctive clay signatures (for example, Emerson 1988: 45–46). Using petrography, archaeologists have found that the red clay pipes from early colonial New England were made locally, rather than being centrally produced or even coming from the Chesapeake (Capone and Downs 2004). Archaeological chemistry reveals that during the pre-contact period in the Middle Atlantic, decorative motifs cross-cut compositional groups *and* cultural groups (Bollwerk 2012). My study uses simpler, indirect evidence to study the choices made in selecting and manipulating clay.

Little is known about techniques for procuring and preparing pipe clay in the early Virginia colony. Emerson cites the example of John Bennett, called to court in Charles City County, Virginia, for collecting clay on a Sunday, in violation of the Sabbath (1988:167). In Maryland, Luckenbach has found what appear to be prepared blocks of clay and clear evidence that Emanuel Drue skillfully manipulated his materials and firing processes to produce pipes in a wide variety of colors (Luckenbach et al. 2002:54–55; Luckenbach and Kiser 2006).

English pipemakers began with white-firing ball clays[18] like those of Kent, Devon, and Dorset (Oswald 1975:11). The clay was often shipped considerable distances, as manufacturing centers weren't necessarily near suitable clay beds. The sole seventeenth-century text (Houghton 1693/4 in Walker 1977) to discuss English pipe manufacturing states that clay was dug out of the ground in square blocks weighing about half a hundred-weight and sold in that form. The pipe maker would have the clay dried and ground, then soaked in water, then dried again to a pasty consistency, and finally beaten to create a homogeneous mass. The process removed impurities and undesirable inclusions. At this point, the clay could be used or set aside to macerate for a period of several months.

So attributes like texture can indicate more labor-intensive processing of the clay, a higher quality clay source, or both. With ceramic objects, it is often not possible to determine whether inclusions have been deliberately introduced to a clay matrix. Furthermore, the pipes are almost entirely made of fine-grained clays. Therefore, relative fineness or coarseness and inclusions are used in the ensuing analysis, primarily in conjunction with other variables, to characterize the clay (as recommended in Shepard 1956:118,164).

Techniques of Manufacture

"Techniques of manufacture" is used here in Rouse's sense to indicate attributes having to do with the manner of shaping, finishing, and firing pipes. Given the problem focus on who controlled the production and distribution of locally made pipes, and in light of the preceding discussion about styles of technology, these manufacturing techniques form the majority of the modes analyzed.

Molding

Archaeologists frequently report finding locally made pipes manufactured using only hand tools, rather than molds. In this collection, however, very few bowls were made in the manner of "pinch pots," using only the hands and fingers to form the pipe. Likewise, few pipes exhibit the kind of eccentric marks, possibly even with visible gouges, that would indicate carving with a blade.[19] Such evidence would be in the form of surfaces with flat planes and parallel striations from dragged inclusions, or cut marks.

Many pipemakers in Virginia apparently had knowledge of techniques and access to specialized tools like those used across the Atlantic. In the European pipe industry, workers rolled the clay into blanks, which they then set aside until they judged the blanks dry enough to mold. Just prior to insertion into the mold, a wire lubricated with oil would be inserted into the smaller end of the blank, stopping just short of the fatter end, which was to become the bowl. This step took some skill, as one had to keep from piercing the sides of the stem with the wire. Some pipes in the sample had been bored more than once in an effort to place the bore in the correct location, and not pierce the side of the stem accidentally. The fact that some pipe stems had to be pierced more than one time might be used, in the aggregate, to point to more- and less-proficient workshops. One might also think of this variable in terms of makers with less expertise and/or who execute fewer repetitions of this difficult task.

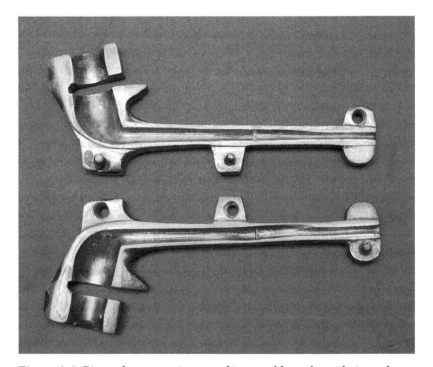

Figure 2.8 Pipemakers sometimes used iron molds to shape their products. This mold dates to the nineteenth, or possibly even twentieth century. Note the shape of the bowl compared with the imported pipes shown in Figure 1.4.

In the seventeenth-century industry, most molds were of brass, although some inventories and apprenticeship agreements describe molds of "tinn," and by the eighteenth century, most molds were of iron (Figure 2.8).[20] Randale Holme's 1688 *The Academy of Armoury* includes the tools of the tobacco pipemaker's craft. His illustration of a mold (see Figure 2.9) depicts "the one halfe of a Pipe Mould, the other side being clapt to it, with the clay betweene them makes the perfect form of the pipe according to the fashion and proportion of the mould, for they haue seuerall Molds for seuerall fashions" (Alcock and Cox 2000:Book III Chapter 21 section 4). Molders could use their tools to impart impressed or relief decoration, as well as marks that identified the products of different master pipemakers. The mold could be mounted in a device that Holme called a pipemaker's screw "by which the Molds are screwed together and the mouth of the pipe made all at a time, as it were" (Holme 1688, cited in Oswald 1975:16). He is describing a vise that simultaneously clamps the halves of the mold together and braces it for the insertion of an attached stopper that hollows out the bowl ("e" in Figure 2.9). Only a few of the Virginia-made pipe fragments show evidence of interior vertical scraping suggesting the use

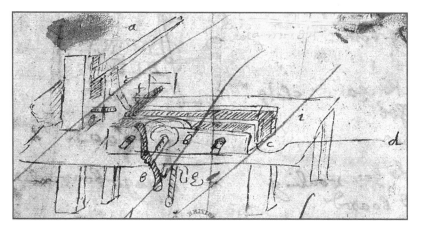

Figure 2.9 This seventeenth-century illustration of a pipe mold shows how it could be used with a larger device which clamps the two halves of the mold together and includes a tool for hollowing out the bowl. *Illustration from Alcock and Cox 2000. Copyright the British Library Board.*

of this kind of stopper. Most have bowls with identifiable traces of hollowing out using a twisting or rotating/reaming motion as with the type of tool marked "S" in Figure 2.10. The use of a separate bowl-forming tool was more common among continental European pipemakers of the eighteenth century (Peacy 1996:10.1; Walker 1977:84–85, 97). The device could be held in the hand and forced into the bowl; a handle allowed the worker to twist the stopper before removal.[21] A distinct minority of the pipe bowls had been cut or hollowed out using a blade. After hollowing out the bowl, by whatever means, the wire used to make the stem hole or bore could be pushed the remainder of the way into the bowl to open the pathway for smoke.

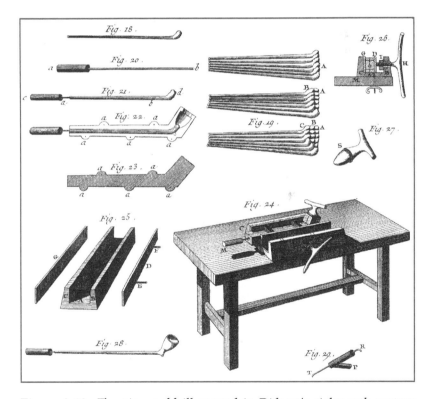

Figure 2.10 The pipe mold illustrated in Diderot's eighteenth-century encyclopedia depicts a continental apparatus. Note how the device for hollowing the bowl differs from the seventeenth-century English tool kit. *Supplemental Plate 2, "Art de faire les Pipes" (Diderot and d' Alembert 1777).*

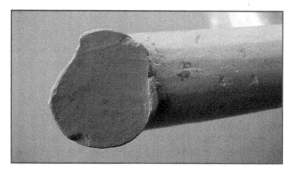

Figure 2.11 The pipemaker who produced the pipe on the left (Green Spring) scraped the mold scar clean away, but did not smooth the heel afterwards. The pipe on the right (Rich Neck) still retains its mold scar, on the lower side of the stem and the front of the bowl, though on the heel the scar is partially obscured by a mark.

"Trimming"

Over 10 percent of the pipe fragments I examined had mold scars. Virginia pipe makers could have removed most of the mold scars from the pipes they produced, so the scars are a conservative measure at best of how many fragments came from mold-made pipes. All mold scars appeared in locations typical of a "vertical-half" mold (Arnold 1977) (as depicted in Figure 2.8). The most common manner of treating a visible mold scar was simply to smooth it down slightly. In some cases it was clear that the maker had used a bladed tool to trim away some of the excess clay prior to, or instead of, smoothing. On some of the pipe fragments nothing was done to eliminate the scar at all, particularly in less visible parts of the pipe. And indeed, the most common locations for the identifiable mold scars are in low-visibility parts of the pipes—on the underside of the bowl and stem. In Figure 2.11, on the right is a pipe heel with the mold scar scraped away. The fragment on the left has only been partially trimmed.

Trimmers did this work with the aid of a tool Holme called a "head scraper," saying that "it is like a knife with a bended point and as if an halfe round nick where broken neere it, or in some the hook end supplying that nick. It is to scrap away all the Mold marks and make the head smooth" (Alcock and Cox 2000: Book III Chapter 21 section 4). With this, a pipe-maker trimmed away the longitudinal seams that would appear on the pipe.

A head scraper could also be used to finish off the lip of the bowl and the mouthpiece. However, most of the artisans whose work appears here seem to have used a tool or jig in order to create a flat, smooth, and uniform lip profile. Some pipe bowl lips even show chattering marks from the rotation of the tool around the pipe bowl. Other pipes appear to have been merely wiped smooth after shaping or simply cut straight across. In some instances, the exterior surface of the lip of the pipe was given a milled pattern. The milling could be done with a "button" that either fit inside the mouth of the pipe to smooth the interior of the bowl or could be attached to a rouletting tool. Otherwise, a milled effect could be imparted with a denticulated knife (Oswald 1975:18–19; Walker 1977:188). The techniques used to trim the mouthpieces identified in this collection were nearly evenly divided among leaving them completely untreated (and therefore slightly rounded), cutting them flat, and cutting followed by smoothing to erase the knife marks.

The great majority of the pipe fragments studied here have a smooth, even slick, surface. The effect was obtained primarily by burnishing at the leather-hard stage (when the clay was mostly dry, just before firing), although some pipes were clearly smoothed while still damp.[22] Historic descriptions of manufacturing note that following trimming, a member of the workshop could further polish the pipe, using a "shanking tool" on the stem and a "burnisher" (described as a highly polished steel with a round end), "rubber," or "trimming smoother" for overall surface treatment. Apparently, the trimming and polishing could be accomplished in as little as six or seven seconds (Walker 1977:122). All of the techniques represented in this assemblage reveal how many specialized pipemaking implements were available in the colony and, simultaneously, that not every pipemaker used them.

Firing

The color of fired clay cannot be used as an indicator of raw clay characteristics, because color depends not just on clay composition, but also on the atmosphere, temperature, and duration of firing. Impurities, primarily iron compounds and carbonaceous material, interact with the characteristics of the clay itself and the firing atmosphere to produce the final color.[23] Color can also be influenced by a range of post-manufacturing factors (Rice 1987:333, 343–345; Shepard 1956:103). Nevertheless, a workshop that regularly uses the same raw materials and subjects them to routinized procedures should produce, in the aggregate, a predictable range of colors for the finished products (Orton et al. 1993:138). The colors of the pipes from the sites in and around Jamestown fit within a narrow range: from light yellowish brown, through light brown and very pale brown, to pink (Munsell Color Company 1975). These are all in the middle of the chromatic range and are not very intense colors. The five most common colors account for 50 percent of the pipe fragments. This generalization makes all the more fascinating the evidence from Swan Cove in Maryland showing that Drue, the pipemaker, deliberately sought out materials and employed techniques that would produce a wide range of colors in his wares (Luckenbach and Cox 2002).

Fired clay is not always a consistent color in cross-section. The fragmentary nature of the artifacts allows a clear section view of the fabric of the pipes. The majority of the fragments show no core at all, indicating that they were fully oxidized. Another quite large proportion has a faint core with diffuse margins, also oxidized. Other fragments have very sharply delineated cores, more typical of ceramics that have been fired in an oxygen-poor environment and then rapidly cooled in the open (Orton et al. 1993:134).

Another clue about firing comes from the fact that nearly one fourth of the pipe fragments bear a *firing cloud*, where the pipe was unintentionally smudged in the process of firing. Firing clouds are generally caused by contact with fuel or hot gasses during the firing process (Orton et al. 1993:223). These are more likely to occur in an open firing setting—where fuel is piled around the ceramics—than during kiln firing, though firing clouds may also be caused by poor draft (low oxidation), overly tight packing of a kiln (Shepard 1956:92), or contact with oily fingers prior to firing.

For the most part, pipes made in Europe were fired in purpose-built kilns, although references to non-specialists (notably tavern keepers and bakers) making pipes, as well as potters producing pipes as a sideline (Walker 1977:183,251), suggest that a specialized structure was not necessary. Excavated examples of seventeenth-century British kilns reveal small (1–1.5 m in diameter) updraft kilns made of brick, ceramic tile, or stone, with the ash pit and flue below the ground surface and a raised firebox and firing chamber, sometimes topped by a chimney. The pipes were fired while placed inside of *muffles*, containers made of fired clay designed to keep kiln products out of direct contact with flames or soot.[24] A firing lasted between five and sixteen hours at temperatures ranging from 850 to 1000 degrees Celsius (Peacy 1996:11.3–11.5; Walker 1977:185).[25]

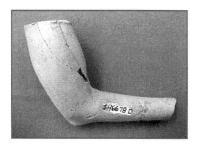

Figure 2.12 Neither a spur, nor a true heel, projections like the one at the base of this pipe (Green Spring) are here called "pseudospurs."

Shape

With Rouse's "shape," we begin to tackle attributes that have formal as well as technological implications. The Virginia-made pipe bowls came in a fairly limited range of shapes: conical, biconical, simple restricted ellipsoid, and cylindrical shapes. Some of the complete pipe bowls in the sample are versions of the forms identified by Henry in her study of locally made pipes from the St. John's site in Maryland (Henry 1976; 1979). The nuances evident in the identification keys developed for imported pipes (see Atkinson and Oswald 1969; Oswald 1975) are more difficult to discern.[26] Still, nearly 50 percent of the relatively complete bowls are shapes commonly produced in European molds, and the three most common bowl shapes account for more than half of the identifiable bowls.

A majority of the pipe bowls were heeless. Those with heels primarily had round ones, as was traditional in the European pipe-making industry, though there were a limited number of square-heeled pipes as well. A handful of pipe bases have a small protuberance that is neither a heel nor the kind of spur usually seen on industrially-produced ball clay pipes, here called a "pseudospur" (Figure 2.12).

Decoration

"Shape" and "decoration" are a bit hard to separate. Here, the latter term applies only to alterations to the surface of a pipe, rather than decorative forms. In this sense, over one fifth of the pipe fragments studied bear some evidence of decoration. The most common forms of decoration are linear motifs, abstract groupings of a single small stamp impressed repeatedly into the clay, carved facets, the "running stamps" described earlier in this chapter—which apparently were set into a wheel that was then rolled over the pipe surface—and geometric shapes such as triangles or diamonds rendered in incised or impressed lines. Decoration appeared most frequently at the juncture of the stem and bowl and encircling either the bowl (particularly at the lip) or the stem. A notable number of motifs were centered on the back or the front of the pipe bowl, or appeared along the stem. The vast majority of the motifs were rendered with toothed implements creating a dotted line. Other common methods included incising with a fine point or blade, or using a small circular stamp, often in the shape of an "O," asterisk, or flower.

Although archaeologists have reflected at length on the significance of white slip on locally made pipes (Mouer et al. 1999:102; Emerson 1988:131–132), few of the specimens studied here show any white slip or paint in recessed areas where decoration had been incised or impressed. Analyses have proceeded from the premise that the white pigment was intended as infill, rather than being the remnants of an overall white wash. White infill does not typically occur on imported ball clay pipes, although white slip was observed on a few imported pipes encountered in the course of this study.

In the European pipe tradition, pipes were sometimes glazed (DAACS 2014). However, the few occurrences of glaze on these locally made pipes seem to be accidental rather than intentional. On several specimens, glaze even occurred on the fractured end of broken pipes. It is possible that these artifacts found a second use as kiln props in the firing of glazed ceramic vessels.

Use

There are two ways to explore "use" with this dataset—by considering which pipes were never usable because of some manufacturing flaw, and by looking for alterations to the pipes indicating that they *had* been used. Rice (1987:179–180) uses the term *waster* to mean ceramics damaged in the firing process, but here I include any trait that renders a clay pipe unusable or otherwise defective. Such fragments are held to be indicative of manufacturing sites because there is little practical motivation to transport goods that are unusable. A few of the pipes represented here appear to have been mis-handled prior to firing. In some cases, the stem or bowl was breached as the pipemaker created the stem bore. Some pipes were pinched or otherwise malformed from being grasped too tightly or moved before they were sufficiently dry. Such traces are particularly noticeable in cases where the pipe maker has left fingerprints in the clay. However, only a very few fragments in the collection could reasonably be argued to be truly "wasters"—totally unusable pipes that would have been discarded immediately after making. Most of these simply have incomplete bores, rendering them useless for smoking.

Two other variables—"post-manufacturing modification" and "smoked"—are the inverse of wasters insofar as they demonstrate that the pipe in question was useable. Post-manufacturing modification can offer some details about *how* the pipes were used, and their disposal as well. Attributes include eroded/worn surfaces, tooth wear, and reshaped or repaired mouthpieces. Fragments that are charred on the interior surface of the bowl, or appear to have charred material still in the bowl, are considered "smoked." Only a small proportion of pipe fragments show clear evidence of smoking. Many more are highly abraded, or have some tooth-wear on the stem.

◌

In ensuing chapters, the modes that reflect pipemakers decisions about materials, techniques of manufacture, shape, and decoration will demonstrate heterogeneity within the local pipe tradition, both within and across plantations. They will reveal the nature of the relationship between those plantations and the capital city at Jamestown. Modal analysis allows us to argue that, unlike other goods, pipe production and distribution fell outside the purview of land- and labor-owning elites. Methods that emphasize category over attribute make the comparisons necessary to support these arguments impossible. Why do we continue to use such methods; where do they come from?

Linnaeus's Legacy

These questions about how and why to create categories, and what they ultimately mean, have specific local significance to be sure, but they also resonate well beyond Virginia and its archaeology. As this chapter has shown, the distinct ways that archaeologists can organize artifacts (taxonomy, paradigmatic classification, and modal analysis) have very different requirements, strengths, and results, but archaeologists do not always make clear distinctions among them. For example, we have seen in the local pipe literature a tendency to refer to all analytical units as "types" and all groupings as "typologies." Another set of difficulties (and much of the "typological debate" in archaeology as a whole) is rooted in the conflation of empirical units (things) with theoretical or conceptual units (analytical tools) (Dunnell 1971a; 1986:152–154). Both of these challenges are a legacy of archaeology's borrowing from the biological sciences. Specifically, we model our treatment of artifacts on the species concept (Brew 1971 [1946]) and its associated classification system: Linnaean taxonomy.

Recall that taxonomic classification includes two key assumptions. First, higher order units encompass lower order ones. For example, the genus *Nicotiana* encompasses several species, including *N. rustica* and *N. tabacum*. Second, members of a taxon are more similar to each other than to members of another taxon of the same rank. For example, tobacco and jalapeño (both family *Solanaceae*) are more similar to each other than either is to a pumpkin (family: *Cucurbitaceae*). These ideas, developed for understanding the biological characteristics of living species, have been taken up by anthropologists interested in cultural phenomena. For example, Pawson's taxonomy (a fragment is mapped out in Figure 2.3) implies that pipes categorized as III 9 are more like III 3s than they are like IV 9s. This matters because significant archaeological faith is invested in the idea that "'typological similarity is an indicator of cultural relatedness'" (Willey 1953:363, cited in O'Brien and Lyman 2003), even if the unit of "culture" is a workshop rather than an ethnic group. We see this line of reasoning shaping the effort to associate locally made pipes with "parent" traditions rooted in Native North America or Africa. Not coincidentally, these ideas about categories and their relations *also* underpinned generations of anthropological efforts to understand biological variation among humans, variations whose salience emerged at a particular historical moment, and have come to be called "race."

In *Race Is a Four-Letter Word: The Genesis of the Concept*, Brace argues that prior to the Renaissance, Western observers—philosophers, historians, scientists, explorers, and artists—treated human difference as graded, rather than categorical (2005:21–29). But that view changed during the age of exploration and colonization that followed, and in the definitive tenth edition of *Systema Naturae*, Linnaeus himself divided the species *Homo sapiens* into several varieties: *Homo sapiens ferus; H. sapiens americanus; H. sapiens europaeus; H. sapiens asiaticus;* and *H. sapiens afer*. With the exception of the first ("Wild Man"), each variety corresponded to a geographical unit. The distinguishing attributes included complexion, hair color and texture, eye color, facial features and expression, temperament, clothing style, and political structure. The varieties are all encompassed within *Homo sapiens*, but members of one category were understood to be more similar to each other than to members of another category. While neither the categories nor the criteria originated with him, Linneaus's *system* has shaped the means by which the diversity of human characteristics could be understood.

Centuries of scientific effort have been expended on the attempt to perfect the categorization of humanity into racial groups. Scientists and philosophers endeavored, for example, to determine the correct number of classes and identify which attributes to use. Less attention was paid to the problems of how to establish a class, or what a class was, or if classes existed. Leaving aside the fact that many measureable forms of variation are shaped by environmental factors as well as heredity (Boas 1912; 1963), human biological variation does not behave typologically. If we start, as many have, from the groups that we "know" to exist, we find that they can contain as much variability within the group as between groups. If we start from the characteristics, we see that some traits cluster together, but groups created using one set of variables cannot be expected to corral another set of variables. This non-correspondence of traits has led many researchers interested in human variation to abandon the quest to characterize individuals (and groups) as belonging to (or comprising) definable varieties (that is, races) and instead to study *clines* or the graded variations of measureable characteristics within a population. Clines, like modes, are examined one at a time. No attribute (for example, facial features) is made to stand in for any other (hair color and texture, or temperament). Biological anthropologists have abandoned biological races, not as a political gesture, but because the concept often doesn't help us understand anything but "race" itself. The groups that our intuition (ideology [culture]) tells us are so desperately important to define, delimit, and examine serve only as impediments to our larger understanding (Livingstone 1962).

I am making a similar argument with respect to the pipes. To paraphrase Livingstone, "There are no types, there are only modes."[27] The analyses in the following chapters examine the distribution of individual variables, unlike previous work on locally made pipes that emphasized recognizing co-occurring attributes, identifying these as "types" and then, perhaps, examining their distribution. This typical approach works, to a point, if one uses a limited number of attributes and/or one presumes the nature of the relationships among them. Bowl shape (usually treated as a higher order variable) and decorative style (a lower order variable) are useful for characterizing a tradition, looking at change over time, or decoding symbolic meanings from the pipes, but aren't much help in investigations of technological styles with an eye towards identifying exchange relationships. "More rather than fewer classifications, different classifications, always new classifications, to meet new needs…"

This detour into races and their classification has another purpose. While the race concept was refined in scientific circles in Europe, the Americas were its crucible and testing ground. As Chapter 6 explores in more detail, Virginia in particular has been held up as an important site for the practical development of an ideology that undergirded colonialism, racial slavery, and white supremacy (Haney López 1995; Morgan 1975; Parent 2003), the consequences of which are still felt worldwide.

So, no, this is definitely not a pipe.

"The Subberbs of James Cittie"
Chapter 3

All he wanted, George Burley claimed, was a smoke. He went into the kitchen for a light, when

> on a sudden I heard a combustion behind mee in the house & turning my self saw Mr Brownings Taylor John Mecarteye & Mrs. Vaulx's Negro all in a heap on the Ground together, & with that I putt up my Pipe & layd hold of the first I could, & that happned to bee the Negro & itt was as much as I could doe to keep him off of Jno Macartie but at last he burst out of the dore from mee, & tore my shirt sleeve half of I went forth into the yard & there was Jno Macartie standing & Mr Brownings Tayler lyeing on the Ground. (York DOW 1634:6:363)

The incident took place in the fall of 1681 at the plantation of Mrs. Elisheba Vaulx,[1] and is documented in the Orders of York County (York DOW 1681:360–364). I use the York County records here, and again in Chapter 6, because even though the plantations in this study are located

Tobacco, Pipes, and Race in Colonial Virginia: Little Tubes of Mighty Power
by Anna S. Agbe-Davies, 71–106. © 2015 Left Coast Press, Inc. All rights reserved.

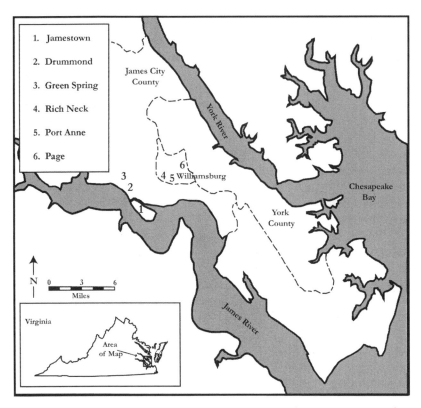

1. Jamestown
2. Drummond
3. Green Spring
4. Rich Neck
5. Port Anne
6. Page

Figure 3.1 The plantation sites included in this study are concentrated at the upper end of James City County, which shares the James-York Peninsula with York County. They are near the seventeenth-century capital at Jamestown and the eighteenth-century capital at Williamsburg. *Illustration by J. Eric Deetz adapted from Agbe-Davies 2010.*

in James City County and the City of Williamsburg (see Figure 3.1), the records of York (unlike those of James City and many other Virginia counties) survived the American Civil War.[2] In any event, the details of this particular story shed considerable light on the individuals who peopled Virginia's plantations, as well as on their relationships with each other and their movements across the landscape.

We have no testimony from any of the three principals: "Taylor" (alias Peter Wells), John Macarty, and "Mrs. Vaulx's Negro" (a man named Frank). However, the outline of what happened can be pieced together from the somewhat contradictory accounts of eight witnesses with varying degrees of knowledge of, and involvement in, the episode. The whole mess had started the night before when Frank, on an errand to speak to Macarty, found him socializing at the plantation of Edward Thomas. Thomas (obviously a landowner) and Macarty (another free man) "told the said Frank the Negro that they were not company for Negroes, soe Frank coming downe somewhat late that Night declared if John Macartey came downe the next day hee would fight with him."

The next day, Macarty visited Vaulx's plantation, drinking with a company that included Burley and three other free men. It was then that Frank somehow got Wells, a servant indentured to Humphrey Browning, involved. Macarty and Wells exchanged heated words.[3] One witness claimed that Wells ended with a curse, "God Damne Humphrey Browning & you [Macarty], for hee [Wells] said hee was as good a Man as Humphrey Browning." Accounts vary over who struck the first blow, and whether anyone tried to diffuse the situation. Wells was grievously injured—the doctor who examined him testified that he would not be able to work for several months. After Wells was carried away and Macarty persuaded to leave, Frank pursued him wielding a fencepost like a club, and they came to blows one last time. Despite the witnesses who described Macarty kicking Wells in the face as he lay on the ground, Macarty was acquitted of the assault charge.

This much *is* clear: Frank and Wells, whether welcome or not, mingled with free people away from their home plantations. Each proclaimed his fitness to associate with, even get drunk with, the owners of plantations far from home. The two appear to have been friends, or at least allies. Macarty, far from secure behind the social barrier of his free status, felt the need to assert explicitly that a "Negro" did not belong with his circle of companions. He furthermore felt compelled to back that claim up with personal force, rather than rely on official sanction. Frank, who "standing in the Kitchin & seeing the People in the Parlour swore (by God) hee would goe to them & make one amongst them," affirmed his common humanity with equal force.

Bondage clearly did not preclude one from visiting other plantations. Social barriers were not a given and needed to be policed. Nevertheless, the outcome of Macarty's hearing shows the consequences for bound laborers who crossed wills with free men. While the sections that follow treat each plantation in isolation, this anecdote reminds us that movement among them was likely frequent and varied. Even people who had no rights—not even to their own time or persons—might be found traveling on official business (as Frank was) or for recreation (which seems to have been what brought Wells into contact with Macarty) or to work (as the injured Wells attempted before Browning ordered him to see the doctor). If Burley's pipe had been made in Virginia, who knows what route it might have taken to get into his hands in Vaulx's kitchen that fateful day…

Plantations and Pipes

Plantations were hubs of economic activity. Men like Frank and Wells—as well as women like Betty Mullin, whom we'll meet later—produced not only tobacco, the colony's cash crop, but other goods as well: pottery; bricks; silk; and indigo. They also produced many of the items needed to maintain a plantation's infrastructure and its residents. What we'd like to know is, were local clay pipes commodities, exchanged across plantation boundaries, or were they made on a plantation primarily for the use of its residents? Either scenario could explain the available documentary record or the traces of production identified at the five plantation sites included in this study (see Table 3.1). However, the pipe fragments themselves can help us to solve this puzzle.

Site name	Number of pipe fragments studied	Features included	Date range
Green Spring	601	Manor house, outbuildings, kiln	ca. 1643–1700
Drummond	862	Outbuilding cellar, kiln, sawpit, possible privy	ca. 1650–1680
Rich Neck	1543	Borrow pit/pond	ca. 1665–1704
Page	160	Manor house, outbuildings, brick kiln, borrow pit	ca. 1662–1720s
Port Anne	517	Borrow pit	ca. 1650–1700

Table 3.1 The pipes in this study came from six structures at Jamestown and five seventeenth-century plantations in James City County and Williamsburg, Virginia. The Jamestown structures are summarized in Chapter 4.

Following from the points made about classification and modes in Chapter 2, it should be clear that the distribution of pipe *attributes* (not kinds of pipes) is key to understanding the pipes' circulation, or lack thereof, in the Virginia colony. If each assemblage were relatively homogeneous and distinctive, then there would be reason to believe that sharing of the pipes was restricted to individual plantations. If the assemblages show internal diversity, however, we then need to ask whether this pattern represents the work of many casual makers or the output of multiple specialists. So, after dealing with the questions of uniformity and representativeness, the analysis of the pipes turns to standardization more generally, and particularly evidence for manufacturing techniques that produce standardized attributes, which would suggest production by specialists.

It is possible that, as was presumed for many years, locally made pipes were *extremely* local, with the pipes being made, used, and discarded all within the same social millieu. If plantations were such closed systems—with pipes neither coming in nor going out—modal analyses will show any plantation assemblage to be internally coherent, and distinct from the others. The documentary record lends some support to this interpretation. The plantation labor regime concentrated much of Virginia's population into sizable "households."[4] An oft-cited account by a European observer explains that the number of dwellings and outbuildings on a plantation meant that "when you come to the home of a person of some means, you think you are entering a fairly large village" (Chinard 1934). The lives of planters, and perhaps their bondspeople as well, were oriented towards these places, resisting provincial policies that sought to centralize tobacco trading, support town building, and promote colonial infrastructure such as frontier forts. The plantation was a unit of sociability and economic activity; it might also have been the unit of pipe production (and consumption). Consider as well the evidence that local pipes were smoked in times of economic distress (Henry 1979; Miller 1991), or by those of lesser means (Emerson 1988; Neiman and King 1999). Might not the very nature of the plantation have encouraged people to make and smoke pipes on site, as it were?

Yet the written record *also* gives some support to the alternative view—that pipes moved well beyond the place where they were made. The evidence shows incessant interaction between plantations. It might consist of bondspeople like Wells and Frank traveling to fulfill their duties or for reasons of their own. One of the factors encouraging elite movement was the density of familial ties across plantations, and the extent to which family relations shaped economic and political cooperation.[5] There is also the much-remarked-upon "visiting" among elites. A planter who, like Governor Berkeley, tried to branch out beyond tobacco might take advantage of those existing networks to profit from the production of other commodities or craft items. Such collaborative ventures leave traces in the written record, as well as the archaeological record.

The plantation sites selected for this study—Green Spring, the Drummond site, Rich Neck, the Page site, and Port Anne—share several important characteristics. First and foremost is their general contemporaneity. One can only expect to identify pipe exchange networks among sites that were actually occupied at the same time. These sites and their features date to the second half of the seventeenth century, a time of social upheaval that was also the beginning of the end for this artifact tradition. Second in importance is the sites' proximity. Several of the plantations are close enough to each other to expect neighborly ties and frequent social interaction among the inhabitants. Even so, as a group, the sites cover a significant portion of upper James City County—the "subberbs" of Jamestown (Rowe letter 1621, quoted in Forman 1940) (Figure 3.1). Third, many of these sites show clear evidence of ceramic manufacture. People at these plantations had the skills and infrastructure, and perhaps the inclination, to produce the pipes studied here. Finally, the owners of the plantations were enmeshed in the dense social web that connected elite inhabitants of late seventeenth-century Jamestown and its surrounds.

Each one of these themes has to do with the *context* of the pipe fragments under examination. In archaeology, as in pragmatism, context is an essential component of meaning. So, the brief site descriptions that follow outline key elite relationships, review the evidence for ceramic manufacture, and establish temporal and spatial context for the pipe fragments. Archaeological and historical evidence combine to give a context that tells us what life was like on these seventeenth-century plantations: the built environment and furnishings among which people lived; the tasks that people undertook; the networks that connected them; and the standpoints that motivated their actions.

Imagine our problem as a classic whodunit. The following overviews of the plantations, their archaeological traces, and their inhabitants establish "means, motive, and opportunity." More importantly, they serve as essential context for our analysis. After introducing the sites, I describe the evidence for uniformity and specialization among the pipes. The analysis shows considerable diversity within individual plantations (low uniformity), but also strong evidence for specialization. The evidence comes in the form of nominal traits—the modes introduced in the preceding chapter—and also a series of measurements that capture the pipes' dimensional variability. These reveal the heterogeneity that characterizes each plantation assemblage, but not in a way that suggests haphazard or amateur production and distribution of pipes. There were, in fact, many ways to make a pipe, and the critical approach to systematics employed here uses the aggregate evidence of thousands of individual choices to reveal the contours of that industry.

Green Spring

Sir William Berkeley, Governor of Virginia, became the first documented owner of Green Spring in the summer of 1643.[6] Whether by accident or design, this plantation, his personal property, abutted the "governor's land"—a 3,000-acre parcel described next under "The Drummond site." Green Spring was Berkeley's primary base of operations during his two tenures as governor, 1642–1652 and 1660–1677. The Council often met at Green Spring instead of the official and semi-official facilities that were sporadically available at Jamestown. The plantation was the symbolic center of the eponymous "Green Spring faction."[7]

Berkeley was a planter as well as a colonial official. However, unlike many of his fellow planters, he saw clearly the perils of building a regional economy on a single export crop. Charles I instructed him to, among other things, promote the cultivation of various staples—hemp, flax, rapeseed, pitch, and tar—as well as more stylish cultivars—grapes for wine-making and silkworms. Berkeley was also to encourage Virginians to plant orchards and produce pig iron. An account from 1649 refers to his acres of tobacco, fruit trees, and his silkworms, while his own writings reveal a man always experimenting with alternatives to tobacco: rice, lumber, flax, and wine, among other schemes (Billings 1996:441–442; Carson 1954:4–5). Based on the archaeological evidence from Green Spring and other sites nearby, he also sponsored pottery production using an on-site kiln (Straube 1995). If any planter were inclined to get involved in pipe production, it would be he.

As a royalist, Berkeley was relieved of the governorship during the interregnum. However, he retained Green Spring and continued as a private planter until his reappointment in 1660. He spent the 1660s attempting to reform the Virginia economy and building the capital at Jamestown. His actions in the 1670s contributed to the disastrous Rebellion described in detail in Chapter 5. After his death, his widow, Lady Frances Culpepper Stephens Berkeley, married Berkeley's cousin and political crony Philip Ludwell, who had recently been made the second most powerful man in the colony by the death of his brother Thomas. The Ludwell couple rented Green Spring to the colony as a temporary residence for subsequent governors. It is not clear how much time Philip and Lady Frances spent there themselves, as they also owned Rich Neck, described below after the Drummond site (Carson 1954:6–7; Smith 1993:2).

The archaeological remains of Green Spring plantation are located roughly three and a half miles north and west of Jamestown. Although early twentieth-century landowner Jesse Dimmick was the first to expose the foundations at Green Spring, the artifacts studied here are from the National Park Service re-excavation, led by archaeologist Louis Caywood (1955:18; Dimmick 1929).[8] The excavators at Green Spring uncovered a substantial dwelling house foundation with at least two periods of construction. The earliest phase consisted of a large square structure with brick and sandstone underpinnings (the "Old Manor House"). The foundation for this structure was overlapped by the foundation for a linear structure running east-west with a small ell to the rear of the western end (the "Mansion House") (Caywood 1957).

In addition to the main house, excavators uncovered two rows of small outbuildings forming a courtyard centered on the Mansion House. To the east of the dwelling house complex, behind the Old Manor House, was the brick foundation of a small pottery kiln (Figure 3.2). Most of the material excavated from the kiln consisted of wasters and kiln furniture. Vessels from the kiln are found throughout the region: red-bodied earthenwares both with and without interior lead glazing (Caywood 1955; Straube 1995). An archaeologist revisiting the kiln in the 1980s made note of the unusual combination of a single firebox plan with a rectangular shape, the latter being more typical of kilns with multiple fire boxes, and also more typical of brick and tile kilns. He further suggested that, given the foundation, the Green Spring kiln may have been an open-topped kiln,[9] as a permanent dome would have been unstable and a temporary dome highly unusual for a rectangular kiln such as this (Smith 1981). As pipe kilns are often open-topped structures, the kiln at Green Spring may have been designed with multiple products in mind.[10]

Figure 3.2 The conventions of scientific reporting mean that today we say that "Louis Caywood excavated a kiln at Green Spring" in much the same way that we might say that William Berkeley built the manor house at Green Spring. Though I have not discovered the name of the man in this picture, I want to make sure that we remember his role in the archaeological endeavor, just as we ought to remember the people who built Berkeley's manor house, and possibly made pipes in that kiln. *Photo number COLOJ11645, Courtesy of Colonial National Historical Park, National Park Service.*

Historical archaeology was in its infancy at the time of the Green Spring excavations. The methods employed have made it difficult to attribute precise dates to distinct phases using archaeological data. The initial construction of the main dwelling house probably dates between 1643, the year of Berkeley's patent, and 1648, when he described the bounty of his plantation to an English pamphleteer. Smith dates the use of the Green Spring kiln to the earliest years of occupation at the site (mid to late 1640s), combining tile production for the dwelling house with small-scale pottery production for the household as a secondary development (Smith 1981:103–104). Sir William and Lady Frances both complained that Green Spring had been ruined in the course of the Rebellion (1676–1677), and she later noted the expense of repairing the house to make it fit for habitation—suggesting a date for the alterations to the Old Manor House. Caywood's attribution of the "Mansion house" to Frances Berkeley's ownership, either on her own or jointly with Philip Ludwell, seems likely.

All of the pipes made of local clays that were recovered from Green Spring during the 1954–1955 excavation season are included in the present study—with the exception of a small group for which no provenience data survive. The pipes were concentrated in a midden deposit behind the Old Manor House. The distribution more likely reflects smoking than making. At this site, unlike those studied by Neiman and King (1999), there is no noticeable difference between the distributions of imported pipes and locally made pipes. Of perhaps even greater significance, there was no concentration of locally made pipes associated with the kiln; only eight local pipe fragments came from the area of that foundation. Furthermore, of the eight pipes from the entire site that could be wasters, based on manner of fracture, incomplete bores, and warping or burning, only one came from the vicinity of the pottery kiln (Agbe-Davies 2001; 2004a).

Though few in number, the Green Spring pipes make a major contribution towards understanding pipe production in seventeenth-century Virginia—both because of the plantation's association with Berkeley and Ludwell and because of the clear signs of mass-production among the pipes. What is not clear, from archaeological evidence, is that whoever made clay vessels and building materials at Green Spring used those skills and facilities to produce tobacco pipes, too. The lack of irrefutable evidence for pipemaking on-site contrasts sharply with what was revealed at the home plantation of Berkeley's neighbor and rival, William Drummond.

The Drummond Site

The site of Drummond's plantation was identified in 1975 by the Virginia Research Center for Archaeology. It is located two miles from Jamestown, along an early road that connected the capital city with "the governor's land," of which Drummond's homesite was a part.[11] The main dwelling house was at the center of a large plantation complex. The local pipes at this site are too numerous to include all of them, so I selected four features from which to draw fragments. All of the features date to the second half of the seventeenth century and reveal traces of pipe manufacture.

A large brick-floored cellar to the north of the main dwelling house[12] included the usual household refuse. Archaeologists recovered coarse utilitarian earthenwares,—but also a range of "Delft" (tin-glazed earthenware) table vessels, such as tea bowls, bowls, and plates; stoneware bottles; table glass; case and wine bottle glass; hinges; and nails. Most of the material dates to the late seventeenth century, though some of the artifacts may

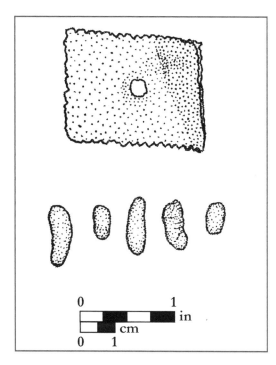

Figure 3.3 The toothed tool shown here could have been used to create a dentate decorative pattern on the surface of some of the pipes recovered from Drummond's plantation. The little lumps of clay produced when a wire is threaded through the stem were accidentally fired, too. *Courtesy of Alain C. Outlaw and Merry A. Outlaw, Wheatland Foundation, Inc., Williamsburg, Virginia*

be early eighteenth century. Cross-mends connecting the lower layers with the upper layers show that the cellar filling episode was rapid rather than gradual. One might say that these objects were all "in circulation" at approximately the same time, meaning that heterogeneity in the pipe assemblage is not likely due to change over time, but represents a diversity of options available at the same time.

The cellar contained an unusually large number of local pipe fragments, and among the finds are objects that appear to have been used in the manufacture of local pipes. Pieces of scrap metal with toothed edges were likely used for creating dentate decoration. Other intriguing finds include marbles made of local clay, miscellaneous fired clay objects, and clay shavings that seem to have come from the trimming and boring of pipes (see Figure 3.3).

In the northeast portion of the site archaeologists found a craft area, with a preponderance of iron-working tools, scrap iron, slag, coal and other industrial materials not commonly found on purely domestic sites. A possible kiln feature dates to approximately 1650–1660. Associated features containing locally made pipes range in date from 1650 to 1710. One of these pits contained burned clay and spalled fragments of ceramic material. Another contained a marble made of local clay. Some of the artifacts found in the kiln feature had domestic functions, but they were not nearly as posh as those from a sawpit at the western edge of the site. Although it too appears to be a work area, much of the fill from the sawpit contained household rubbish—some of it quite fancy for seventeenth-century Virginia, including a Chinese porcelain tea bowl, window and mirror glass, glass tumblers and fragments of a Venetian wine glass or glasses, as well as an iron lock plate. Many artifacts, including imported pipes, point to a date range of 1650–1680. The cross-mend record also suggests that the layers in the pit were rapidly deposited and are roughly contemporaneous.

A small pit, possibly a privy, was located just outside the fence that surrounded the core of the Drummond homelot, to the northeast of the main house. It is also not far from the structure identified as a kitchen. Among the usual domestic debris—drinking glasses, wine and case bottle glass, straight pins, and bones—archaeologists found clay shavings from the manufacture of local pipes, as well as miscellaneous fired clay fragments. The layers span the years 1650–1680. All of this evidence indicates that the associated pipes were all being produced and used at approximately the same time and that any differences were due to factors other than gradual changes in style.

The Virginia Company had established the governor's land in 1618, mandating that 3,000 acres be set aside for the use of the governor of the Virginia colony. Governor Argall selected an area between Jamestown and the Chickahominy River, perhaps envisioning it as a buffer zone between the capital and the wilderness.[13] Initially, tenants were to pay the governor a barrel of Indian corn per 25-acre parcel, per year, with leases running twenty-one years. In 1671, the lease length was extended to ninety-nine years, in part due to campaigning by William Drummond (Forman 1940:480; Nugent 1934:177; Outlaw 1990; the William and Mary Quarterly 1906:288). Drummond was the first tenant to build a homestead on his leasehold, with his first lease commencing in 1648 (Nugent 1934; the William and Mary Quarterly 1898b).[14]

Drummond had the social and political connections that usually went with wealth. He was high sheriff of James City County in the late 1650s and early 1660s. He served as a James City County justice of the peace in the year 1655, and as a burgess (Billings 1976:136; the William and Mary Quarterly 1902:38; the Virginia Magazine of History and Biography 1900:108; 1901:188). In the patent records of the 1660s he is referred to both as a "Mr." and a "Gentleman" (Nugent 1934:400, 403). He was well connected with other elites in the colony, even if those connections were not always harmonious.

While Drummond owned land throughout the colony, including lots in Jamestown,[15] the dwelling at this site was his home. An inventory taken after his execution by Berkeley (more on this later) described it as a "most commodious plantation in James City County were Mr. Drummond lived: with mutch housing and mutch pasture ground" (Washburn 1956:369, citing CO 5/1371 459–460). In a lawsuit his widow, Sarah Drummond, alleged that Berkeley had illegally taken crops (tobacco, corn, wheat, barley) from the fields, as well as hogs, a grindstone, three bedsteads, two cupboards, and a table, to a value of £ 144/10/0. While Berkeley had claimed these were seized for the king's service, Sarah Drummond contended that he had kept them for his own use, and that Lady Frances Berkeley had taken further crops (corn and tobacco) from the leasehold after Berkeley's departure for England in later 1677 (CO 5/1371:523–530, cited in Washburn 1956:371).[16]

Sarah Drummond's petition for restitution was successful. Furthermore, she remained at the property with her children. Eventually their son, also named William Drummond, was reintegrated into the colony's power structure, serving as a messenger for the House of Burgesses and a James City justice of the peace in the 1690s and early 1700s. The land appears to have remained in Drummond hands at least until 1753 (Forman 1940; the William and Mary Quarterly 1905).

Rich Neck

If William Drummond was a thorn in the side of the governor, then Thomas and Philip Ludwell of Rich Neck were among Berkeley's closest allies. Their plantation was partway between Jamestown and "Middle Plantation" (later called Williamsburg). George Menefie, Council member and merchant, held the first patent on Rich Neck, receiving the 1,200 acres in 1635 as his headright for transporting twenty-four people— including "Antho. [an] Eastindian" and "Anth. [a] Turk"—to the colony (Nugent 1934:54). Menefie then sold Rich Neck, almost immediately, to Richard Kemp, secretary of the Virginia colony. Kemp added 840 acres to the property in 1638, claiming headrights for himself and sixteen others, namely "Henry Fenton, Thomas Cooke, Robert Sumers, John How, George Harrison, Francisco, Mingo, Maria, Mathew, Peter, Cosse, old Gereene, Bass, young Peter, Paule, [and] Emmanuell, Negroes" (Nugent

1934:104). Unlike Menefie, Kemp actually lived at Rich Neck, describing himself in his will as Richard Kemp "of Rich Neck," and requesting that he be buried in his orchard (the Virginia Magazine of History and Biography 1894b:174). Brick architecture being rare in the colony at this time, Kemp's four-room dwelling and brick service building speak to his relative wealth and elevated position within society.

After Kemp's death in or about 1650, his widow, Elizabeth Wormley Kemp, married Thomas Lunsford, a royalist who had emigrated in the aftermath of the English Civil War. They lived together at Rich Neck until approximately 1653, at which point records indicate that Elizabeth Wormley Kemp Lunsford was again a widow. She moved to Lancaster County (closer to the Wormleys) and continued to manage her various properties on her own behalf until her marriage to Robert Smith in 1659. The Smiths deeded Rich Neck to Thomas Ludwell in 1665 to cover a debt.

Ludwell had arrived in Virginia in 1646 as a headright of his cousin Governor Sir William Berkeley, a relationship that eased his passage into positions of significant power. Like Richard Kemp, Thomas Ludwell was secretary of state for the colony, achieving that office in 1660. Although Thomas Ludwell owned thousands of acres of land in several different counties, he maintained Rich Neck as his residence. Among the people Thomas Ludwell claimed as headrights was his younger brother Philip, who also rose to prominence, becoming deputy secretary of state by 1677. When Thomas died in 1678, Philip succeeded him as secretary of state for the colony. As a measure of their integration with the colony's power structure, recall that after Berkeley's death, his widow married Philip Ludwell, and the two may have lived at Rich Neck after quitting Green Spring.

Succeeding generations of Ludwells divided themselves among the family's plantations, with Philip Ludwell's son from a previous marriage, also named Philip Ludwell, making his home at Rich Neck, certainly arriving there no later than 1698, when his first child was born at Rich Neck. Based on the location of subsequent births, it seems that that he moved away between 1704 and 1706 (Smith 1993:2). After that, it was never again the family's primary residence. This unusually detailed and complex ownership history shows that, first, except for a brief span, Rich Neck was the home plantation for its seventeenth-century owners. Second, it demonstrates how many individual owners' social networks may need to be considered once we turn (in Chapter 5) to the problem of whether elite networks influenced the exchange of pipes.

Rich Neck is located in what is now the City of Williamsburg.[17] The core of the seventeenth-century plantation complex covers an area smaller than 100 meters square and includes several structures—both brick and post-in-ground—as well as fences, ditches, middens, and a large pond— the feature from which the pipe sample for this study was drawn.[18] The brick manor house began life as a hall and parlor structure. It was renovated at least three times, though, including the addition of rooms at the back, as well as end chimneys to replace the earlier central stack, and also re-roofing with pan tiles. The other major structure at Rich Neck was a brick service building, which probably served as a combination quarter and kitchen.

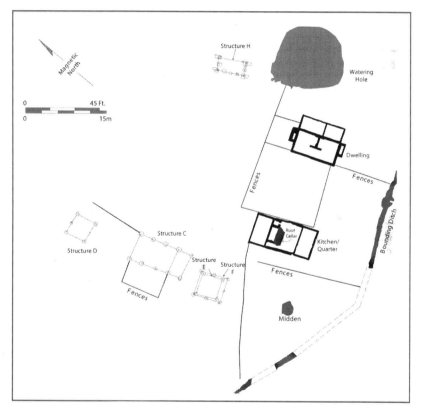

Figure 3.4 The plantation at Rich Neck underwent many transformations between its initial settlement and the abolition of slavery. This plan map shows the core of the plantation during the years that it was owned by Thomas Ludwell. *Illustration adapted from Muraca et al. 2003:47, figure 49. Courtesy of the Colonial Williamsburg Foundation.*

This building was also renovated with matching cellared additions on either side. Other structures were post-in-ground buildings and are interpreted as quarters, service buildings, and storage. Muraca et al. (2003:23) also identified and tested, but did not fully excavate, a brickmaking kiln.

The pond, measuring over fifty feet across and nearly five feet deep in places, was located to the east of the main house. It began as a borrow pit, a source for clay with which to make the bricks used in construction at the site. The lower layers of this feature consist almost entirely of sterile silt. After a period of exposure and use as a water-filled feature, the western portion of the pond was filled with brick rubble that probably derived from the extensive renovations to the two brick buildings. Indeed, the expansion of the manor house *required* the filling episode, which shrank the size of the pond and offered a solid footing for the additions to the building's east side (Figure 3.4).

Construction of the manor house and the kitchen/quarter dates to the Kemp occupation, as do the pond, in its initial incarnation as a borrow pit, and the kiln. The alterations date to Thomas Ludwell's ownership (1665–1677).[19] Some of the renovations may have been to repair damage sustained during Bacon's Rebellion, as Ludwell had made a claim for restitution following the revolt (His Majesties Commissioners 1677). Residents partially filled in the borrow pit/pond around this time. After Philip Ludwell inherited his brother's plantation, he apparently made a few alterations to the plantation's buildings himself.[20] At roughly the same time, the pond was finally filled in completely, situating the pond deposits solidly during the tenures of Thomas and Philip Ludwell, when they were at the height of their powers.

Rich Neck and plantations like it made up the community of Middle Plantation, the loose cluster of households that would ultimately become the City of Williamsburg and Virginia's capital for much of the eighteenth century. At the time of Rich Neck's initial settlement, however, it was still the frontier, approximately four and a half miles to the northeast of the colony's first capital and only seventeenth-century city, Jamestown. On the other side of Middle Plantation, archaeologists with the Colonial Williamsburg Foundation found the homelot of John Page.

Page

Prior to John Page's occupation, the area of the site was a kind of no-man's-land between the English and the Powhatan.[21] In 1634 the English had erected a palisade across the James-York peninsula, from near the mouth of Archer's Hope (College) Creek to Queens Creek, six miles away. Its purpose was both defensive, to protect the down-river settlements from attack, and expansionist, to help make permanent the English invasion of the James-York peninsula. Part of this palisade passed through what later became the Page property. His deed of 1655 gave him "All that One hundred Acres of Land being freehold scituate lying & being upon the Pallizadoe of the middle Plantation...Bounded Northwest upon the Pallyzadoe (York DOW I:159–60, cited in Metz et al. 1998:34).

The brick manor house at the Page site had a cruciform plan, similar to House 5 of Structure 144 at Jamestown (described in Chapter 4). The Page dwelling house, either one-and-a-half or two stories, was constructed entirely of brick with a tile roof. Both the bricks and the tiles were manufactured on the property. Each of the ground floor rooms had a full basement under it, entirely paved with brick and tiles. The house was even adorned by a custom-made brick cartouche with the initials of John Page and his wife Alice Page, along with the date 1662. The other major building on the property was a large structure to the northwest of the manor house. It was also of brick with a tile roof, but without a cellar. Artifacts recovered from the associated trash pit led Metz et al. (1998:65–66) to conclude that it was probably a combination kitchen and quarter for servants and/or slaves. To the east of the main house were two fences enclosing a rear yard. Documents from the period mention other generic "houses," a bread oven, a malt house, and two brick barns.

Brick and tile production facilities located on Page's home-lot yielded building materials not just for the manor house and the substantial brick kitchen/quarter, but also several other structures, at least one in the heart of Middle Plantation, and one other at Jamestown, six and a half miles away (Galucci et al. 1994; Metz et al. 1998:43, 49–50). The archaeological remains of Page's brick and tile works consisted of an irrigation trench, three clay tempering areas, a possible pug mill, as well as one post-in-ground building, a borrow pit, and, of course, the kiln. The rectangular up-draft kiln is a form common to European brickmaking until the eighteenth century. The kiln was semi-permanent, with the arch structure and benches being reused with each firing, but the remainder of the structure would be built of green bricks and dismantled each time the kiln was fired.

Page was the first Englishman to build a dwelling on the property he purchased at Middle Plantation. He arrived in the colony as a young man in 1650, and within five years was a member of the York County House of Burgesses. Later in life, he served as York County sheriff, and was a member of the Bruton Parish vestry. However, Page's greatest honor was an appointment to the Council of State in 1680. During his lifetime, Page owned two other plantations, two brick houses at Jamestown, and several properties in what became downtown Williamsburg. But he also owned shares in several merchant ships (York DOW 1691/2:9:103–107), and he was often described as a merchant, rather than a planter. For a time he acted as a *factor*, or local agent, for London merchant John Jeffries (McCartney 2000b:260–262). The church for Bruton Parish was built on land that he donated. In sum, Page was a well-to-do and powerful man, though not necessarily a member of Governor Berkeley's inner circle (Metz et al. 1998:31–33; Sprinkle 1992:164).

Page's will makes clear that his plantation was home to a number of servants and slaves, as well as his family. He mentions none of these bonded men and women by name, referring only to "servants, slaves, livestock, and household goods" (York DOW 1691/2:9:103). Other documents in the York County records shed more light on the "servants." Page registered the ages of young servants with the county; the information had a bearing on the length of their indenture. Humphrey Davis (aged 16), William Gurant (19), and Sarah Gibson (16) all appeared before the court between 1667 and 1670. "An Indyan boy called Jacke" was only seven in 1672, when Page claimed credit for his transportation into the colony (York DOW 1667:4:154, 157; 1669/70:4:279; 1672:5:27). It is sobering to think of these children and contemplate their likely fate. The rare privilege of having even this scant information about their lives is purely an accident of the location of Page's plantation. As Page's seat was on the "York" side of Williamsburg, the associated records are well-preserved and offer a more detailed account of his household than the others profiled here. Page's will instructed that his home and the associated property (human and otherwise) be shared equally between his wife Alice and son Francis (York DOW 1691/2:9:103). It seems that descendants of John and Alice moved away in 1705, but that the plantation was still owned by their great-grandson—another John Page—when the manor house burned in the late 1720s.

A significant number of the artifacts from the Page site were recovered from the large borrow pit located northeast of the main house, adjacent to the work-yard for the brick and tile kiln. In fact, Metz et al. (1998:72) suggest that the upper layers of fill in the borrow pit date to Bacon's Rebellion and its aftermath, based on the preponderance of architectural hardware and ash. Page *had* claimed damage to his property during the Rebellion, though apparently his house was not completely destroyed at that time. The earliest deposits at the site confirm the manor house construction date suggested by the brick cartouche, indirectly dating the brickworks as well. The many dated window leads may indicate post-Rebellion repairs.[22]

The locally made pipe fragments constituted approximately 10 percent of the entire pipe assemblage (Metz et al. 1998:79). Unlike at Green Spring, at Page the greatest number of locally made pipes *did* come from the areas devoted to ceramic production—the kiln, work-yard, and borrow pit. So Page's brick and tile works is a slightly better candidate for a pipe operation than the kiln at Green Spring. A smaller concentration of the pipes was associated with the kitchen and its transposed midden. The much later manor house cellar fill contained only three fragments of locally made pipes, further evidence that the local manufacture of pipes was really a *seventeenth*-century tradition.

Port Anne

The site at Port Anne is located on a terrace just east of College Creek, known in the seventeenth century as Archer's Hope Creek.[23] The dwelling site appears to have been abandoned in the last quarter of the seventeenth century, and was not reoccupied during the area's "College Landing" heyday, when it was a landing for sea-going commerce via the James River. The small complex of features included several fence lines, trash pits, and a small shed, flanking a large, irregularly shaped borrow pit from which the site's inhabitants mined clay.[24] The small building to the northeast of the borrow pit likely dates to the seventeenth century, based on the use of post-in-ground construction. Its size suggests an outbuilding for a main dwelling that apparently stood to the northwest.[25]

The large borrow pit was the most substantial feature uncovered at Port Anne, measuring approximately twenty-nine feet long, and as wide as eleven feet in some places. Traces of the original seventeenth-century excavators of the pit appear in the form of their shovel marks at the bottom of the feature. Archaeologists have interpreted the feature as a source for clay for making bricks or daub to be used in construction. The fill of the pit was not uniform and seems to consist of rubbish from the nearby dwelling. The filling of the pit occurred rapidly, with artifact fragments from the bottom of the pit mending with fragments from the uppermost layers (Lester and Hendricks 1987). Edwards (1987:34) suggests a filling period of months, as opposed to years, sometime in the middle to later seventeenth century (Brown 1986:119–121).[26] Edwards also notes that over 80 percent of the pipe fragments from the borrow pit were locally made rather than imported pipes—an unusually high ratio.[27] Only pipe fragments from the borrow pit, the feature containing the preponderance of *all* the artifacts recovered from Port Anne, were included here.

The earliest occupation of the site at Port Anne might be associated with Dr. John Pott, of Jamestown (Brown 1986). Pott acted as the colony's physician-general from the time of his arrival in 1621. In addition to his earnings for performing duties for the colony, Pott drew income from the labor of servants that he seated on a leasehold in the governor's land. Though he served briefly on the Council, he was removed for unethical conduct, seemingly a pattern throughout his time in the colony, based on the testimony that survives. Pott got into quarrels with many of his peers, and even his superiors, including Governor Harvey, whom he eventually helped oust from office. He served as deputy governor in 1629 (McCartney 2000b:287, 27–29). Later possible owners of the land at Port Anne include Richard Brewster[28] and William Davis[29] (Edwards 1987:42). However, because of the destruction of Williamsburg and James City County's records, the exact history of the site's ownership is unknown.

The power struggles that characterized Pott's career in the colony were not so unusual for prominent early Virginians. His antagonism with Governor Harvey—a principal associated with several of the Jamestown sites in this study—helps to make Port Anne a particularly interesting case, even beyond the high proportion of local pipes. Once the heterogeneity of the individual plantation assemblages is established, and we have seen how distinctive the Jamestown pipes are compared with the plantation pipes, we will be equipped to tackle the question of whether the networks of elites had any bearing on the distribution of the pipes, suggesting their participation in the enterprise.

$$\therefore$$

People residing on each of these five plantations may have had the means, motive, and opportunity to make clay tobacco pipes. Some households, at first glance, seem more likely candidates than others. Whoever was making pipes and wherever they were based, what the following "first pass" at analysis shows is: First, there were several "schools" of pipemaking—not every maker used the same techniques. Second, pipemakers were quite proficient and some had access not only to specialized ceramic facilities, but to tools and techniques specific to *pipe* making. And finally, these diverse styles were found intermingled at every plantation. The differences within each plantation's assemblage cannot be explained away as the development or evolution of the industry. We are left with either people working side-by-side on the plantations using profoundly different pipemaking strategies (not just different decorations) *or* we must conclude that the pipes from the plantations were not necessarily all made on-site. This makes the problem for the "next pass" one of exchange.

Uniformity, Standardization, and Specialization

A systematic understanding of the pipes and the social relationships they reflect requires the use of three related concepts: *uniformity, standardization,* and *specialization. Uniformity* results from many different processes, which have different implications for the study of production. Social learning, or "culture," is often cited as both a force for continuity of decorative style and an explanation for the very existence of locally made pipes. And it is true that styles—usually taken to mean "decoration"—that are transmitted among members of families, households, or other social groups are responsible for a great deal of the uniformity found within archaeological assemblages (for example, Deetz 1965). So the factor that has historically received the most attention in the local pipe literature is the social learning of distinctive decorative attributes. However, other important processes, including individual motor habits and mass-production methods, also standardize artifacts.

Standardization may be thought of as the relative degree to which products are made to be "the same," or the process by which relative variability among products is reduced (Blackman et al. 1993:61; Eerkens and Bettinger 2001:493).[30] If a limited number of individuals made pipes for use within the same plantation household, the similarities within a plantation assemblage should be greater than those between assemblages, and the pipe fragments from a single site may furthermore differ from the overall population of pipes. We have reason to believe this assertion—regardless of whether or not these pipemakers knew what they were doing—because replication studies reveal uniformity even in objects made by non-specialists. This fact also means that uniformity is not, in and of itself, an indicator of *specialization*, in which some individuals undertake to produce goods for use by others who make none. Specialization can be supported through evidence for uniformity, to be sure, but can also manifest through signs of standardized production that used specialized toolkits and techniques. So, low variability within a site's pipe assemblage could mean that a limited number of makers, casual or specialist, made the pipes. High variability within a site, on the other hand, likely signifies pipe procurement from a number of different "hands."

Ethnoarchaeological and replication studies demonstrate that objects produced by a single individual tend to be more similar than items produced by others. When producing objects, individuals are likely to differ from one another in patterned ways. Their own corpus will be relatively consistent. Some part of this uniformity is due to subconscious motor patterns, particularly fine motor techniques, which are noticeable over the long run (Eerkens 2000, or examples from Hill 1977). It is also true that a task performed repeatedly increases the skill level of the performer, so that if there is any motivation to produce standardized products, that capacity is enhanced. Finally, the methods and goals associated with mass-production—molds or patterns, compact storage and transport options, and other "cost-saving" measures—encourage uniformity as well. So uniformity in general potentially conflates the effects of a small number of makers—skilled or unskilled—with the effect of technologies that facilitate mass production. This problem means that we need to examine variability along multiple attributes and distinguish forms of variability that indicate the use of mass-production strategies from those that reflect variation among individuals from those that suggest varying levels of skill.

So far the discussion has emphasized the need to consider technological as well as decorative variables. In addition to these named or *nominal* traits, we can also use measurements, *metric traits*, to compare pipe fragments and assemblages with one another. Archaeologists have devised a number of techniques for recognizing, quantifying, and comparing relative degrees of uniformity in archaeological assemblages. In some cases, researchers have graphed the relative frequency of various attributes in a sample and inferred from the skew, peakedness, and/or sample means the number of producers represented by the sample (Alden 1982; Espenshade 2001; Rice 1981). Another method is to apply statistical tests[31] to artifact attributes as a way to determine whether the samples are drawn from a single population (that is to say, produced by "the same" individual/workshop/social unit) or several (Hantman and Plog 1982:249). More common in recent years has been the use of the techniques that compare within-sample variability with population variability (for example, the coefficient of variation [CV] and the F test) (Costin 1991:31; Rice 1981:220).

Metric and nominal traits provide complimentary ways to compare artifacts and assemblages. As Rice explains (1981:221; 1984:51), an analysis based on multiple attributes, carefully chosen and distributed among the different classes—stylistic, metric, material—is more robust than one relying on fewer lines of evidence. Such a strategy counteracts the tendency to emphasize certain characteristics of the pipes, specifically decorative style and form, at the expense of others, such as technological attributes and metric traits (Blackman et al. 1993:61; Costin 1991:34; Hantman and Plog 1982:238; Rice 1996:167–181).

In sum, while uniformity can indicate standardization, a hallmark of specialized production for wider use, uniformity alone cannot prove the presence of specialist pipemakers. Internal consistency can occur in isolated groups of producers, regardless of skill level. If isolation were the primary reason for uniformity among the pipe fragments studied here, there should be greater similarity within individual plantation sites than among them. The analysis in Chapter 2 showed that the entire collection does contain a diverse and non-homogeneous group of pipes. Here we investigate the *internal* variability that the sites themselves contain and the extent to which that variability is explained by the association of pipe fragments with their site.

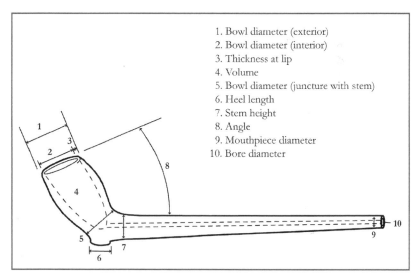

1. Bowl diameter (exterior)
2. Bowl diameter (interior)
3. Thickness at lip
4. Volume
5. Bowl diameter (juncture with stem)
6. Heel length
7. Stem height
8. Angle
9. Mouthpiece diameter
10. Bore diameter

Figure 3.5 Each pipe fragment in this study could be measured along a variety of dimensions, depending on how complete it is. *Illustration by J. Eric Deetz.*

Metric Attributes

Within limits, metric traits are epiphenomenal, at least to the extent that a pipe's *precise* dimensions have little bearing on a pipe's basic utility as a vehicle for tobacco smoke. However, metric traits also resemble technological style, insofar as they capture information about functionally equivalent ways of shaping a pipe. A number of measurements were successfully used by Alvey and Laxton in their studies identifying individual pipe molds from measurements of pipe dimensions (Alvey and Laxton 1974; 1977; Alvey et al. 1985). Here, measurements were collected to create a record of the shape and size of the bowls suitable for statistical testing, reducing the need to rely only on "stylistic" descriptions of shape and form (Figure 3.5).[32]

The coefficient of variation (CV) has proved to be a very useful statistic for assessing and comparing the variability of these metric traits. A CV score can characterize an entire batch of measurements with a single number expressed as a percentage. (Blackman et al. 1993; Eerkens and Bettinger 2001). Then it is possible to compare, for example, the variability of pipe bowl thickness and the variability of the exterior diameter of the bowl at the lip. Bowl thickness is more variable with a CV of 27.1%. At 6.2%, the exterior bowl diameter is noticeably more uniform. They can be compared even though one dimension is nearly ten times larger than the other (2.33 mm vs. 20.61 mm; see Table 3.2).

Ethnoarchaeological observations of specialists and non-specialists alike demonstrate that they can consistently produce a CV range of 2.5–6% (Eerkens 2000:667; Longacre 1999). On the other hand, a CV greater than 10% should be interpreted as encompassing two or more smaller groups (Thomas 1986:84). So variability greater than 6–10% is likely due to factors besides the limitations of the medium or of the artisans. High variation can represent, among other things, a high tolerance for variability. Makers and users are not always interested in consistently sized objects, particularly if a dimension does not affect the functioning of the object (Eerkens and Bettinger 2001:499). More meaningfully, a high CV may be the result of a sample containing the handiwork of many different producers.

Table 3.2 The coefficient of variation allows us to examine the metric variability of the pipes, even comparing dimensions that are very different in scale, such as thickness and bowl diameter. For the most part, the individual sites are less variable than the entire study collection, as is shown by their lower CV values.

Measure-ment	All sites	Drum-mond	Green Spring	James-town	Page	Port Anne	Rich Neck
angle	41.4	14.9	56.6	42.8	—	32	32.7
thickness	27.1	35.5	29.6	26.6	1.9	26.3	21.5
volume	20.9	12	11.5	19.7	22.6	18.5	20
stem diameter (indeterminate location)	16.4	17.4	16.7	14.7	19.1	14.1	13.4
bore diameter	15.8	16.5	12.4	14.3	15.4	14	14.1
mouthpiece diameter	12.7	12.5	11	13.3	1.4	11.4	10.6
heel length	11.6	12	6.8	11.2	—	4.1	14.8
bowl diameter (juncture)	11.2	11.1	11	10.7	15.2	9.7	9.9
stem height	9	11.1	8.4	8.1	15.1	8.4	8.2
bowl diameter (interior)	7.9	7.6	5.5	6.9	8.5	6.5	7
bowl diameter (exterior)	6.2	8.3	4.8	4.9	7.4	6.2	6.8

	non-Jamestown	Str 100	Str 112	Str 127	Str 144	Str 19	Str 26/27
angle	41	56.1	10.9	41.7	8.6	40.2	59.5
thickness	27.3	23.5	46.3	37	32.6	22.2	29.7
volume	21.3	18.6	10.3	22.3	—	16.8	—
stem diameter (indeterminate location)	17.1	12.7	14.9	12.3	14.4	15.1	13.9
bore diameter	16.5	13.6	12.6	15.8	12.3	11.1	15.3
mouthpiece diameter	12.5	11.7	9.7	12.2	11.6	11.9	5.9
heel length	12	11.9	11.1	—	6.1	7.2	13.4
bowl diameter (juncture)	11	11.1	7.1	4.3	15.4	12.1	5
stem height	9.5	7.3	8.3	7.3	7.9	8	9.7
bowl diameter (interior)	8.1	7.8	0.7	5.3	—	2.1	5.3
bowl diameter (exterior)	6.5	5.1	3.2	1.6	—	5.3	—

Several interesting possibilities and problems are suggested by the findings summarized in the first column of Table 3.2. First, the high value of many of the CVs demonstrates the internal variability in the total assemblage of 4,971 fragments. This variation reinforces the findings of Chapter 2 in which the pipe modes suggested a heterogeneous study collection. Most of the measurements show variability exceeding the 10% threshold. Bowl angle,[33] bowl thickness, and bowl volume are the most variable. Stem exterior diameter, mouthpiece diameter, and bowl diameter at the juncture with the stem are all above 10% as well. The only attributes that come in below the mark are stem height and two measures of bowl diameter at the lip (interior and exterior). These still show greater variability than is usually found in assemblages produced by a limited number of individuals, particularly if those individuals are specialists, let alone talented amateurs (Eerkens 2000).

The CV scores of the individual sites are, for the most part, lower than scores for the combined assemblage (Table 3.2), though for bowl angle, thickness, and stem height at least one site is noticeably more variable than the collection as a whole. Only Port Anne is consistently *less* variable than the combined assemblage across multiple measures. It might be a good candidate for a site where smokers relied on a "single" producer. The Drummond site, on the other hand, is more variable than the overall assemblage for the majority of the recorded measures. So at that site, we might argue for many hands. The data in this table give us reason to question the idea that residents of a plantation would rely only on a single source for their pipes. But on the whole, the sites show a comparable, rather than significantly lower, degree of variability. None appears to be obviously the handiwork of a small subset of producers. Even the smokers at Port Anne appear to have been getting their pipes from more than one maker. Though none of the site assemblages reflects the kind of homogeneity that would suggest reliance on a single specialist producer, the pipes from any one site may still be more homogeneous than the assemblage as a whole.

An analysis of variance test (also known as ANOVA and discussed in greater detail in Chapter 4) shows that for every measure but one—bowl angle again—the variance of the entire assemblage is greater than the variance within each site.[34] This pattern suggests that even if any site includes the pipes of more than one maker, its residents likely had access to only a subset of the producers active in the region. The pipe modes reinforce this tentative interpretation, and we address them now. Measurements will feature again when we turn to the question of how mold manufacture influences metric variability.

Nominal Traits

Analyzing the modes site by site is another process that reveals diversity within the plantation assemblages.[35] The decorative evidence for on-site production is ambiguous at best. The decorative repertoires of the pipe fragments from each plantation are neither homogeneous nor distinctive. The variety and character of manufacturing techniques found at each site undermines the argument that people made pipes casually for their own immediate use—or the use of their associates on the same plantation.

Decorative Style

Remember that the measurements for the Drummond pipes generally resulted in CV values similar to or greater than (that is, more variable than) the study population as a whole. Well, the Drummond site pipes also showed a diverse range of decorative motifs—more than any of the other plantations. For example, the pipes at that site came from makers who used both linear and stamped motifs. These two decorative strategies are negatively associated with each other on individual fragments; they seldom occur together. Some of the motifs unique to the site are variations on the linear theme, such as banded lines set at a diagonal rather than the standard horizontal orientation, or a zigzag line instead of a straight one. But these and other unique motifs were quite rare and do not distinguish the site in any quantifiable fashion. The broad range of motifs hints, even if it doesn't prove, that the assemblage represents the work of many pipe-makers. One could assign somewhat more weight to observations about the design of the base of a pipe (for example, the presence or absence of heels, as well as heel form), because these attributes are produced by, and correlate with, distinct shaping strategies—mold manufacture (pseudo-spurs) versus hand-shaping (square heels). Unlike the surface decoration, this set of heel variables presents a slightly more homogeneous picture of the Drummond site; neither pseudospurs nor square heels appear in this collection. Whereas, the variants that do occur at this site (heelless and round heel) speak primarily to the maker's design sense, as they can be produced using multiple manufacturing strategies.

There is little to distinguish the Rich Neck pipes from others in the study collection. Despite being a much larger assemblage than any of

Figure 3.6 The archaeologists who excavated the Page site identified this botanical motif as a possible tobacco plant. If so, it would be a fitting decoration for a pipe.

the others, Rich Neck has no unique decorative motifs. One might expect a relatively large assemblage to contain more variety simply by increasing the odds that an unusual variant would be included. The few distinctive motifs, such as triangles, bowties, and chevrons, are not unique, but shared with the Drummond site. That said, the Rich Neck pipes are far from homogeneous. There are fragments both with and without paint or slip. Motifs include the usual spectrum of linear decorations at the lip and at the juncture between bowl and stem, but many fragments have stamped designs rather than linear motifs. It is perhaps telling that even within the large assemblage from Rich Neck, still no pseudospurs appear, and only one pipe fragment has a square heel. Thus, while the decorative repertoire was fairly wide-open, the technologies used to produce formal variation were somewhat constrained.

Page, unlike Rich Neck, has very few pipe fragments, so the homogeneity of heel types is not surprising. The one unique motif is a single instance of what the excavating archaeologists have interpreted as a depiction of a tobacco plant (Metz et al. 1998:75) (Figure 3.6). Otherwise, the site presents the full range of linear decorations around the bowl, as well as stamped motifs. Fragments appear both with and without paint or slip. At Port Anne, too, the standard range of motifs appears, with only a couple of unique additions: a pattern best described as "argyle," and a linear band of slash marks that, only at this site, appears vertically on the surface of a pipe fragment.

Like most of those at the other plantation sites, the pipe fragments from Green Spring include a variety of decorative motifs. Most dominant are single and banded lines of dentate decoration at the lip of the bowl and at the juncture between the pipe and the bowl (see Figure 3.7).[36] There are pipes with and without white slip or paint, and decorations created with stamps as well as with rouletting tools or bladed implements. Not a very homogeneous assemblage. At Green Spring these standard motifs are also joined by some unusual designs, such as bands of diagonally cut lines, notches, and the use of a panel to surround text, the latter two designs being unique to this site. Each motif represents multiple fragments of the same object, rather than a repeatedly rendered motif—that is, a pattern. The only decorative commonality suggesting that the Green Spring pipes might come from "the same" (or a limited number of) hand(s) is that all of the pipe heels are round. Overall, though, the assemblage seems to reflect the sensibilities of several makers.

In sum, there is little in the decoration or form of the pipe fragments studied to suggest that smokers at any given plantation relied on a limited number of resident pipemakers. Of course, decorative motifs readily transfer and may be imitated by many makers, either to appeal to users or for any number of idiosyncratic reasons. Therefore, decorations that occur across multiple sites—such as a starburst motif, or a geometric shape I have called "bowtie" (and that others have interpreted as stylized depictions of animals/skins [Mouer 1993:141])—are not necessarily indicative of a single pipe maker. Technological attributes, on the other hand, are less likely to vary once a maker hits on a successful routine for creating pipes, and therefore would be less susceptible to innovation than surface decoration, thereby being an even better indicator of an assemblage of pipes coming from "the same" workshop.

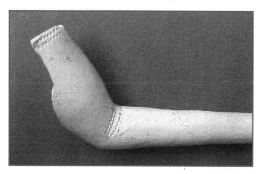

Figure 3.7 Many of the pipes from Green Spring had dentate decoration not only at the lip of the bowl, but also at the juncture where the bowl meets the stem.

Technological Style

The distance between decorative and technological style is bridged via an examination of the tools used to create decorative motifs. For example, pipemakers created linear motifs using several tools that produced slightly different dentate effects (refer back to Figure 2.5). "Tool 1" is more commonly found associated with the characteristics of handmade pipes. "Tool 4" occurs more frequently with characteristics common to mold-made and/or mass produced pipes. The difference in the distribution of tools 1 and 4 is significant when the six sites (the plantations plus Jamestown) are compared, but no site yields one tool or the other exclusively. In other words, every plantation's assemblage contains pipe fragments using both dentate tools. They are used to create the same kind of decoration and are used interchangeably, but in only two instances out of nearly 5,000 did they occur together on the same fragment. If they are interchangeable, and not used together, then a maker would use one or the other, but not both, so the presence of both, on separate fragments, in each assemblage suggests multiple "hands" at work.

As far as the non-decorative aspects of technology are concerned, Page is a good site to examine in detail. Page's assemblage is the most homogeneous and distinctive when examining technological style. For example, two variables (clay type and handmade versus mold-made) showed significant differences among the plantations when their frequencies were compared statistically. Page is homogeneous in the sense that there are no agate-bodied pipes, and the only recognizable bowl forms are those that are customarily identified (following Henry 1979) as hand-modeled rather than mold-made. However, this homogeneity is not unambiguous proof of narrow sourcing for the Page assemblage. Many of the variables which make the Page site distinctive (lack of pseudospurs, lack of square heels, absence of wiping at the lip) were insignificant when the sites were compared to each other. Simply put, they did not distinguish one site from another more generally. When we examine other variables, ones that are found at similar rates at all of the plantations, even Page's small number of fragments encompasses the range of available techniques. For example, all of the techniques for forming a mouthpiece were found at Page, as were all of the techniques for forming a bowl. In sum, even Page—with its on-site ceramic facilities which should by rights mean on-site manufacture by specialists without pipes coming in from "abroad," and its tiny assemblage, in which one would expect few of the rarer variables to occur—looks like a hodge-podge of tool kits and manufacturing styles. Its pipes are not at all typical of an assemblage that comes from a single, on-site workshop.

The other plantation assemblages also show telltale signs of coming from more than one or two on-site pipemakers. These observations, while not modal analysis per se because they are not comparative, can nonetheless be organized according to the themes identified by Rouse: materials; techniques of manufacture; and use. With respect to materials, each assemblage shows evidence of pipemakers employing a wide range of clay preparation techniques. Every site includes both fine and coarse textured clay bodies and the full range of visible inclusions. Take, for example, a site like Rich Neck with its clay borrow pit and kiln likely used in the production of brick and tile for the main house. Someone with a working knowledge of ceramic production spent time at Rich Neck during the initial construction of the manor house, and perhaps during its renovation when the pond was filled, burying the pipes studied here. It is hard to imagine that person having any reason to experiment widely with different clays and preparation regimes, once the right preparation was established. Again, a variety of producers offers an alternative explanation for the variety of clays present.

As for techniques of manufacture, diversity of shaping technologies used to form the bowl and to finish the lip and mouthpiece appear in each plantation's assemblage. At the Drummond site, for example, the pipe bowls show traces of being formed using a tool inserted vertically into the pliable clay, as well as a tool that employed a twisting or reaming motion. Several other bowls appear to have been hollowed out with a knife or other blade. There would be little reason for either an individual with limited skills or knowledge or for a workshop set up to make large numbers of pipes to switch back and forth among these very different techniques for forming pipes. More likely is the possibility that the pipes came from more than one operation. It is still possible that these multiple operations could have persisted on a single plantation, but that would not explain the diversity of *materials* that are also present. Imagining multiple independent makers producing large numbers of pipes within the same household also presumes an individualism on the part of workers that seems unlikely given what is known about the organization of labor in the colony and in pipe production, as we shall see in Chapter 5.

Surface treatment is another area where every site showed internal variation. At Page, as at every other plantation, the assemblage was divided among specimens that had been quickly smoothed and others burnished to a high gloss. With respect to technologies used in firing, these can only be inferred from the evidence of coloration, including cross sections, as well as the presence of firing clouds. Port Anne is typical in that the pipes recovered from that site had experienced a variety of firing environments. Some pipes are clear through the cross-section (oxidized). Others have cores or are completely gray in cross section (reduced). Firing clouds appear on many of the fragments. These variations could be explained by poorly controlled firing conditions. They could also indicate widely divergent firing conditions, and thus multiple sources for the pipes.

Standardization (and Specialization)

While the assemblages of pipes from each plantation are not homogeneous, many do show evidence of being made in ways that produce standardized objects and suggest that they are the handiwork of specialists. Here, we turn to the evidence for specialized production and its relationship with processes of standardization. The fact that specialization often correlates with standardization, combined with the variety found in each plantation's assemblage, suggests people in the past not only making, but exchanging pipes. What we need is further proof that the pipemakers whose products we see were in fact using specialized tools and techniques.

The connection between specialization and standardization has been a foundational assumption in archaeology for many years (Earle 1982:5; Rice 1996:177). While much of the standardization in artifact assemblages can be attributed to some degree of specialization, not all specialized production is standardized. Nor, as replication research shows, are all standardized assemblages produced by specialists. Direct evidence of specialized production would include finds such as tools, particularly those that imply mass production (that is, molds or stamps), or facilities specifically associated with production (that is, kilns), and perhaps wasters or raw and scrap materials. In the case of these plantations, only the Drummond site seems to have irrefutable evidence of pipe*making*—with the clay scrapings and other incidentally fired detritus. However, all of the other sites have direct evidence of some other ceramic production—including kilns (Green Spring, Page, Rich Neck, as well as Jamestown—see Chapter 4) and clay borrow pits (Port Anne and Rich Neck). Direct evidence being rare, though, archaeologists are often forced to rely mostly on indirect

Measurement	CV (%) all fragments	CV (%) mold scar absent	CV (%) mold scar present
angle	41.4	47.2	27.8
thickness	27.1	23.5	31.7
volume	20.9	23.4	11.7
stem diameter (indeterminate location)	16.4	16.6	14.3
bore diameter	15.8	16.1	13
mouthpiece diameter	12.7	12.8	10
heel length	11.6	12.7	10.4
bowl diameter (juncture)	11.2	10	6.9
stem height	9	9.6	7.5
bowl diameter (interior)	7.9	7.9	7.7
bowl diameter (exterior)	6.2	6.4	5

Table 3.3 A comparison of the CVs of all of the dimensions in one batch (leftmost column) shows that the difference between the scarred and not scarred fragments is significant. The chances of the scarred pipes having lower CVs for so many measurements at random are less than 1 percent.

evidence, especially standardization and stylistic similarity (Hantman and Plog 1982:237; Rice 1996:174; Sinopoli 1998:163). Inferences drawn from the final products themselves are the most common form of indirect evidence for ceramic production. These include implied skill or specialized knowledge, high concentrations of finished products (so much the better if they are unused), and evidence of standardization.

Lack of standardization could be rooted in the eccentricities of individual pipe makers, particularly when analysis includes the handmade pipes. Are the handmade pipes more variable than the mold-made ones? At the assemblage level, pipe fragments with mold scars *are* generally less variable than those without (Table 3.3). For most measurements, pipes with mold scars are more uniform than other fragments. For example, pipemakers using molds exerted much better control over bowl volume and angle than those not using molds. Yet the *average* measurements for volume and angle show little difference between scarred and not-scarred fragments. In other words, mold-users made more standardized pipes, but not differently proportioned ones.

The same dimensions are at or below the 10% CV threshold for pipe fragments with mold scars as for all pipes. For dimensions that are well controlled in general, mold-manufacture also produces standard-sized pipes. However, the less well controlled variables are *still* quite heterogeneous, including very high CV scores for bowl angle and thickness. Notably, the one exception to the rule of higher uniformity among molded pipes is the attribute, bowl thickness. The exterior and interior diameters of pipe bowls show remarkably little variation, but the thickness at the lip—which is, after all, dependent upon the relationship between paired interior and exterior diameters—is highly variable. The molding process should adequately control this dimension. Molded pipes, hollowed with a specialized pipemaker's tool (refer back to Figures 2.9 and 2.10), should show a fairly uniform thickness, if only one mold was used. The best explanation for this variability is that the sample contains the products of multiple pipemakers' kits.[37]

Despite the role of molds in specialized production, neither the proportion of mold scarred fragments nor the proportion of mold-made bowl shapes seems to be associated with a site's CV values. Sites with many molded pipe fragments still show high CVs, and site samples showing little evidence of mold manufacture can have very low CVs. These patterns suggest that mold technology is not the only way to produce pipes with standardized measurements. And it's not just molds. Sites where many signs point to specialized production, like Green Spring—and as we shall see in Chapter 4, Jamestown Structure 26/27—have high CVs, and sites like Port Anne, where there is little evidence of specialized production, have low CVs. Although the sites do vary, statistically speaking the differences in CV from one site to the other have little significance.[38] A further test confirms this finding: when all of the attributes are considered together, no site stands out as being significantly more variable than any other.[39]

∷

Rather than trying to trace the origins of a decorative motif to a specific symbolic tradition, my study compares the distribution of attributes in assemblages and uses characteristics they share as indices that signify the circumstances of their manufacture. Whether the variability we're discussing is nominal or metric, the key thing to remember is that most of these distinctions point to distinctive individual motor habits and/or particular kinds of tool kits. Therefore, the variety at the plantations should be understood as a variety of technologies and, presumably, makers. These data do not allow us to speak to what "variety" of person those makers might have been.

These plantation assemblages show evidence of both specialized production and diversity of style (decorative and technological). For example, at Green Spring the pipes range from the most conventional mold-made pipes in the imported style to exuberantly decorated and eccentrically shaped handmade specimens. So it seems that variation within a site might have less to do with the ad-hoc production of one-offs by plantation residents and more to do with being the product of multiple specialized producers, on-site or off-. The answer to the question about the impact of specialization on these assemblages is suggested by the modal data, especially the widespread presence of attributes indicating the use of specialized tools, and is strongly reinforced by metric analyses. The plantations, collectively and individually, show the tools for specialization combined with variable assemblages. The heterogeneity of metric traits, as well as decorative and technical style, individually and in combination, point to many makers.

Say for the sake of argument that Burley's pipe was Virginia-made. The evidence is piling up that he did not make it himself. It also seems that he and other members of his household could have obtained pipes from a range of sources, and were not dependent on a single (group of) maker(s) within that same household. Even though "everyone smoke[d] while working and idling," it seems "everyone" did not resort to pipe making in order for that to happen. In fact, the evidence suggests that while the capacity for making pipes was widespread, that capacity was also fairly specialized.

If Burley's pipe suffered the same fate during the melee as his shirt, and eventually got carted out to a midden with the rest of the kitchen trash, its presence at Mrs. Vaulx's plantation may have been emblematic of the kinds of processes that could create the intra-site heterogeneity seen in this chapter. But that movement may also have been much more systematic. So, now that we have examined variability *within* the sites, next comes an analysis of variability *among* sites in the sample—with a focus on the different structures at Jamestown—again, in terms of both nominal and metric attributes. Specifically, we turn to the question of whether the capital served as one half of an exchange dyad, either as the recipient of pipes produced—like the tobacco that filled them—on the surrounding plantations, or as the primary center of a craft industry—as the powers-that-were so ardently hoped the town would become.

Jamestown, Cities, and Crafts
Chapter 4

Charles I was not impressed with the way the Virginia colony was shaping up. He decreed:

> And also [you are] not to suffer men to build slight Cottages, as heretofore hath been there used, And to remove from place to place only to Plant Tobacco, That Tradesmen and Handycrafts men be compelled to follow their Severall Trades and occupations and that you draw them into Towns.

In his instructions to Governor William Berkeley in 1641(cited in Billings 1975:56), the king accurately described—and found wanting—the material world of the colonists. He dismissed the vernacular architecture that had developed. He knew that tobacco planters shifted from field to field, constantly clearing new land. He worried that too many artisans, seduced into tobacco farming, abandoned their trades and their rightful place in the capital city.

Tobacco, Pipes, and Race in Colonial Virginia: Little Tubes of Mighty Power
by Anna S. Agbe-Davies, 107–138. © 2015 Left Coast Press, Inc. All rights reserved.

But Virginians had reasons for not conforming to the ideals set forth by the king and his advisors. His "slight Cottages," what other contemporaries called "Virginia houses," offered many advantages. They used readily available materials and skillsets. They were inexpensive, allowing settlers to redirect investment toward land and labor. With the need for constant upkeep, they may even have contributed to social cohesion (Carson et al. 1981; Deetz 2002; Graham et al. 2007; Neiman 1993; St. George 1996; Yentsch 1991). With respect to planting strategies, tobacco thoroughly depletes soil nutrients. Shifting cultivation with long fallow periods was the only way to maintain productivity with seventeenth-century agricultural techniques and technologies.

As for Charles's "Tradesmen and Handycrafts men," the earliest artisans in the colony were the carpenters and coopers who provided critical support for the tobacco planters and factors (Carr and Walsh 1988:145). It made sense for them to settle outside the capital, amid their clients and close to sources of timber. As the colony became more established, other craft specialists found opportunities to practice their trades. Metz notes, for instance, that during the seventeenth century many of the craft specialists in York County supported the tobacco trade: coopers, carpenters, and builders. By the early eighteenth century, they had been joined by an equal number of "artisans" such as blacksmiths, silversmiths, and glaziers (Metz 1999). Some of these people operated in towns, but archaeological evidence shows that many plied their trades on plantations. Thus, we have evidence of distilling at Martin's Hundred (I. Noël Hume and A. Noël Hume 2001), pottery making at Green Spring, brick and tile production at the Page family seat, and pipe manufacture throughout the Chesapeake.

Brown and Samford's analysis shows that even into the early eighteenth century, Virginia's new capital at Williamsburg lacked the kind of urban patterns preferred across the Atlantic. Chesapeake towns were so small that residents seemingly felt no need to confine to non-residential or outlying sectors whichever noxious industries happened to spring up. Archaeological evidence shows a gunsmith along the green leading to the governor's "Palace," and other messy industrial enterprises near private homes and upscale taverns (Brown and Samford 1994). Excavations at Jamestown have revealed a similarly promiscuous landscape for the seventeenth century (Cotter 1958; Wehner 2006).

So, even though early Virginia governors complained that the fast money in tobacco drew even settlers with specialized skills into cultivation, and they resorted to tax incentives and legal sanctions in order to keep craft-workers from abandoning their trades (Billings 1996; Horning 1995:150–151); shoemakers, blacksmiths, gunsmiths, potters, weavers, and their like *did* contribute to the colonial economy, if only by lessening the dependence of the planters and factors on manufactured goods imported from Europe. Residents of the Virginia colony equipped their homes with a combination of items imported into the colony from overseas and from their Algonquian and Iroquoian neighbors, along with goods produced within the colony itself.

As the early colony's capital and only (barely) urban center, Jamestown *could* have been a locus of production or distribution for craft products like tobacco pipes, fulfilling the desires of the king, his policy makers, and his agents. However, the commercial pattern established by Virginia's planting elite had dispersed tobacco sales and exchanges to the plantations and small landings along Virginia's many rivers and creeks. This, despite the best efforts of colonial administrators who fought the diffusion of economic activity and sought to regulate the tobacco trade by concentrating it in the capital. So, it is therefore also possible that pipes, like other crafts produced in the countryside, might have found their way to Jamestown. In either case, the pipes from Jamestown would be representative of the pipes recovered throughout the region.

Perhaps trade relationships were far too complex to be glossed as "from Jamestown" versus "to Jamestown." If the Jamestown pipes do not mirror the aggregate assemblage, or if they are distinctive when compared with the plantation assemblages, then other possibilities arise. It may be that the Jamestown fragments represent a distinctly "urban" style of pipe production. The key to unraveling this puzzle is careful attention to the contexts from which the Jamestown pipes came, along with comparisons among the individual assemblages.

Chapter 2 showed that distinctive stylistic characteristics crossed multiple assemblages of pipes. Analysis in Chapter 3 showed that individual plantation assemblages contained significant variation. Furthermore, the technological styles of the pipes, their standardized features, as well as evidence uncovered at several of the sites, demonstrate that the pipemakers used specialized tools and technologies. This is not what it looks like when smokers make a few pipes for their own (household's) use. As pragmatist analysis proceeds not from first principles, but premises, I position the conclusions of the preceding chapters as the premise for this next phase of analysis: in early Virginia people with expertise and experience made pipes and distributed them beyond the borders of their own households. From this position I can tackle the next problem, which has to do with the relationship between people in Virginia's capital city and those in the countryside.

Again, we can imagine competing scenarios: Jamestown as the source of the region's pipes versus Jamestown as a place towards which the handiwork of outlying plantations and settlements flowed. In an analysis of bowl forms and bore diameters, Monroe and Mallios (2004) appear to favor the Jamestown-as-production-center interpretation. My analysis of a selection of Jamestown pipe fragments alongside the plantation artifacts suggests something more complicated: the pipes from Jamestown, rather than mirroring the plantations—as would be the case with exchange between town and plantation dwellers, regardless of the direction of the exchange—instead show their own distinctive characteristics.

To address these questions, I examine the Jamestown pipe fragments at several different scales. Treating them as a single assemblage allows the town site to be compared with the plantations introduced in Chapter 3. Variability among the Jamestown pipes shows quite clearly that town residents, just like their rural peers, drew on a range of pipemakers. So, I also disaggregate the Jamestown pipes into the individual structures from which they were excavated. This further highlights the variability of the Jamestown assemblage. Finally, I contrast Jamestown on the one hand with the plantations on the other. How meaningful is the category "Jamestown" when set against all plantation sites at once; does it work as well as "Jamestown" as a site among five others? This sequence sets up the comparisons in Chapter 5 between elite social networks that encompass both town and rural sites. In order to contextualize these comparisons, it is important first to understand how Jamestown fit into the colony as a whole and second to review the individual histories of the structures selected for this study.

The Meanings of Jamestown— from Colonial Capital to Archaeological Site

In the spring of 1607, a group of men and boys arrived at Jamestown Island with the express purpose of establishing an English foothold in North America; 104 of them stayed. They were settlers on behalf of the privately owned Virginia Company of London. Their mission was to improve the land and send raw materials and commodities back to England. The colony was meant to be a permanent settlement, designed to enrich the investors and form a bulwark against Spanish expansion in the New World. The initial fortified settlement was erected near the present Jamestown Church (Kelso 2006).

Powhatan, leader of the local, eponymous Algonquian chiefdom, had left that particular low-lying, swampy part of his domain unsettled for a reason (Fausz 1985:237; Rountree 1989:26–27); the colonists died of "bloudy fluxes" and "fevers," as well as malnutrition and, increasingly, in skirmishes with those self-same Powhatan. At the end of the first six months, barely one third of the settlers remained (Billings 1975:5). The colony survived its initial decades largely because a stream of immigrants—including, eventually, a few women—constantly replaced those that continued to succumb at a horrifying rate (Earle 1979). Despite concerted efforts by the Powhatan to drive them off (particularly in 1622 and 1644), the Europeans stayed, having spread out from Jamestown Island, settling along the James and, later, York rivers.

In the second decade of the seventeenth century, settlers began to establish communities away from Jamestown Island, and also began to build out from James Fort. Communal farming was phased out, and individual settlers became responsible for feeding themselves by growing crops on individually assigned plots of land (McCartney 2000a:34). New policies made it possible for individuals to own land, rather than working land for the Company. With the land came the responsibility to improve it, usually by building a house upon it, within a given period of time. The "headright" system insured that those who owned land also had the means (labor) to make the land profitable. It linked land with labor by granting fifty acres to any individual credited with the arrival of a new member of the colony, free or not. Ironically, perhaps, a parallel enclosure of the commons in Britain was what drove most English servant migration in the first place. The same cannot be said for bound laborers from Africa.

A 1618/9 muster counted 892 "En[g]lish and other Christians," 32 Africans and 4 Native Americans living in the various European settlements of Virginia. According to the muster, 117 of these people lived in "James City," which may have included a few other settlements besides Jamestown Island proper (Thorndale 1995:160, 168). Two narrative sources describe an event later in 1619 in which the settlers traded provisions to a passing ship in exchange for a group of twenty or so African people (see Sluiter 1997; Thorndale 1995). These accounts demonstrate how quickly Virginians began to participate in the international trade in bound labor, even though the emphasis remained on English indentured labor for several more decades.

Not long after the first Powhatan uprising, factionalism and misman-
agement of the Company reached a critical mass and Virginia ceased to be
a private colony; it was reorganized as a crown colony under King James.
As late as 1625, the population of James City was still only 125 people
(Noël Hume 1994:369). Laws encouraged development in the town with
an eye toward the creation of an urban setting with commercial and residential aspects. Other laws made it illegal for ships to open their cargoes
or sell any goods before landing at Jamestown, in the hope of encouraging
commercial activity (Hening 1819–1823:I:166–167). On the plantations,
heads of household were required to plant commercially valuable crops
(mulberry trees for silk and grape vines) in addition to the corn they grew
for food (McCartney 2000a:74). By the time Virginia had become a crown
colony, however, tobacco was clearly king (see, for example, Morgan
1975:108–130).

Archaeology reveals the early Virginia colony to be a world in which
most people lived in small post-set buildings, with earthen or wooden
walls and floors. As time wore on, people increasingly partitioned these
"Virginia houses" and their associated landscapes, designating specialized
work spaces while increasing privacy and segregation within the house-
hold (Carson et al. 1981; Deetz 2002; Graham et al. 2007; Neiman 1993;
Yentsch 1991). Only major public buildings, such as those at Jamestown,
and an occasional elite dwelling were built of locally manufactured brick.
Drummond, for example, for all his social stature, had an earthfast house.
All of the Jamestown structures yielding pipes for this study were of brick.
In part, this is because the town had a high proportion of brick buildings.
It also reflects the methods of the earlier excavations, which were better
suited to locating brick foundations than the soil stains that mark former
post-in-ground structures.

Building in brick was important technically—bricks resisted fire and
damp better than wood—but it also mattered symbolically. Brick structures
required a greater initial outlay, and their relative permanence implied a
greater investment in the project at hand, whether that be seating a plantation or housing political institutions. Furthermore, brick buildings might
have helped to make a place like Jamestown look like a "real" town in the
eyes of men and women whose ideas of cities were based on European examples.[1] To this end, the General Assembly passed laws prohibiting wooden
buildings at Jamestown and in 1662 mandated that each county raise funds
for the construction of its own brick edifice in the capital (Hening 1823
II:172–178). These "country houses" were a bone of contention in many of

the counties because of their cost and the fact that well-connected elites like Matthew Page (brother of John) often got the contracts for their construction. If the settlers' complaints are taken at face value, the country houses were a significant contributor to the Rebellion against the government in 1676–1677 (His Majesties Commissioners 1677).

So Jamestown, even as a living town, was a bit of a shifter. Depending on where one stood, it could embody the colony's inability to live up to expectations or symbolize overreach and domination on the part of the provincial government. Periodic reports back to England stressed the need for artisans, noting the opportunities for profit by those with manufacturing skills. Individuals such as Governor John Harvey were ardent promoters of local industry and manufacture (Horning and Edwards 2000:90–92). The demands of tobacco planting may have kept the colonists from fulfilling their leaders' urban aspirations. According to John Smith, when he wrote in 1629, "Their Cities and Townes [were] onley scattered houses, they call plantations, as are our Country Villages" (Smith 1986 [1629]:218). Even in 1642, when Sir William Berkeley first became governor, his instructions admitted that "the Buildings at James Town are for the most part decayed" (Billings 1975:54). Acting on further instructions in 1662, which compared the Virginia colony unfavorably with those of New England, Berkeley developed a program for urban renewal. He and the Assembly mandated that only brick buildings were to be constructed at Jamestown; in fact, existing wooden structures were to be permitted to decay. He also promoted the construction of the aforementioned "country houses." Every county was responsible for organizing and sponsoring the construction of at least one brick structure at Jamestown (the Virginia Magazine of History and Biography 1895:16; Hening 1819–1823:II:172–176). Whether the counties followed through on these requirements is unclear, though complaints by the counties suggest that the structures were begun, if not completed or maintained (McCartney 2000a:119–120, 143).

As the colony grew in size and population, administrators divided it into counties and vested these with significant authority on local matters. The modern limits of James City County were established in the mid seventeenth century. Jamestown during the years of interest to us—the second half of the seventeenth century—was described as "close upon the river, extending east and west, about 3 quarters of a mile; in which is comprehended some 16 or 18 houses, much as is the church built of brick, faire and large; and in them about a dozen families (for all the howses are not inhabited)" (Anonymous 1846:25). When Bacon's Rebellion raged in 1676, brick architecture, though valued for its air of permanence and solidity as well as its resistance to fire, was of little use. The town burned just the same. In 1692, another spate of construction was prompted by yet another royal mandate, this time that every council member keep a house at Jamestown. Yet near the turn of the eighteenth century, several eyewitnesses concurred that Jamestown still consisted of only twenty to thirty houses (McCartney 2000a:164). Still, Jamestown remained the principal "city" in the colony.

Jamestown seems to have reached its peak as an urban center in the late seventeenth century, as a village of only twenty or thirty houses. Despite the efforts by a series of governors to build a lasting city, maintaining viability was a constant struggle. A major fire in 1698 seemed to be the last straw, and in 1699, the capital and administrative center was finally moved to Middle Plantation (Williamsburg). Despite losing the infusion of money and population that goes with being a colonial capital, the town remained an official port. However, after the removal of the capital, the consolidation of Jamestown real estate that had been going on for some time began to pick up steam. Land on Jamestown Island was gradually consolidated into the hands of a few families who would gradually convert it from a town to a collection of plantations. From 1831 onward the parcels were united into a single farm (Horning 1995; Horning and Edwards 2000; McCartney 2000a; McCartney and Kiddle 2000).

From time to time, people made pilgrimages to Jamestown to honor Virginia's early beginnings. The farm became a place for veneration, tourism, and nostalgia. This new meaning of Jamestown really began to take over in the later part of the nineteenth century. Landowners Edward Barney and Louise Barney hoped to capitalize on the historic significance of Jamestown Island by building facilities for a visiting public. The Barneys sponsored some exploratory digging among the "ruins" associated with their farm, but Mary Jeffery Galt was the first person to direct a semi-systematic excavation of archaeological remains in 1897 (Galt n.d., in Cotter 1958:222). Galt confined herself mostly to the churchyard and its associated graves. Colonel Samuel Yonge located and excavated a number of structures in 1903—including Structure 144, discussed later in this chapter—during the installation of a seawall to prevent erosion along the James River shore of the island.

These early excavations mark yet another set of changes in Jamestown's meaning. The efforts of Galt, Yonge, and their unnamed assistants represent an epistemological shift: Jamestown could be known scientifically, using material evidence. This attitude—we could call it empiricism—continues today, despite significant changes in specific excavation or analytical techniques. The reports from the earliest projects are minimalist, as are the artifact collections, which precluded their analysis here. But the work that these early excavators did shaped the archaeological record that later archaeologists encountered. And to the extent that pragmatism sees science as a dialog among researchers (Baert 2005a; Preucel and Mrozowski 2010), these early scholars were part of a conversation about Jamestown's meaning(s) that continues to this day.

The bulk of Jamestown Island passed from private to public hands in 1934 with the establishment of Colonial National Monument, becoming a part of Colonial National Historical Park in 1936. Modern archaeological practices arrived at Jamestown Island with J. C. Harrington, who led excavations there from 1936 to 1942. Prior to Harrington's tenure, the government had hired John Zaharov, Frederick Parris, and H. Summerfield Day (the only archaeologist in the group) to supervise Civilian Conservation Corps excavators and direct their search for the original settlement. Proceedings were complicated by turf wars between the archaeological team and an architectural team, led by H. Chandlee Forman. The greatest casualty of these conflicts was the archaeological record, as large portions of Jamestown Island were excavated during this period, but there was little adherence to normal archaeological procedures, such as systematic trenching, recording stratification, cataloguing artifacts, or retaining artifact provenience data (as described in Cotter 1994:26–29). The permanent archival and artifactual record reflects these problems. The situation improved markedly when J. C. Harrington was hired to oversee the archaeology. He introduced new standards in excavation techniques, data recording, and artifact analysis. Excavations resumed between 1954 and 1957 in preparation for the 350th anniversary of settlement in 1957, with John L. Cotter directing research.[2] With the exception of Structure 144, the Jamestown material discussed here was excavated and curated under the direction of researchers working for the park.

Cotter wrote an exhaustive summary of archaeology at Jamestown (Cotter 1958). At the time, the site included over 150 structures and hundreds of other unassociated pits, ditches, postholes, and other features. Seven structures are included in this study, chosen for a combination of their dates of occupation, the characteristics of their local pipe assemblages, and their possible associations with known individuals. Structures 19, 26/27, 100, 112, 127 and 144 are indicated in Figure 4.1. The local pipe

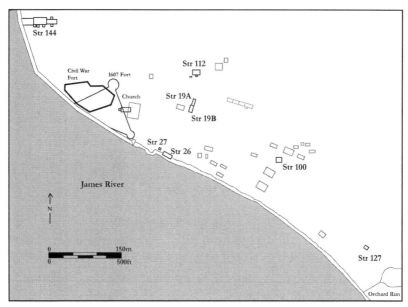

Figure 4.1 Over a century of excavation at Jamestown Island has meant that a significant portion of Virginia's seventeenth-century capital has been exposed. The Structures contributing pipes to this study are labeled. *Illustration by J. Eric Deetz, adapted from Agbe-Davies 2010.*

assemblage from Jamestown includes every fragment associated with these structures.

Following the large scale efforts of the mid twentieth century, excavation picked up again at Jamestown in 1993 and has been ongoing since that time. The National Park Service sponsored a multi-year assessment of existing archaeological collections and remaining unexcavated resources (see Horning 1995; Horning and Edwards 2000). The park also funds cultural resource management work to identify and protect as-yet-undiscovered sites (for example, Agbe-Davies 2000). Since 1994, the Association for the Preservation of Virginia Antiquities (now Preservation Virginia) has been engaged in a project to discover and study the remains of the first fort at Jamestown, located on their own portion of the island, which includes Structure 144 (Kelso 2006; Kelso and Straube 2004). The Structure 144 pipes used here were excavated under these auspices.

The foregoing genealogy serves several functions. It situates our scientific understanding of Jamestown among others that preceded it (let alone what the island meant for the people who lived in the area before anyone thought to call it "Virginia"). Most crucially, it makes clear the debt we later researchers owe to our predecessors, without whose field records and observations the pipe fragments would be but so much rubbish. It also establishes context, essential from the pragmatist's point of view. The context of archaeological research at Jamestown sets the stage for a more detailed consideration of the individual structures from which the pipes came.

The Jamestown Structures

Specific criteria guided the selection of these specific structures from among the scores that were excavated over many decades. Like the plantation sites in Chapter 3, these structures fall within a specific time span in the later seventeenth century. Any differences among them should not be due to changes in pipemaking over time. These dates were established using Harrington's method for dating imported pipe stems (see Chapter 2) and corroborated by date ranges for other artifacts, as well as stratigraphic evidence. Particular ownership histories also influenced my selections. Structures associated with individuals who owned the plantations discussed previously were given special priority in the expectation of capturing evidence of connections between linked town and country properties. Structures with large numbers of locally made pipes—either in absolute terms, or relative to imported pipes—were also favored. Two structures appear to be facilities for ceramic production and speak to the pipemaking potential of the town.

The portraits that follow describe the evidence for attribution to a particular time in Jamestown's history, for connecting a specific structure with a known individual, and for ceramic production in the capital. I refer to the structures by the numbers used by Cotter (Table 4.1) to ease reference to his comprehensive report of 1958 (Cotter 1958), and also because—as will soon become clear—the function of any structure, and its associations with any one ownership history, is in most cases a matter of ongoing interpretation. Therefore, I think it best not to refer to these structures by a particular interpretation, or owner's name.

Pipes from the individual structures are compared against the "norm" of the entire study population. All of these sources of information underwrite the effort to understand what the ensuing similarities and differences *mean*. A pragmatist approach to linguistic meaning emphasizes discursive moments over "language" in the abstract. So, too, the meaning—indeed the very identity—of these artifacts is inextricable from their context. To put a materialist spin on a familiar phrase: the medium is the message. Each portrait includes a summary of the archaeological and archival (and therefore also social) contexts for the pipes, as well as a brief description of the stylistic tendencies that characterize the pipes from each structure.

Structures 26 and 27

The early excavators of Structure 27 identified it as a flight of steps. It was only later that Cotter recognized it as a pottery kiln. It consisted of a small central firebox, roughly five feet by one foot, flanked by two chambers. The small size of the opening at the front means that the kiln was probably unloaded from the top, in a fashion similar to that described for pipe kilns in Chapter 2, as well as the kiln at Green Spring. Several floor tiles with glaze on both surfaces, and in one case running down the side, may have served as kiln props. No locally made pottery vessels were recorded from within the kiln itself. The small brick structure shares an orientation with nearby Structure 26, suggesting they stood at the same time.

Structure 26 was much larger. The fifty-two by sixteen foot brick and stone foundation was only just above mean low tide when it was excavated in 1935.[3] It was oriented along the river, and the foundation, rather than being cut into the soil of the shore to make it level, stepped down towards the river. Long and narrow, with few interior partitions and no chimney base, it differs in size and layout from most of the dwelling houses uncovered at Jamestown. The shape, location, and orientation all suggest a warehouse or storehouse.

At the time of excavation, most of the artifacts from Jamestown were stored and analyzed according to 100 by 100 foot excavation areas termed "lots," so that the artifacts can only be attributed to "Structure 26 *or* 27" at best. But the opportunity to include a kiln which closely resembles contemporaneous pipe kilns in the study overrode the lack of precise provenience information. The pipe stem histogram technique developed by Harrington shows that a reasonable estimate for the assemblage that includes both Structure 27 and Structure 26 is the latter half of the seventeenth century (refer back to Figure 2.2). The date ranges of other artifact classes suggest an early (first-quarter seventeenth-century) initial occupation of the area, perhaps before the construction of these buildings, with Structures 26 and 27 persisting to the end of the seventeenth century.

Analysis of the documentary record links the land on which Structure 26 stood to a William Parry of Kecoughtan, who patented it in 1638. He had substantial holdings elsewhere in the colony, and may never have resided at Jamestown. It is also possible that a member of the Bland family owned this land later in the century.[4] The Blands, as we will see in Chapter 5, fell afoul of the Green Spring faction, and including pipes from a holding of theirs would permit a comparison with both establishment and rebel groups. Structure 27 was on land contained within a different parcel, at one point owned by John White, a merchant. Perhaps he was a party to the nearby "warehouse"?

The pipe fragments from Structure 26/27 and vicinity capture in microcosm the stylistic universe of fragments selected from the five plantations and six Jamestown structures. The Structure 26/27 pipes differ very little from the norms of the larger set in terms of materials, techniques of manufacture, and use. The few attributes which make this subassemblage stand out hint at mass production: an abundance of mold scars, a larger proportion of smoothed rather than burnished surfaces, and a tendency toward finer, as opposed to coarser, clays. We cannot conclude from these characteristics that this assemblage necessarily includes a site of pipe production because other indicators call that interpretation into question. Excavators recovered few wasters or flawed pipes, such as one might expect to see at a production, as opposed to use, site. If the people who built and operated the one structure interpreted as an open top pottery kiln weren't the ones sending pipes from the city to the countryside, was anyone?

Structure 127

Cotter described Structure 127 as a brick kiln or, more precisely, a brick *clamp*. Clamps are constructed of the raw bricks about to be fired, so, unlike kilns, they are almost entirely dismantled when the firing is complete. Here, the clamp was built in a rectangular pit approximately eleven by nine feet. Portions of two firing chambers remained at the time of excavation. Facilities for brick and tile making at Rich Neck and Page invite comparison. Cotter dated the structure to the first quarter of the seventeenth century, based primarily on the large number of square "case" bottle fragments (early seventeenth century) and the absence of round wine bottle glass fragments (post-1650).[5] He also evoked the bore sizes of the imported pipe stem fragments, though the proportions he reports actually suggest a date range of 1620–1650.[6] A recent reassessment of the entire artifact assemblage reinforces a mid-century date (Horning and Edwards 2000:89).

The large number of locally made pipes (over 60 percent of all pipes) from Structure 127, caught Cotter's attention, leading him to state that they "strongly suggest the identity and location of a small but determined tobacco pipemaking effort at Jamestown" (Cotter 1958:145). He continued,

> Anyone of modest means who worked with clay and wanted to smoke would have fashioned clay pipes by hand and devised a simple way of utilizing the heat of the kiln to fire them—anticipating the blossoming of American ingenuity. Doubtless such a workman would have few scruples about neglecting to contribute to the Crown the duty imposed upon imported pipes—nor would his companions, to whom he may have sold pipes in excess of his own needs.
> The brown clay pipes have very characteristic construction details, while showing a wide latitude in ingenuity of design. Three of the bowls are 8-sided, giving them a unique design which rarely appears elsewhere in the Jamestown collection—they are undoubtedly from the hand of a single workman. The other bowls are decorated, one with elaborate stippling which has been filled in with a white paste. The rounded bowls are subconical and of a shape often described as "Indian..." However, it is likely that any white settler's handmade pipe would have come closer to the Indian prototype than would the delicately rounded bowl of the molded import types. The heels of the Structure 127 brown stems also have several examples of a Maltese cross crudely modeled in relief. One heel has had the initials "BR" incised by hand in the wet clay. (1958:145–146)

Subsequent excavations in this area reinforce Cotter's points about Structure 127 possibly being the site of a pipemaking venture. More recent testing along a stretch of the Jamestown waterfront revealed a noticeable concentration of locally made pipes in the vicinity of Structures 126 and 127 (Agbe-Davies 2000:42–43) (Figure 4.2). But even though it seems clear that someone was making pipes here, pipemaking wasn't the principal activity at the site. It was not an operation designed for pipemaking.

What about Cotter's observations about the pipes themselves; do they hold up when the collection of pipes from Structure 127 is compared systematically with a large population of pipe fragments from many sites? A modal analysis of the "8-sided" bowls serves to illustrate. In this case, Cotter's initial impression is confirmed. The faceted bowls *are* quite rare at most of the other sites, including the plantations. At Jamestown, only one other structure (144) yielded more than a single fragment with

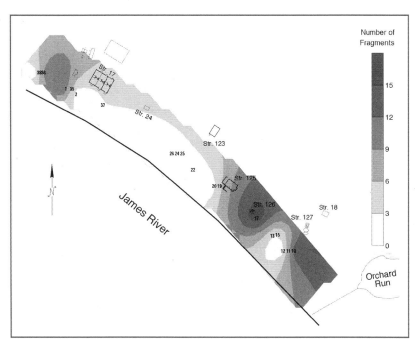

Figure 4.2 A shovel test survey of the Jamestown shoreline demonstrates that local pipe fragments were concentrated at the end closest to Structures 126 (a "brick structural remnant" [Cotter 1958]) and 127. *Adapted from Agbe-Davies 2000:45, figure 32. Courtesy of the Colonial Williamsburg Foundation.*

this design. Rich Neck—with which Structure 144 is connected via the Ludwells—also has a number of faceted bowls. This coincidence makes for a tempting narrative about connections between Structures 127, 144, and Rich Neck (all within the Berkeley/Ludwell sphere of influence), but a closer look reveals significant differences among the sites in terms of the number of faceted bowls.[7] Structure 127 really does stand out, and in a way that doesn't fit with the patterns found at outlying sites—at least in terms of decorative style. The decorative similarities that exist between the pipes from this structure and, for example, Rich Neck, Drummond, and Green Spring—all with faceted bowls—reflect a more general, technological pattern, rather than direct connections. The same holds for the infilled stippling (Emerson 1999; Mouer et al. 1999) and modeled heels. Any pipemaker working at Structure 127 was working outside of the traditions that used molds and other tools that facilitated mass production.

So the pipes themselves stand out like the proverbial sore thumb when placed alongside the other fragments from Jamestown, which means that there was likely little exchange (of pipes or of ideas) between people at this structure and the others. As Cotter noted, the pipes show all the hallmarks of being made without the benefit of specialized tools (disproportionately fewer mold scars, as well as heavily faceted burnishing marks, heels and bowls shaped by cutting or scraping with a blade). Paradoxically, though, Structure 127 *also* stood out for yielding plenty of fragments of bowls shaped using an apparatus like Holme's highly specialized pipemaker's screw (refer back to Figure 2.9) This is unlike the other sites with bowls that have reaming marks on the interiors. In terms of decoration, more of the Structure 127 fragments also bear traces of white slip or paint than is common on the sites included in this study. These measures speak to the comparison between the individual structures and the study assemblage as a whole (not to comparisons between the structures, which appear toward the end of this chapter). Clearly the "brick clamp" pipes are very different from the pottery kiln specimens, and they differ in ways that suggest entirely distinct processes of pipemaking.

With what additional information can we supplement these patterns to try to contextualize them? Documentary research identifies Sir John Harvey as the first English owner of the land on which Structure 127 sat. In 1624 he patented a six-and-a-half acre lot bounded on the east by "the Swamp lying on the East side of the said New Towne" (interpreted as a reference to the modern Orchard Run). When Harvey's property was seized and sold in 1640 (more on Harvey's troubles below, in association with Structure 112, and in Chapter 5), the six and a half acres were divided into several parcels, each with its own history. The portion that eventually included Structure 127 reached the hands of Thomas Hunt no later than 1655. Thus, the kiln might show Harvey's influence (he was a great promoter of local industry) *or* Hunt's. Hunt appeared often in the official records of the colony, including several times for allowing the assembly to meet at his house.[8] In 1662 and 1663 Hunt appeared as a contractor responsible for whomever was to produce the necessary bricks and lime for and then construct Nansemond County's brick "country house" at Jamestown.[9] Hunt died in 1670 or early 1671, and the documents associated with the settling of his estate note that he also had a leasehold in the "governor's land," making him not only someone with access to a ceramic specialist, and someone intimately involved in the efforts to build a brick Jamestown, but also a possible associate of William Drummond and/or William Berkeley.

Structure 100

Structure 100 is a bit of a mystery. Its shifting meanings exemplify the pragmatist model of scientific knowledge as an ongoing conversation (Baert 2005b). The structure straddles a line that separated two early seventeenth-century lots[10] and has definitive associations with several plantation owners introduced in Chapter 3. Richard Kemp, William Berkeley, and John Page were all owners at some point in the seventeenth century. At the turn of the eighteenth century, the lot was purchased by William Drummond, son of the notorious rebel.

"Structure" 100 is, essentially, a single brick wall slightly longer than forty-four feet, presumed to be the north wall of a building when first excavated in 1940. Eight to nine courses of brick survived, buttressed on the north side by small columns of bricks attached to the wall by mortar, but not bonded into the brick matrix, and therefore presumably later than the original construction. The only evidence of any east or west walls consists of filled trenches in which the brickwork could have sat. The walls were either never laid or were entirely removed after abandonment. Researchers re-examined the feature in 1992 as part of a larger reassessment of the architectural evidence uncovered by the mid-twentieth-century excavations (Bragdon et al. 1992). These scholars suggested that the feature was in fact a terraced garden, with the brickwork acting as a retaining wall for the soil on its northern side.[11] The architectural re-analysis prompted additional archaeological testing of Structure 100 in 1993. In this case, the archaeologists concluded that Structure 100 was most likely a retaining wall, but that neither the garden feature idea nor the structural hypothesis could be disproved with the available information (Horning and Edwards 2000).

The artifacts from Structure 100 place it in the mid seventeenth century. For example, the bottle glass was from square-sided case bottles, rather than the later round bottles. Cotter noted that the preponderance of imported pipe bowls suggests a date from the 1640s to the 1660s (refer back to Figure 1.4).[12] The Harrington histogram in Figure 2.2 suggests that the deposits fall into the time span 1650 to 1680. Cotter also wrote of the smaller number of locally made pipes, "[a] majority were molded rather than modeled" (Cotter 1958:96).

With the addition of the pipes from Structure 100 we can begin to see how there is no single Jamestown "type." As with much of the rest of Jamestown—including the assemblage from Structure 26/27, but unlike that from Structure 127—smoothed surfaces and mold scars are overrepresented at Structure 100. In fact, such variables occur disproportionately frequently there compared to the study collection as a whole. These characteristics are typical of pipemakers with specialized tools and facilities. On the other hand, Structure 100 *shares* with 127 (unlike other Jamestown structures) an abundance of square heeled pipes and evidence of incomplete oxidation during firing. These are characteristic of pipes produced using a more generalized tool kit. So if the pipes recovered from the two kilns (26/27 and 127) represent the products of two different pipemakers, both would have been contributing to the collection recovered from Structure 100. Structure 100 is an amalgam. We see nothing like an exclusive relationship with one possible "source" or the other.

Structure 19

Structure 19 also appears to bring together the products of multiple makers. The pipes could easily be lost in either the Jamestown subassemblage or the larger grouping that includes the plantation sites as well. Many distinctive characteristics, such as tooled bowl lips, mold scars, and the ambiguous protuberances that are neither heel nor spur (refer back to Figure 2.12), all indicate mold manufacture and, likely, specialized production as well, despite the relatively rough and coarse texture of the clay itself.

Structure 19 is represented by two overlapping foundations (19A and B), including a forty-three by sixteen foot brick cellar. Due to the circumstances of excavation, the two buildings must be treated as a single structure, just like Structures 26 and 27. Both 19A and 19B are oriented along a north/south axis, perpendicular to the James River shore. The entire complex has been interpreted as a tavern, based, first, on the vaulting of the cellar in Structure 19A ("a use for the old foundation hole for a wine cellar is indicated" [Cotter 1958:53]) and, second, on the large number of (imported) tobacco pipes that excavators recovered.[13] Because so little attention was paid at the time of excavation to stratification or the provenience of artifacts, they are not much use for establishing a date of occupation for either 19A or 19B individually. Excavators found many fragments of round wine bottles but few square case bottles. This impression of a late seventeenth-century date is corroborated by the evidence coming from the imported tobacco pipes. Harrington's technique shows that a reasonable estimate for the entire assemblage is 1650–1710. Such is the archaeological context for the more than 200 local pipe fragments found there.

The historical context is no clearer. Little definitive is known about the ownership history of the lot on which Structure 19 sat. Unlike some of the other structures, I chose it primarily for the size of its local pipe assemblage (see Table 4.1) and the timing of its occupation. Over the years, researchers have linked this structure with a range of seventeenth-century individuals, including John White, or the rebel Richard Lawrence—with subsequent ownership by loyalist Nathaniel Bacon, the Elder (cousin of the rebel who shared his name), or Thomas Woodhouse (Cotter 1958:57). Thomas Swan has also emerged as a potential owner (McCartney and Kiddle 2000). However, these connections are based only on interpretations of the structure's function as a tavern, rather than on chains of title linked to reliable landmarks. Structure 19 illustrates how very limited both the archaeological and documentary record may be, even at a site as comparatively well-studied as Jamestown.

Structure 112

At Structure 112, on the other hand, the archaeological and documentary records present a fairly straightforward picture, at least for the early years of the structure's use-life. All of the information about possible owners or residents of Structure 112 relies on the interpretation of the building

Jamestown Structure number	Number of pipe fragments studied	Interpreted function	Date range
26/27	108	Warehouse, pottery kiln	ca. 1650–1700
127	83	Brick clamp/kiln	ca. 1620–1680
100	233	Retaining wall	ca. 1640–1680
19	221	Tavern? Dwelling house?	ca. 1650–1710
112	266	Dwelling / Statehouse	ca. 1620s–1690s
144	378	Dwelling / Statehouse	ca. 1664–1698

Table 4.1 Six structures from Jamestown comprise the sample used in this study.

as the dwelling of Governor John Harvey, and therefore the "statehouse" during his terms of office (1628–1635, 1636–1640).

Among the many complaints made by Harvey back to the metropole was that he was forced to be Virginia's official host, and that his dwelling house was being used as the colony's statehouse. When Sir Francis Wyatt replaced him as governor in 1640, Harvey was ordered to settle his debts and compelled to sell all of his Jamestown holdings, though he retained life rights to the property. His estate was sold to the colony and included "all of that capital, messuage or tenement now used for a court house late in the tenure of Sir John Harvey Kn[igh]t, situate and being within James City island in Virginia with the old house and granary, garden and orchard, as also one piece or plot of ground lying and being on the west side of the said capital" (McCartney and Kiddle 2000:116). After Sir William Berkeley arrived to take over the governorship in February 1642, the colony presented him with "the orchard with two houses belonging to the colony" at a time when the colony seems to have only owned three tracts, including the churchyard (McCartney and Kiddle 2000:117). So it was likely Harvey's former lot that, when Berkeley died in 1677, he passed on to his widow, Lady Frances. Upon the occasion of her next marriage in 1680, the tract would have become the property of her new husband, Philip Ludwell. At his death (following hers) his properties descended to his son, also Philip Ludwell.

The written record, therefore, firmly places the property in the hands of establishment figures. It also shows that Structure 112 straddled the line between public and private: it was a dwelling, but also served as meeting place for provincial functions. We might expect, then, a more heterogeneous pipe assemblage than at any of the possible production sites. A collection of pipes representing the statehouse aspects of the structure's purpose might be as variable as what we see in a possible tavern such as Structure 19. The pipes would represent the various means by which the assembled smokers obtained them. Pipes accumulated while the structure served as a dwelling might be slightly more homogeneous, to the extent that the occupants of the house could have relied on a narrower range of pipe producers.

The ways in which the Structure 112 pipes stand out from the overall population of pipes in this study cause them to resemble the assemblages from the other Jamestown structures. As at Structure 19, the pipes from Structure 112 differ from the norm in ways that point to well-equipped pipemakers with distinctive materials (coarse clays with red inclusions) as well as distinctive ideas about design (the pseudospurs). Fewer than normal errors in stem-boring may indicate the skill of the maker(s). More likely, however, they reflect Structure 112's status as a point of use, but not manufacture. Production sites could be expected to yield both functional and defective pipes. The latter would be rare at a site without pipe*makers*.

The other artifacts are typical of a well-appointed dwelling of the period rather than a commercial structure such as a warehouse or ordinary. The architectural embellishments of Structure 112 include roofing tiles, roofing slate, lathe-impressed plaster, and ornamental plasterwork, as well as hardware such as nails, hinges, and locks. The windows were glass panes set in lead cames, a fitting setting for a governor.

At the time of Cotter's excavation, a layer of architectural debris and charcoal under some portions of Structure 112's brick floor led him to suggest that "the original building may have burned. Afterward, the foundations might well have been enlarged and strengthened when the house was rebuilt. At any rate, two stages of construction are evident" (Cotter 1958:117). Immediately above the second-phase brickwork was a layer of charcoal, covered with a layer of building rubble (bricks, mortar, plaster, and some building hardware), evidence that the final version of Structure 112 was also destroyed by fire. Imported tobacco pipes found under the brick floor of the cellar suggest an initial occupation in the first or second quarter of the seventeenth century. Above the brick floor (and therefore probably dating to the latest occupation of the structure and its immediate aftermath) artifacts including pipe fragments and round wine bottle glass are more typical of the third quarter of the century (1650–1680).

Bragdon et al. further suggest that the evidence for renovations marks the conversion of the structure from a private dwelling to a public building, namely one of Jamestown's many statehouses (Bragdon et al. 1992). Archaeologist Audrey Horning revisited Structure 112 in 1993. She concurred that the artifacts point to an initial construction date in the 1620s. However, she takes the statehouse argument further. She concludes that the final fire took place in 1698 and links it to written records testifying that the Jamestown statehouse burned in that year (Horning 1995:242). The lack of fourth-quarter-seventeenth-century artifacts is attributed to the light use of the structure during its final phase and/or selective recovery methods (Horning and Edwards 2000:56–57). As we will see now, subsequent scholarship asserts that *Structure 144* was the statehouse that burned in 1698 (Carson et al. 2002).

Structure 144

The foundations of Structure 144, a five-unit building otherwise known as "the Ludwell-Statehouse Group," were first exposed by engineer Samuel Yonge in 1903. Thus, it has been an archaeological site for a period significantly longer than its use-life.[14] Yonge was the one who first identified the multi-unit structure as the building that included one of Jamestown's seventeenth-century statehouses. Additional excavation in the 1950s was by Park Service archaeologists in cooperation with the landowner, the Association for the Preservation of Virginia Antiquities (APVA). In 2000, the APVA returned to Structure 144 with its own archaeological team, led by Jamie May for principal investigator William Kelso (May 2003).[15]

These twenty-first-century archaeologists paid careful attention to the little evidence that remained regarding construction sequence and use. The latest assessment concludes that "the preponderance of evidence points to the easternmost of the units that comprise Structure 144 (House 5) as having been the statehouse that was built in 1665, burned by Bacon's rebels in 1676, and rebuilt in 1684 to serve as the final statehouse at Jamestown" (Carson et al. 2002:iv).[16] Given the artifacts recovered from the site and the dimensions of the various houses, which conform to the requirements set forth in the 1662 town-building act, a late third-quarter seventeenth-century construction date is likely.[17] Structure 144's House 5 may pre-date 1665, which means it could be the statehouse mentioned in documents of that date. Although Carson et al. subscribe to the statehouse interpretation, they note that House 5 is similar enough to such brick manor houses as Green Spring, Bacon's Castle, and Arlington (one might also add the Page house) to be interpreted as a private dwelling that was later repurposed as a statehouse (Carson et al. 2002:1–13).

The oldest portion of Structure 144 (Houses 1 and 2) probably dates no earlier than 1662, the year of the town-building act that specified the dimensions and materials to be used in transforming the community on Jamestown Island into a proper "city." Carson et al. (2002:3–8) suggest that House 5 is the building indicated in documents dating to 1664/5 referring to a newly built "State House," with additions made perhaps sometime between 1664 and 1685. Some, if not all, of the units of Structure 144 were damaged within a timeframe consistent with Bacon's Rebellion (1676). In 1685, House 5 was rebuilt, again as a statehouse. In 1694, Philip Ludwell[18] repaired and added to Houses 3 and 4. But in 1698, a fire "broke out in a house adjoining...the State-house," (cited in Carson et al. 2002:3–11), providing the Council with the rationale they needed to implement their plan for moving the capital to what would become Williamsburg.

In addition to clarifying the construction sequence at Structure 144, the most recent archaeological excavations confirmed Yonge's original interpretation that the houses were destroyed by fire, and furthermore that the fires occurred after the chimney-work and porch additions. The artifact assemblage taken as a whole points to an occupation in the second half of the seventeenth century. The artifacts are typical of domestic sites of that era, including wine bottle glass, and imported and local tobacco pipes. Tellingly, House 5—thought to be the statehouse—yielded little in the way of household artifacts.

The Structure 144 pipes, like those from other Jamestown structures, differ from the norm in ways that suggest specialized manufacture. They have more mold scars, and like those found at Structure 127, more fragments with evidence of bowl formation using a tool inserted vertically, rather than rotated. The Structure 144 fragments include fewer than normal pinched or scraped surfaces, and so forth. Interestingly, there are fewer parallels with Rich Neck than with Green Spring, despite all of these sites having Ludwell connections.

The contested history of Jamestown's statehouses needn't cause alarm. Fallibilism—acknowledging that one has to begin one's investigation somewhere—means that new information, new clarity on this question, will simply continue the scientific conversation and further refine foregoing analysis. It is enough for our purposes that, whether the Council met in Structure 112 or Structure 144, both were securely within the orbit of the Green Spring faction. What this portrait of Structure 144 and those of the other structures with their pipes show is that the pipes from Jamestown—whether considered by structure or collectively—do not represent a random sample of the universe of pipe variables predominant in the early Virginia colony, as they might if they were either the source of the plantation pipes or the recipient of pipes from the plantations. Rather, the Jamestown structures present collections with some distinctive stylistic qualities. Important characteristics distinguish among them and show important contrasts with the pipes from the Green Spring, Drummond, Rich Neck, Page, and Port Anne plantation sites.

Pipes, Jamestown Style

Far from replicating the larger assemblage in microcosm—as we might expect if the town were a single source of pipes for the hinterlands, or if it were a collection point for the output of plantation-based makers—the pipes found at the Jamestown structures, collectively and individually, have their own style. To be clear, there is nothing like a Jamestown "type." No attribute or combination thereof appears always and only among the Jamestown specimens. There is no marker for "Jamestown." And the characteristics of the Jamestown style, which trends towards the mass-produced, are lacking in the one assemblage (Structure 127) that is most distinctive and seems most likely to represent a production site. The fact of Jamestown's distinctive style matters because the technological differences in the way that many Jamestown pipes were made suggests that they were not made by the same people who made the pipes recovered from the planation sites.

We can begin the comparison with a familiar criterion, namely decoration. The pipemakers whose wares were recovered from Jamestown were no more, and no less, decorated than pipes at the other sites. To put it more precisely, there was no significant difference in the frequency of decoration when the pipes from Jamestown were treated as the equivalent of one "site" and compared with the plantation assemblages. Likewise, Jamestown yielded similar proportions of pipe fragments on which the maker had picked out decorations in white paint or slip to the proportions found on the plantation sites. Cotter was right to state that Structure 127 had a notable number of such pipes. It was the only structure at Jamestown whose assemblage differed significantly from the norm, and in that regard resembled Page (another brick manufacturing site) and Port Anne (which had a clay borrow pit, but not much else in the way of evidence for ceramic production). So in terms of the rate of decoration, Jamestown is not substantially different from the study collection as a whole.

If we turn to the style of technology, rather than the style of decoration, there are again some ways in which Jamestown pipes could be simply a subset of pipes in the region, rather than a distinct category. For example, as a group, the Jamestown firing cores fit neatly into the overall assemblage, but examining the assemblages of the six structures individually shows that "Jamestown" consists of divergent subsets. So, Structure 127 yielded disproportionately more fragments fired in oxidizing atmospheres or in a reducing atmosphere with rapid cooling in an oxygen-rich environment (Rye 1981:figure 104), whereas the Structure 26/27 fragments disproportionately were fired in reducing environments without later exposure to oxygen. So, the two structures differ from the norm, but they also diverge from the Jamestown "norm," and in different directions from each other. As with several other attributes, when combined into one

"Jamestown," these firing core distributions cancel each other out, revealing that the conformity of Jamestown as a whole to the rest of the study population is a product of its hybrid nature. Like the study collection itself, "Jamestown" is an amalgam of different pipe styles.

The different techniques that pipemakers used to finish the lip and mouthpiece of each pipe tell a story similar to that told by the kiln conditions. Taken as a group, the Jamestown pipes don't differ significantly from the norm when one considers whether pipemakers used specialized tools to finish the pipes. So it is not impossible that pipes could be moving from town to countryside or vice versa. Yet, examined individually, the structures at Jamestown *do* diverge from the norm. Some show the use of specialized tools. The pipe fragments from Structures 19 and 112 have more traces of the use of a bottering or other shaping tool at the lip. On the other hand, many of the Structure 100 pipes were simply cut across the top as they were finished. At Structure 127, there is less evidence of specialized equipment. There, rounded mouthpieces predominate, a characteristic typical of pipes made without molds. And furthermore, when Jamestown is used as the reference point, all but one of the Structures (127) resemble the town's norm.[19]

Some variations do cause the Jamestown pipes to stand out—as a group. For example, there are more firing clouds on the Jamestown pipe fragments. This difference is due primarily to the influence of the fragments from Structure 100. The only other site with a significant number of firing clouds is Drummond's plantation, which in other respects shares very little with the Jamestown assemblage. More telling, perhaps, is the greater evidence for the use of specialized tools to make the Jamestown pipes. For example, significantly fewer traces of cut or scrape marks appear on fragments in the Jamestown assemblage. And more pipe bowls appear to have been made with a tool that was fixed to a mold and inserted with a plunging motion into the pliable clay. The makers of the Jamestown pipes smoothed, rather than burnished, their wares. The fragments show significantly more pipes with heels, especially round ones—an aspect of decorative style, but one that tracks closely with production in molds. Finally, the Jamestown pipe fragments are characterized by an abundance of mold scars. The only plantation to show a similar pattern is Green Spring, which was both near to Jamestown and closely linked with the capital through the ruling elite. These technological differences, more numerous than the technological similarities, call into question the idea that the pipes from the plantations and the pipes from Jamestown came from the same makers.

The larger pattern—of Jamestown *as a whole* replicating the characteristics of the total population of all pipe fragments included in this study,
while the individual structures diverge from each other—can still be accom-
modated by a scenario in which pipemakers at Jamestown distributed their
wares to the plantations. But the lack of wasters and other mis-made pipes,
which should be found in a production setting, is difficult to overcome.
Jamestown should have more wasters, more fragments of pipes that were
misshapen, and perhaps more examples of pipes with more than one bore,
but there is no significant difference between the Jamestown collection and
that of the larger population. Those individual structures which show significant differences, for the most part, have *fewer* "seconds" than the overall
norm. These characteristics underline the argument that even though they
appear to be made differently, the Jamestown pipes don't really look any
more like a production assemblage than the plantation groupings do.

It seems unlikely that any one Jamestown structure—like the kilns
26/27 and 127— or the town as a whole could have been a source for pipes
on the plantations. The pipes from Jamestown are just too out of step with
the rest of the assemblage, with all of the hallmarks of large-scale production. The Jamestown sites—and the plantation sites for that matter—are
not simply components of a single heterogeneous tradition. Rather, the
attributes reveal patterns that distinguish the individual sites. This knowledge sets up the next inquiry: Are any sites similar to each other based
on more particular criteria? It is possible that Jamestown and the other
sites were enmeshed in more complicated exchange relationships based
on proximity or social networks (the subject of Chapter 5). The tasks that
remain here are to show whether the variation among the sites (rather
than between the individual assemblages and the aggregate assemblage)
is due to chance and whether that variation indicates a rural/urban divide.

"Jamestown" as a Category

Another angle from which to approach the pipe fragments from Jamestown
is to group them. Here, I analyze these artifacts as one assemblage among
six, the other five being the plantations from Chapter 3. This analysis
reveals the extent to which these sites are really different from each other.
Once the extent of difference among the six sites is established, it can be
used as a baseline for the final comparison, in which I consider whether
the Jamestown assemblage is viable as a category (urban?) to be contrasted
with another which includes all of the plantations (rural?).

Some of the variation among sites/structures is random, but most clearly isn't. The only variable for which we see no significant difference among the six sites—Green Spring, Drummond, Rich Neck, Page, Port Anne, and Jamestown—is the presence or absence of white paint or slip. A similar picture emerges when one compares individual sites or structures to the overall assemblage. (The details for this variable are shown in Table 4.2, and repeated again in Table 4.3). So the white slip, which has received much attention (Emerson 1999; Mouer et al. 1999), appears to be randomly distributed across the sites and not characteristic of any particular pipe assemblage(s). The white slip is something of an anomaly, though; many other attributes *do* discriminate effectively among the sites and structures. The distribution of modes, representing both decorative and technological style, is not random, but patterned.

Whether the attributes are related to materials, techniques of manufacture, shape, or decorative style, the sites—including Jamestown—do seem to be meaningful units of pipe style. The first column of Table 4.3 shows all of the attributes for which the sites differ significantly from each other. The "Ns" in the third column, for "no significant difference," show that the Jamestown structures are more similar to each other than the six

	Paint/ slip	Not		Round heel	Square heel
Drummond	30	832	Str. 100	20	6
Green Spring	16	585	Str. 112	13	2
Jamestown	37	1252	Str. 127	2	7
Page	10	150	Str. 144	15	—
Port Anne	26	491	Str. 19	16	—
Rich Neck	47	1496	Str. 26/27	10	1

Table 4.2 The chi-square statistic shows that presence or absence white paint or slip decoration does not adequately distinguish among the pipe fragments from the six sites studied here (x^2 = 10.97, df = 5, p >0.05). The difference between round heels and square heels does vary significantly among the Jamestown structures (x^2 = 30.654, df = 5, p < 0.001; note: the expected values are quite low, meaning that the true significance is debatable).

	Site <0.05?	Site Cramer's V	Structure <0.05?	Structure Cramer's V	Jamestown vs. plantations <0.05?	Jamestown vs. plantations Cramer's V
scar	Y	0.29	Y	0.18	Y	0.17
bowl base	Y	0.39	N	—	Y	0.32
heel shape	Y	0.28	Y	0.58	Y	0.19
surface texture	Y	0.27	Y	0.16	Y	0.17
mouth-piece	Y	0.24	n/a[1]	—	N	—
lip forming tech	Y	0.22	Y	0.42	N	—
surface treatment	Y	0.20	Y	0.18	Y	0.14
bowl forming tech	Y	0.19	n/a	—	Y	0.09
multiple bores	Y	0.19	Y	0.15	N	—
inclusions	Y	0.15	n/a	—	Y	0.06
dec motif presence	Y	0.14	N	—	N	—
firing cloud	Y	0.13	Y	0.13	Y	0.06
fabric texture	Y	0.09	Y	0.24	Y	0.03
core	Y	0.09	Y	0.16	N	—
pinching	Y	0.05	Y	0.11	N	—
paint/slip	N	—	Y	0.05	N	—

[1] "Expected" values too low for accuracy; if the contingency table contains too many "expected" values of less than five, or any values less than one, then the chi-square results should not be viewed as entirely reliable (Drennan 1996:197).

Table 4.3 At what level of aggregation do assemblages differ from one another? This table records whether the sub-assemblages show significant differences ("Y" for "yes") among themselves, using a range of technological and decorative modes. The statistic Cramer's V is a measure of the strength of association between a variable and the unit of aggregation. For example, the sites may be distinguished from one another based on the presence or absence of mold scars. Reading from left to right, the same variable also shows statistical differences between the Structures at Jamestown. Finally, the presence or absence of mold scars is also a way in which Jamestown differs from the plantations. Furthermore, the association between individual sites and presence/absence is stronger than between Jamestown structures and presence/absence.

sites are. What is really interesting is where the lack of difference shows up. The Jamestown assemblages are similar to each other, for example, in the proportion of fragments with a heel or spur, and the proportion of decorated fragments. Any Jamestown "style," then, is a purely decorative one. The pipemakers whose handiwork archaeologists recovered from the Jamestown structures made pipes that looked alike—sharing superficial decorative similarities—but were not necessarily made in the same way. This is not to say that the similarities are meaningless, only that they are a kind of style that is easily imitated and can move quickly and consciously from one maker to the next, through deliberate imitation. Such similarities, therefore, are poor indicators of manufacture by the same individual(s). The pipes from Jamestown were made by people who had seen one another's efforts and replicated popular decorative characteristics, but the pipemakers did not work together or share technological expertise.

Returning to Table 4.3, we see in the second and fourth columns a statistic called Cramer's V, which measures the strength of association between variables (for example, presence or absence of mold scars) and categories (sites or structures).[20] A quick scan of these columns shows that the sites are not necessarily distinguished from each other by the same attributes as the structures are. For example, the presence or absence of a heel or spur ("bowl base") discriminates well among the six sites, whereas heel *shape* is what matters most among the Jamestown structures. So to the extent that we consider presence/absence to be a bigger difference than shape, the Jamestown pipes are less different from each other with respect to heels than the plantation site pipes are from each other.

Where the strength of association gets really interesting is in the comparison of these two kinds of groupings—sites and structures—with another kind of grouping, one which pits Jamestown against the plantations. As it turns out, sorting the pipe fragments into the categories of "Jamestown" and "plantation" produces weaker results than sorting the pipes into groups defined by the individual sites and structures. As shown in the "Jamestown vs. plantations" columns of Table 4.3, that comparison yielded fewer significant differences and lower strengths of association. For example, differences in lip forming technology, that had proved a *good* discriminator among sites and among structures, showed no significant difference between "Jamestown" and "plantation" pipes. In every instance but one (surface texture), the "Jamestown" versus "plantations" comparison produced a Cramer's V score *lower* than that obtained with comparisons among sites or among structures. In other words, the differences between the groups "Jamestown" and "plantations" are less strong. Sorting the pipes into these two categories creates a distinction without a difference.

Comparisons of pipe dimensions lead to a similar conclusion. Measurable pipe dimensions allow one to distinguish the six sites (the plantations plus Jamestown) from one another. A test for variance[21] helps to answer the question: Are the sites' pipe assemblages really different from one another in terms of the dimensions of their pipe fragments? It also offers an answer to another question: Is there more difference *between* the groups than *within* each one? The results show that, for most measures, the differences between sites are greater than those within sites (Table 4.4).[22] So we again conclude that Jamestown makes sense as a category in comparison with the individual plantations, even if it does not when in contrast with them collectively.

Looking at it another way—through the lens of the coefficient of variation (CV)—we can further confirm the idea that the Jamestown pipes stand out among the six groups, but the contrast between "Jamestown" and "plantations" means little. The average CV for the Jamestown sites is lower than that of the other sites, suggesting greater homogeneity (see Table 3.2). A comparison of the "Jamestown" CV to the "plantation" CV shows that the coefficients from Jamestown are generally lower. However, the town assemblage is not significantly less variable than the group consisting of all plantation assemblages. This idea can be further supported by a series of t-tests comparing Jamestown to the plantations. This method shows that there are fewer metric distinctions between these two groups than among the six sites (Agbe-Davies 2004b:316). As with the nominal attributes and the analysis of variance, examining the CV of the grouped plantation assemblages in opposition to the grouped Jamestown structures only succeeds in blurring differences that had been clear before— for example, stem height, mouthpiece diameter, interior bowl diameter, and volume. At the same time, the analysis of variance provides no additional clarity for measurements that fail to discriminate at the site level— for example, exterior bowl diameter, angle, and thickness (Agbe-Davies 2004b: Table 9.7).[23]

	Source	SSQ	df	Variance	F	p<0.05?	% explained
volume[1]	total	85.4972	57	1.4999516	11.512	Y	29.51%
	b/w	25.2299	2	12.61497			
	w/in	60.2673	55	1.0957691			
bore diameter	total	5427.16	3267	1.661205	145.47	Y	18.30%
	b/w	993.366	5	198.67323			
	w/in	4455.04	3262	1.3657373			
mouthpiece diameter	total	269.836	291	0.92727	12.686	Y	15.02%
	b/w	40.54	4	10.13501			
	w/in	229.296	287	0.799			
bowl diameter (juncture)	total	387.656	128	3.0285637	10.891	Y	14.74%
	b/w	57.1358	2	28.567924			
	w/in	330.52	126	2.623177			
bowl diameter (interior)	total	104.477	86	1.2148514	3.679	Y	8.05%
	b/w	8.41459	2	4.2072968			
	w/in	96.0626	84	1.1436027			
heel length	total	176.458	100	1.7645831	3.774	Y	7.15%
	b/w	12.6179	2	6.3089608			
	w/in	163.84	98	1.6718407			
stem height	total	689.396	567	1.2158663	8.428	Y	5.65%
	b/w	38.9481	4	9.7370267			
	w/in	650.448	563	1.1553251			
thickness	total	76.6144	193	0.396966	1.8433	Y	4.67%
	b/w	3.58047	5	0.716094			
	w/in	73.0339	188	0.388478			
angle	total	9712	68	142.82353	0.138	N	—
	b/w	62.7595	3	20.919841			
	w/in	9831.24	65	151.24985			
bowl exterior diameter	total	171.358	114	1.503141	2.293	N	—
	b/w	9.99913	3	3.3330426			
	w/in	161.359	111	1.4536842			

[1]Measurements need to be normally distributed. If not, a site was omitted from the comparison.

Table 4.4 The analysis of variance (ANOVA) allows us to compare the metric variability among sites to the variability encompassed within them. Volume distinguishes quite well among the sites. Angle is irrelevant.

˙˙˙

This chapter has considered Jamestown at a number of scales. Comparisons of pipes from individual Jamestown structures to the population of all pipes included in this study—as well as comparisons of the structure assemblages to each other—have shown that "Jamestown" is not a monolith. Rather, it is a heterogeneous amalgam, much like the population itself. The Jamestown-to-population comparisons undermine the argument that Jamestown, understood generically, could be a source for (or recipient of) pipes like those excavated from plantations. The assemblages of pipes from the individual structures are different enough from each other to not be a single conceptual unit. And the assemblages of individual sites, while not stylistically uniform, are distinct from each other.

And yet, the comparison of a collective "Jamestown" assemblage to the population of all pipes shows that the pipes recovered from the town structures stand out in several ways. Likewise, when treated as one site among others, "Jamestown" holds up reasonably well. The Jamestown pipes differ in terms of superficial characteristics, such as decoration, which might easily have been imitated by many pipemakers. But more tellingly, they also exhibit deep technological differences, including a suite of clay processing, shaping, and firing techniques and technologies. What is striking, though, is the failure of "Jamestown" in opposition to the single category "plantations." The findings come from a series of modal and stepwise analyses, proceeding not from first principles, but from premises as befits a pragmatist approach (Agbe-Davies under review a). Rather than define categories of pipes, I have considered the distribution of variables across populations, populations that have archaeological and social contexts. The variables index specific actions on the part of pipemakers. The pipes are signs of the choices made in their own production.

Still, we have not yet eliminated the possibility that pipemakers at either kind of site—urban or rural—may have had a more specific and less generic relationship to pipe-smokers. In other words, maybe trade didn't move from "Jamestown" to "plantations" or vice versa, but rather along individualized lines established by specific social relationships. So the problem for Chapter 5 is to examine the effect of relationships among elite land and labor owners on the assemblages recovered from the sites.

Moving Pipes through Social and Physical Space
Chapter 5

Tobacco, smoking, and pipes—as global phenomena—epitomized the emerging modern world. We can consider them from the perspective of Virginia's colonizers who introduced tobacco to the people of the Old World, settling the Chesapeake, establishing plantations for increased production, and, when the pace of European immigration couldn't keep up with the demand for labor, conscripting Africans to fill the gap. But we can also contemplate these artifacts and practices from the flip side, from the bottom up as it were, using the pipes themselves as evidence. Matthew Johnson has written about pipes made in Britain as

> artefact[s] of colonialism as well as of popular resistance [because of their association with alehouses and other hotbeds of radicalism]. Like many other commodities, such as tea and sugar, the popularity of these items among ordinary people from the later seventeenth century onwards fueled Imperial trade and colonial domination. (Johnson 1996:186)

Tobacco, Pipes, and Race in Colonial Virginia: Little Tubes of Mighty Power by Anna S. Agbe-Davies, 139–170. © 2015 Left Coast Press, Inc. All rights reserved.

Determining whether this domination included a role for Virginia elites in the production and circulation of locally made pipes concerns the extent to which craftspeople could assert their own power and engage in economic activities beyond the gaze of the great planters.

Investigating this question, however, involves a bit of jujitsu. Just as the martial art redirects the power of an opponent rather than meeting it with an opposing force, this chapter uses the dominance of elite actors in the written record to reveal their lack of control over pipe production and distribution. With few exceptions, available documents do not discuss the principal artisans associated with early Virginian crafts. The aforementioned instances of tools in a probate inventory and the chance description of someone digging "pipe clay" are quite unusual. The artisans in other industries are scarcely better documented. We find even less written about the other people who labored in and otherwise supported these enterprises. For every John Page commissioning bricks and tiles—for his own use, as well as for sale—there was an unnamed master craftsmen directing the operation, and any number of indentured servants and slaves digging the clay, molding the forms, tending the kilns, and carting around the finished product. And this vision doesn't even take into account those whose labor supported the endeavor by maintaining the household and taking up the subsistence tasks that the specialists left undone (Hendon 1996). Historical archaeology, because it uses both the written and material record, gives us an opportunity to understand the contribution of all these unnamed individuals to "Page's" enterprise.

Although historical archaeology traditionally emphasizes domestic sites—and understands people of the past in terms of their possessions, their homes, and their private lives—the fact remains that for many people one of their primary social roles was as a *worker*, and archaeological studies of their laboring places and products can contribute to our understanding of that very important aspect of their lives. Archaeologists going back to V. Gordon Childe have investigated the relationship between social complexity, hierarchy, and craft specialization (Brumfiel and Earle 1987; Clark 1995; Sabloff 1996; Wailes 1996). So while the problem of production is interesting for its own sake, production and distribution patterns (the "modes of production") have broader implications for our understanding of the larger society.

An historical archaeology of production has the potential to tell us a great deal about social relations, technology, labor management, and a host of other important topics (compare Agbe-Davies in prep with Noël Hume

1969:174–175). At the same time, we can investigate specific instances of social learning, analyze community networks, and reconstruct regional economies. We can think of production and exchange as existing in social, as much as physical, space. This chapter considers to what extent social relationships among planters and physical proximity among sites affected the distribution of pipe attributes across these sites.

Social Contexts of Pipe Production

Pipemaking in the plantation setting can be compared with what is known about specialized pipemaking in Europe. For one thing, European pipemaking was highly specialized and tightly controlled. Professional pipemakers chartered a guild in Westminster in the year 1619, forbidding all but guild members to "practice use or exercise the acte or mistery of making of Tobacco Pipes of any matter or forme whatsoever" (Walker 1977:189). They also did not allow non-members to "erect or sett up or mayntayne any furnace Structure instrument [or?] Engyn for the makeinge framinge or workinge of the said Tobacco pipes." But away from the controls of the metropole, the barriers to entry were low. Seventeenth century probate inventories included values for three vices and three molds at £ 2 (1663), and five molds at £ 3 (1691). Such molds could last for a generation, sometimes longer (Oswald 1985:7–8). Equipment, then, was inexpensive and apparently within the reach of the pipemaking families who frequently appeared on relief registers (Arnold 1977).[1]

Pipemaking in proto-industrial Europe was a collaborative effort. According to Walker, a small workshop in the late seventeenth century would likely include a master pipemaker, his wife, two journeymen, and two apprentices.[2] The number of discrete roles that were filled by any one person is not always clear, though according to one early nineteenth-century account of a French factory, as many as fifteen or sixteen individuals would be involved in the manufacture of a single pipe, all prior to the firing stage (Walker 1977:88). H.-L. Duhamel du Monceau's[3] discussion of pipe making in northern France and the Netherlands dating to 1771 describes the various roles, including *batteur, rouleur*, molder, and *trameuse*. A skilled molder in the eighteenth-century French industry could shape perhaps 3,000 pipes a week, and earned a monthly wage about half that of the batteur. A roller, because of the expertise required, earned slightly more than a molder. A trimmer could expect to make one third the wage of a molder (Walker 1977:416). The traces that their work left on the pipes have already been addressed; in this chapter, we situate these workers in their social context.

Of course, not all aspects of a pipe production operation would transfer across the Atlantic. Even if settlers of the Virginia colony thought of themselves as English subjects, life and labor played out very differently on the colonial stage. Pipemaking would have been no exception, and operated differently in a society without guilds, factories, or much of an apprentice system. We can imagine people moving pipes through two parallel landscapes, one physical and one social. Both were products of the colonial enterprise, the tobacco economy, and the colony's insatiable appetite for labor.

Landscapes of the Virginia Colony

After the initial colonization of Jamestown Island, the immigrants spread out rather rapidly along Virginia's rivers. Unlike farmers in England, Virginia's planters did not live in nucleated settlements surrounded by their fields. Tobacco agriculture was partially responsible for this settlement pattern. Without supplemental nutrients, tobacco fields were often exhausted after only a few years. Planters who could afford to would allow a field to recuperate for a decade or more before using it for tobacco again. This meant that new fields were continually being cleared, and that planters' homes were often separated from one another by many acres of fields, fallow ground, and woods.

The people who lived in these isolated households were mostly immigrants newly acquainted with the place and with each other. The majority of European immigrants arrived as indentured servants, who were generally prohibited from marrying and bearing children during the term of their indenture (Tomlins 2001:27). Elizabeth Mullin, for example, indentured to Elisheba Vaulx, became pregnant before her term was up (and before she had entered into the sacrament of marriage). Her punishment was to serve additional time. Vaulx paid the fine, 500 pounds of tobacco, to exempt her from the beating that was also prescribed by law in such cases. People like "Betty," as Vaulx called her, could be contentious members of a plantation household, and in fact, Vaulx had some difficulty getting Mullin to comply with the court order to serve additional time: "she is growne soe high and soe parantory, that I can scarce speake to her" (York DOW 1680/1:6:279, 288).

Mullin was likely an immigrant from England. Other bonded laborers came into the colony "by shipping" (Africans) or "by land" (Native people). As we shall see in Chapter 6, the status of these laborers as what we might now call "indentured servants" (bound for a term) or "slaves" (bound in perpetuity) shifted over the course of the seventeenth century. The matter is somewhat academic, because if Middlesex County, Virginia, was typical, only a minority of indentured servants survived their terms (D. Rutman and A. Rutman 1984b:130). They may as well have been bound for life. A servant who managed to beat the odds, and had the opportunity to form a family in freedom, was older than his or her counterparts across the Atlantic and had fewer childbearing years left. Furthermore, planters routinely brought men into the colony at a higher rate than they did women. All of these factors combined to ensure that the colony depended on in-migration to grow the population.

The demographic structure shaped familial relationships in other ways. Even after the proverbial "seasoning" period, during which new immigrants adjusted to the disease environment and the hard labor expected of most of them, mortality was still high, which affected the social structure as well as the population structure. Few people attained adulthood with both parents still living, a third had lost both parents by the time they were grown (D. Rutman and A. Rutman 1979:153). Men and women whose spouses died often remarried rapidly; it was not unheard of for children to live in a household in which neither "parent" was a blood relation.

The vulnerability of any particular nuclear family was counterbalanced by connections between families. These networks of kinship and friendship were maintained through mutual obligations—for example, lending capital, pooling labor, raising orphans, or assisting in legal matters. Community rituals further strengthened these ties. Court day, religious services, and rites of passage brought together people from different households frequently. Travelers to the colony commented on the mania for "visiting" and the high value placed on giving and receiving hospitality. Though significant, these networks connecting nuclear families were fairly localized. Researchers examining Middlesex County, Virginia, found that 95 percent of marriages brought together partners living within five miles of each other. Friendships occurred most often in areas two to three miles across. As might be expected, immigrants had fewer kin than friends, and the wealthy and well-connected had more friends than the destitute. Individuals with higher status were more likely to have friendships that transcended their immediate locality (D. Rutman and A. Rutman 1984a:110–111; 1984b:120).

Elites weren't the only ones moving about. We have already seen bonded men moving between plantations, seemingly on a regular basis. Peter Wells's and Frank's movements were at least occasionally endorsed by the heads of their respective households. Bondspeople also traveled *without* permission, sometimes with an economic motive. The unnamed servants of Captain Francis Page whom Mary Mills was found guilty of "trucking and tradeing" with may not have come to her with their ill-gotten goods (York DOW 1688:8:121). But there were plenty of cases in which servants absconded altogether, sometimes with contraband. Thomas Ashby's story shows the risks associated with such acts. Indentured at the age of 16 to John Page, Ashby ran away, but was caught mere months from the end of his original indenture, at which time he was made to serve nearly three more years, in part for the crime of seizing his freedom, in part for taking with him "a considerable quantity of goods & money" (York DOW 1675:5:109; 1682:6:410).

The modern adage "it takes money to make money" would have rung true for a seventeenth-century Virginian. Immigrants who came as free people with the resources to secure land and labor had a much greater chance of success than those who arrived as bonded laborers. For ensuing generations, parental wealth was an important predictor of one's own chances for financial success.[4] The odds of achieving a higher level of wealth than one's parents decreased as the century wore on, as land became scarcer, and as the initial cost of obtaining labor rose (Carr and Menard 1979; D. Rutman and A. Rutman 1984a:120–130). This economic immobility is an ironic contrast with the peripatetic tendencies of colonial Virginians.

Becoming a tobacco planter did not guarantee financial success, but it was generally a free person's best option. Despite the efforts of governors like Harvey and Berkeley to diversify the economy, the colony relied on tobacco exports almost exclusively for its income for much of the seventeenth century and, following the classic mercantilist model, imported many of the goods that might otherwise have been produced locally. Harvey, for example, tried to recruit artisans from Europe, but had to resort to legislation to prevent those few that came from abandoning their trades to grow tobacco (Billings 1996; Metz 1999). And despite Charles II's 1662 instructions to Governor Berkeley to encourage the production of silk, flax, hemp, pitch, and potash, he was also clearly aware of the revenue generated by the taxes and shipping associated with the tobacco trade. His mandate seems to be encouraging a shift to some semi-processed commodities, but not a fundamental change in the relationship between

England and its colony, as he omitted local manufacture for local needs (the Virginia Magazine of History and Biography 1895). Immigrants were continually funneled into fieldwork—sometimes in direct violation of indenture agreements. Thus, there were few opportunities for learning trades in the colony, and with start-up costs for planting being so low (at the most basic level, access to land, a hoe, seeds, and sweat equity), most free people tried their hand at planting.

Although it was possible to become a planter relying only on one's own labor, several crucial elements were beyond any one person's control. For example, the international trade on which planters depended tended to favor their partners located in the metropole. Planters were not able to set the prices at which their commodity was sold. They relied on merchants or factors to negotiate prices for them and exchanged the resulting credits for imports for their households. Those who were on the losing ends of these transactions in the seventeenth century had a sense of their exploitation. Bacon's Rebellion was one of many manifestations of their frustration.[5]

Virginia's system of government (examined in greater detail in Chapter 6) was dominated by a small coterie of men, many of whom were related by blood or marriage. Local office was the key to provincial power. This provided important continuity and helped provide experienced officers for the complicated task of governing, but it also tended to perpetuate the power of particular individuals and cliques over long periods of time. The name "Green Spring faction" was used by late seventeenth-century Virginians to refer to the core group of Governor Berkeley's supporters, employing the name of his plantation at Green Spring. Many of these men were his councilors, or had other official roles in the provincial government. In the colony, offices were used to cement friendships and find suitable marriage partners (the daughters, widows, and sisters of one's peers), which tended to concentrate power, wealth, and privilege in the hands of a few related families who, unsurprisingly, looked out for each other's interests.

The degree to which public offices were used for private gain is nothing less than astonishing. In an era where a laborer generated less than £ 7 a year for a planter, Governor William Berkeley received an annual salary of £ 1,000, and made thousands more in fees and other official perks. Many officers were compensated for service with a percentage of the fees they collected, turning an appointment into a moneymaking opportunity. When the General Assembly met—usually for less than a month—even the drummer who called the burgesses and councilors to the statehouse was paid more than a man could make working the fields for an entire year. In fact, the expense of Assembly meetings was a perennial complaint among free Virginians. Tobacco prices headed steadily downward at the same time that fee income rose for colonial officials. People complained bitterly, but their only recourse was to men often engaged in similar profiteering. In addition to outright fraud, a significant proportion of tax proceeds went to projects, such as the "country houses" of Jamestown, that many saw as pointless. Virginians were similarly skeptical of the frontier forts proposed by Governor Berkeley to protect settlers from their Native neighbors (His Majesties Commissioners 1677; Morgan 1975).

In sum, a small group of provincial elites had the authority to tax, manage, and regulate the behavior of their subordinates. The source of their power was familial wealth, marriage and friendship alliances, and patronage. Virginia was a hard place for those who bore the brunt of exploitation by these men—bound laborers, and to a much lesser and indirect extent, freemen and small planters. It was hard in a different way for those who felt that they deserved that authority as much or more than those who held it (Bacon 1893 [1676]; Billings 1970; 1996; D. Rutman and A. Rutman 1984b). All of these elite powers derived—at least officially—from the authority of the king. For some time the Virginia colony had experienced a kind of benign neglect, but in the second half of the seventeenth century things began to change.[6]

"A History of our miseries"[7]

Virginia had become a crown colony in 1624, meaning that it was no longer the private venture of the Virginia Company, but belonged to England in the person of James I. The Crown ruled its American colonies with a pretty light hand in the first half of the seventeenth century. When parliamentarians overthrew the monarchy in 1649, making England a commonwealth, the colonies were ordered to pledge allegiance to the new government, but were in many other respects left to their own devices. In fact, Virginia was able to offer safe haven to loyalists during Cromwell's regime. When the monarchy was restored, one of the punishments visited on parliamentarians was indentured servitude in the colonies. Following the Restoration, Berkeley, Virginia's loyalist former governor, was reappointed, setting the stage for an American revolt against provincial authority that some have compared to the English Civil War, or the American Revolution, in scope and intent (Webb 1995; Wertenbaker 1940).

In the summer of 1675, a minor dispute between a group of Stafford County settlers and their Doeg trading partners escalated out of control, leading to a state of generalized guerilla warfare between a number of Algonquian and Iroquoian polities on the one hand, and the European colonists of Virginia and Maryland on the other. Both sides attacked, and even killed, non-combatants. The atmosphere of panic within the colony was not lessened by news from New England that Algonquian groups allied with the Wampanoag leader Metacom, alias "King Philip," had engaged an all-out war with the colonists there. Governor Berkeley's defensive strategy included diplomacy with "friendly Indians" and the construction of frontier forts. However, he and his government were relatively safe at the heart of the colony. Frontier settlers were less interested in determining which Native groups were friendly; they advocated the extirpation of all Indians from the colony. They also pointed out, correctly, that the proposed forts were of little use for outlying households subject to surprise attacks. To add insult to injury, the frontier colonists were heavily taxed to fund the contracts that Berkeley's political allies obtained to build those forts, men who subsequently located the forts to their own advantage, thus doubly profiting from the misery on the frontier.

Frontier malcontents found their leader in Nathaniel Bacon, a recent immigrant of good family. In fact, he was related by marriage to Berkeley's wife. His cousin, Colonel Nathaniel Bacon, was a member of the Governor's Council. As befit his wealth and status—and in spite of his youth and inexperience—the younger Bacon had been appointed to the Council, but showed little interest in politics. In March of 1676, radicalized by the killing of members of his own Henrico County household, Bacon led a group of his neighbors in retaliatory action against a nearby Indian group (who seem to have been bystanders). Berkeley then declared Bacon an outlaw for undermining the government's official accommodationist policy. After several attempts by Berkeley to co-opt Bacon politically, and by Bacon to get his frontier agenda through the legislature, it became clear that the two programs were irreconcilable, and Bacon escalated the conflict by leading a small army of men to the statehouse at Jamestown and demanding a commission to continue the frontier war.

One of the factors that made Bacon's defiance so alarming was the backing he had among recent freeman, indentured servants, and slaves—people who had little to lose and the most to gain by a change in the social order. In an attempt to recapture popular support, particularly among freemen, Berkeley had declared a new election for the Assembly (the first election in twelve years) and extended the franchise to *all* free men, not just landowners. However, this "June Assembly" reflected the radical tendencies of the electorate, and when it met, just two days after the group of "at least 400 foot they ye Scum of the Country, and 120 horse" besieged the capital (Sherwood 1893 [1676]:171), the Assembly approved much of Bacon's agenda (Morgan 1975:263–264). The major points included a declaration of war against the Indians, a reversal of the frontier fort policy, term limits for colonial offices, a ban on multiple office-holding, and standardization of the fees that officers could collect.

In July, Bacon and his deputies marched to Middle Plantation to administer loyalty oaths and confiscate the property of Berkeley's supporters, calling them "traytors to the people." Berkeley and his closest allies, including Philip Ludwell, fled across the Chesapeake Bay to Virginia's Eastern Shore to regroup. Berkeley's forces returned to Jamestown in September, only to have Bacon attack a second time. After a pitched battle of several days, the loyalists retreated again. This time the Baconian army burned the town, destroying the old center of government, as well as the private property of several elite families (two rebels, William Drummond and Richard Lawrence, set fire to their own houses). The "country houses" were another casualty. The rebels moved their center of operations to Berkeley's mansion at Green Spring, arguing that Berkeley was a traitor for "abandoning" them to the Indians.

In mid October, Bacon's army moved to consolidate its hold on the interior. According to Webb (1995:83), the rebels controlled over two thirds of English Virginia by then. That, however, was the peak of their power. Nathaniel Bacon died in late October, not in combat, but of disease, according to eyewitnesses. His lieutenants, particularly Richard Lawrence and Joseph Ingram, carried on, but by January 1677, Berkeley was re-ensconced at Green Spring and began his campaign of reprisals.

Berkeley and his Green Spring faction spent the next four months rounding up rebels and punishing them. The most dangerous men were tried before a jury of Berkeley's peers and summarily hung. Among them was William Drummond, thought to be Bacon's councilor and a chief ringleader. Minor players were sometimes given the opportunity to exchange property, future crops, or their liberty for their lives. Aside from the rebels brought before the court, dozens of planters, even acknowledged nonpartisans, had their estates plundered and their families assaulted and terrorized (McCartney and Walsh 2000:69–71). Such actions were often justified as retaliation for the depredations of Bacon's army.

The backlash was only halted by the arrival of 1,000 British troops, sent to put down the Rebellion, and a commission, appointed by Charles II to uncover the causes of the revolt. These men came to the conclusion that by persecuting the rebels, Berkeley was only inviting further trouble, for the colony and the king (the tax on tobacco being a significant portion of the Crown's income), so when Berkeley refused to be recalled, the commissioners forced him out. In early May 1677, Berkeley sailed for England to give an account of what had transpired.

The intra-colonial fighting had lasted less than a year, but Bacon's Rebellion had intermediate- and long-term repercussions. Most obviously, it forced the Crown to pay even closer attention to the colony, leading royal officers to seek more centralized, efficient colonial administration (Billings 1975:247).[8] Berkeley had begun to alienate Charles II with his uncooperativeness on the question of the Navigation Acts and other proto-imperial policies endorsed by the Crown. By the time Bacon's Rebellion came along, the powers-that-were at Whitehall saw no reason to keep him on. Berkeley died without ever having a chance to defend himself before his king.

Why Bacon's Rebellion?

This brief summary may leave the impression that the events of Bacon's Rebellion were driven largely by the personalities of Berkeley and Bacon, or that the causes of the brief revolt were localized. However, the events of 1676 did not occur in isolation. One of the factors that brought Native people and colonists into conflict on the frontier was a shift in the balance of power among Native polities. The expansion of the Iroquois forced the Susquehannocks out of their territory. They, in turn, pushed on the frontier settlers, who then pushed back. In addition, many combatants on both sides of the Rebellion were veterans of the English Civil War. Indeed, much of the rhetoric employed by Bacon to excite support and condemn his enemies was strongly reminiscent of the "country" arguments advanced by Commonwealth political writers. Furthermore, many of Bacon's rebels were freemen and small planters, radicalized by their poverty, which was partially due to the steady decline in international tobacco prices throughout the seventeenth century. Bonded laborers were another major component of the rebel army. In this sense, the rebellion was also a reaction to the international trade in bound labor, and its discontents.

As many as two thirds of Bacon's followers were runaway servants and slaves (Heslep 2001; Webb 1995). One of them was William Baker, who in 1679 appeared before the York County Court and confessed that "he was a soldier in the late rebellion wth Bacon six weekes being his owne voluntary act." The justices, including, on that day, John Page, ordered him to return to serve his bondholder, Elisheba Vaulx (York DOW 1679:6:88). For Baker, and all of the other people swept up in the conflict, Bacon's Rebellion was a local manifestation of much larger scale processes and transformations throughout the Atlantic World.

The primary reason I have elected to study pipes made and used in the years surrounding Bacon's Rebellion is because the conflict highlights important aspects of social relationships, particularly alliances, opposition, and domination. The documentary record establishes the limits of social networks by revealing the fault lines that divided loyal from rebel elites. It also shows how social relationships and structural positions contributed to the shape of the conflict and individuals' participation in it. For example, Sprinkle's (1992) study of the attributes of named rebels and loyalists found that rebels were most concentrated on the James-York peninsula and the Southside of the James, but they were more likely than loyalists to be from frontier counties. Men who rebelled tended to have family ties with other rebels, live in areas threatened by Native attack, or, as we have seen, have preexisting, sometimes personal, grievances against the colony's leadership.

In addition to highlighting cleavages among the colony's ruling elite, the conflict reveals tensions between elite authorities and their subordinates, the smaller planters and freemen. Even though most of the movement's leaders were of middling rank or higher, an elite rebel's average landholding was still only half the size of the average elite loyalist. On average, loyalists owned more labor and were slightly older. They were also more likely to have provincial, as opposed to county, offices. Three quarters of the elite men whose role in the Rebellion is known were loyal (Sprinkle 1992).

One of the things that made Bacon's Rebellion so shocking was the support it received from, and the way it elevated, the most desperate members of society. The leaders may have had relatively high social standing, but the rank-and-file of Bacon's army included many landless men, significant numbers of them indentured servants and slaves (Heslep 2001). In this manner, Bacon's Rebellion returns our attention to the planter-laborer dyad, and the tensions that characterized it. The pipes may offer clues to economic relationships among members of the elite class *or* provide a window into labor negotiations within households. The Rebellion brought the tensions of both kinds of relationships into high relief.

The events of 1676–1677 draw our attention to interactions among Native, European, and African Virginians at a time when relations were undergoing tremendous change. To a certain degree, Bacon's race war against the Indians distracted colonists from their internal differences. Likewise, the class conflict within the European population embodied by events like Bacon's Rebellion became an *ex post facto* explanation for the colony's subsequent shift from indentured servants to slaves. The former were likely to become free malcontents, whereas the latter, theoretically, would never be free to compete with or challenge the planters who owned them (Morgan 1975).

The timing is likewise important, for reasons peculiar to the pipes themselves. Few early eighteenth-century sites show any evidence of the local pipe tradition (Emerson 1988:172–173). New information about modes of production and exchange sheds light on the reasons for this decline. It may not be a coincidence that the latter half of the seventeenth century was the beginning of the end for local pipe production.

Finally, the Rebellion has what we sometimes call "archaeological visibility." Material traces of the conflict remain. Brick structures at Jamestown speak to the rebels' complaints about their excessive tax burden, part of which was poured into a vain attempt to convert the capital from a frontier outpost to a proper brick-built city (His Majesties Commissioners 1677; Horning 1995). In the course of the conflict, rebels and loyalists alike trashed the colony, leaving rubble in their wake. Later, those who could—like Page, Ludwell, and Berkeley—attempted to restore what they had lost. Not every charcoal-rich layer is evidence of marauding armies, nor every building episode evidence of recovery efforts, but the rebellion did have a very real, observable impact on the material world experienced by the residents of sites like Page, Green Spring, and Structures 112 and 144 at Jamestown. The final quarter of the seventeenth century was a time of literal, as well as social, rebuilding.

The major participants in the Rebellion—Berkeley, Bacon, Drummond, the Ludwells, Page, and the rest—are especially visible. They are the men whose homes researchers have sought and studied for decades. The archaeological archive of the Chesapeake has been biased towards the elite, but in this case it is an opportunity, not a limitation. Here, we focus on the elite not for their own sake, but because knowledge about their alliances and social networks can be used as a baseline against which to compare patterns of pipes, lending insight to the lives of early Virginia's "99 percent." This end-around is one way that historical archaeology in the Chesapeake can fulfill the claim that ours is a "democratic" discipline.

Before, during, and after the Rebellion, the Virginia economy centered on tobacco production, but colonial administrators, planters themselves, encouraged economic diversification among their peers. Most prominent in these efforts was the long-serving governor, Sir William Berkeley, one fulcrum upon whom much of the story pivots. Were the pipes like other goods, moving along paths shaped by elite interests and relationships? Comparisons of pipes from sites connected by ownership, family, and economic ties cause us to question the ideology of total control that these labor-owners were in the process of constructing.

Keep Your Friends Close...

Previous chapters have hinted at empirical reasons for thinking that something besides physical proximity guided the distribution of pipes. There are noticeable similarities between Green Spring and most of the Jamestown structures; the nearness of Green Spring to town could be a contributing factor. However, the Drummond site, located midway along the road between the governor's plantation and the capital, seems to have little in common with either. Likewise, pipes from Structure 127 bear little resemblance to the assemblages of other structures in the town.

Based on the degree of elite dominance in society in general, and the prevalence of bound labor in the colony, we might expect elite influence over pipe production to be the missing factor. Elites sponsored specialists in ceramic production of commodities such as pottery, brick, and tile—why not pipes? If pipe production and exchange were under elite control, as several other industries seem to have been (Billings 1996; Horning 1995; Metz et al. 1998; Smith 1981), then we might expect to see evidence that elite landscapes, alliances, and enmities structured pipe distribution networks. The products of John Page's brick and tile kilns were found at a number of his properties in Middle Plantation, and even as far away as Jamestown (Galucci et al. 1994; Metz, et al. 1998). Pipes, being that much more portable, also might have been distributed to sites associated with the person who owned the means of the pipes' production.

All of which means that the path to understanding the relationship between owners and producers (as well as the control of labor and its products) runs through another kind of relationship entirely: the connections among elite families and heads of household. Pipe distribution patterns that seem to honor those of elite relationships (that is, enhanced exchange among sites belonging to friends, less among sites belonging to antagonists) could indicate elite management of pipe production. Absent such evidence, we have greater reason to believe that this enterprise was, as archaeologists have long assumed, an unmediated expression of the aesthetic, entrepreneurial, or economic choices of members of the tobacco colony's large laboring class.

The dense social webs that enmeshed the elite of the Virginia colony are difficult to untangle. And our knowledge of the associations between any site and known individuals can sometimes be tenuous. Another difficulty lies in establishing the character of elite relationships. There is a fine line between "friendship," "patronage," and "exploitation" (Page's connection with Berkeley comes to mind). And finally, the material correlates of the relationships among people are ambiguous. Take the case of Giles Bland.

Bland came to Virginia in part to reclaim his father's estate, which had been seized by Thomas and Philip Ludwell. When his efforts were thwarted, he used the channels available to him as the royal customs collector to report their alleged complicity in misappropriation of provincial funds and other fraud back to the metropole. On top of this, he publicly called Philip Ludwell a coward for failing to show up for a duel. He went on to undertake a crucial mission for Bacon during the Rebellion: bringing back the loyalist party from their Eastern Shore refuge. The price he paid after his ignominious capture was six months imprisonment in a ship's hold, a trial before a panel including Berkeley and both Ludwells, and finally, execution (Webb 1995:50–53, 151–154). The relevance to our story is in the fact that the Bland family may have owned Structure 26. The question becomes, would Structure 26 and Green Spring be *more* or *less* likely to show evidence of shared pipe modes because of this history? We would not necessarily expect cooperation between the Blands and Berkeley or the Ludwells. But then again, perhaps as the elder Bland's estate was appropriated by the Ludwells, Structure 26 *did* make its way into the network that included Green Spring, Rich Neck, and other sites associated with Berkeley's inner circle.

With Bland/Structure 26, and many similar cases, it is difficult to label any of the sites or structures as "rebel" or "loyal" sites. So rather than trying to characterize a style typical of a social network, I examined the distribution of attributes across three categories of site pairs. First are sites at which the owners had positive social relationships and that were close together.[9] Second are sites at which the owners had positive social relationships, but that were located far apart.[10] Third we have sites at which the owners had negative social relationships, but that were close together.[11]

...and Your Enemies, Closer

This last group is important because we might turn the question of alliances on its head and ask who would be *unlikely* to engage in the exchange of goods, given the opportunity? If elite control were an important factor in production and trade, then pairs of sites characterized as the domains of "close friends" and "distant friends" would show greater similarity to each other than would be found between the site pairs that encompass "close enemies," with sites in the "close friends" column having perhaps the greatest similarity because physical and social attractors were working congruently rather than at cross-purposes. If elites did not control the pipe trade, then their relationships would have had little bearing on the distribution of pipes, and we could expect some other pattern, possibly with greater similarities, because of their proximity, between close friends and close enemies versus distant friends. The analysis tests the relative effects of geographical distance and elite social distance on pipe distribution networks.

The social fabric connecting Virginia's power elite was tightly woven, indeed. The connections, both positive and negative, between the planters and provincial leaders we have been discussing in this book were the basis for selecting which pairs of sites should be used in the comparison of pipes. Table 5.1 summarizes documented positive and negative social interactions among plantation and lot owning elites. Favorable relationships manifested as property and other commercial transactions, patronage, friendships, legal assistance, cooperation in political contexts, and marriages. Antagonistic relationships show up as lawsuits, soured political and business dealings, disputes over leases, seizure of one another's property, and of course, open rebellion and prosecution of that rebellion. Endnotes include additional details about the family ties, contracts, collaborative ventures, rivalries, and feuds of the individuals who owned these sites during the critical years preceding and following Bacon's Rebellion. Specifically, they summarize the evidence for friendly relations characterizing the following pairs: Page and Green Spring;[12] Structure 100 and Page;[13] Port Anne and Rich Neck,[14] Green Spring and Rich Neck, and also—because they are so intertwined—Green Spring and Structure 144;[15] and Structure 144 and Rich Neck.[16] The notes also detail hostilities between the landowners at Drummond's plantation and Green Spring;[17] as well as at the Drummond site and Structure 144.[18]

	Drum-mond	Green Spring	Page	Port Anne	Rich Neck	Str. 100	Str. 112	Str. 127	Str. 144	Str. 19	Str. 26/27
Drum-mond											
Green Spring	– – –										
Page	+ -	++									
Port Anne		+									
Rich Neck	--	+++++ &&	++	++ ?							
Str. 100	++ - &	+++ &	++ &	?	++++ &						
Str. 112		&&&&		+ -	+ &&	&					
Str. 127	+			+	++		&				
Str. 144	--	++ &			+++ &		&				
Str. 19	+++ --	++	+		+						
Str. 26/27	+	+ -			--						

Table 5.1 Of the sites studied here, many are linked by the relationships among their elite owners. Some of those relationships were friendly (+), some were hostile (-). Given the high turnover of land—whether because of intrigue, land speculation, death, or remarriage—many of the sites were actually owned by the same individual or immediate family members (&). Site pairs tested here are indicated in bold.

The Effect of Elite Social Relations on the Pipe Trade

Relations among elite owners were no predictor of pipe similarities and differences. Of course, the social relationships themselves were not always perfectly friendly or perfectly hostile. People with grave social and political differences continued to do business with one another. People were cheated or taken advantage of by others whom they rightfully expected to look out for their interests. People who seemingly had little in common socially or socio-politically took up arms together—on both sides of the pivotal conflict. Even with all of these caveats, the overall pattern still argues *against* an elite role in structuring pipe distribution networks.

Similarities can have many explanations: the same maker, makers with similar tastes or training, selection by smokers, imitation, and so forth. Differences, on the other hand, can eliminate the possibility that pairs of

a

Figure 5.1 The pipemaker who pierced the bore of the pipestem on the left placed it too low on the first try. The lower hole would not have connected to the bowl, as would be necessary for the smoke to pass through. The stems below left are marred with the pipe maker's fingerprints. The pipe fragments are from Rich Neck (*a*) and Jamestown Structure 100 (*b*).

b

sites participated in a common pipe distribution network, particularly if the differences are technological. Many of the attributes show significant difference between most pairs of sites, regardless of what kind of pairing. For example, all but one of the site pairs (Rich Neck and Port Anne—a pair of close friends) differed significantly in the proportion of pipe fragments with mold scars. It doesn't prove that Rich Neck and Port Anne shared a source for pipes, but it implies that the other pairs likely did *not*.

Regardless of whether they were close together or far apart, owned by allied or enemy elites, the site pairs showed far more differences than similarities. Differences can be characterized as pertaining to decorative or technological style, materials and firing conditions, evidence of skill (or lack thereof, via errors such as those depicted in Figure 5.1). Summarizing Table 5.2, the ratio of similarities to differences was more pronounced than the simple number of similar traits. Not all attributes yielded usable results, so empty cells may mean "no significant difference" as well as "cannot be determined." Pairs of close sites showed about half again as many differences as similarities. Distant sites, even though "friendly," showed twice as many differences as similarities.

As one might expect, pairs of close friends have the fewest differences in their pipe assemblages. Beyond this simple fact, it is interesting to note the *nature* of the similarities. For example, Rich Neck and Port Anne are strikingly similar in terms of manufacturing techniques, whereas the greatest similarity between Green Spring and Structure 144 lies in their decoration. The latter could be explained by imitation, or the popularity and desirability of certain motifs, whereas the former may actually entail shared sources for pipes. Interesting that for Green Spring and Structure 144 with the highest potential for standardization—where most pipes appear to have been made using highly specialized tools, and with connection to other ceramic industries—these two site assemblages have fewer technological similarities than the pair of Port Anne and Rich Neck, with more handmade pipes.

The technological similarities that unite Port Anne and Rich Neck are also more typical of friendly pairs in general. Even when separated by some distance, friendly pairs tend to share variables associated with the techniques of forming the pipes. But notably, they still differ in characteristics having to do with the clay itself, the firing process, and decoration. These discoveries suggest similar production routines and labor practices, but different personnel, sources for materials and/or facilities.

	"Distant friends"				"Close enemies"		"Close friends"	
	Rich Neck & Green Spring	Rich Neck & Str 144	Page & Str 100	Page & Green Spring	Drummond & Green Spring	Drummond & Str 144	Rich Neck & Port Anne	Green Spring & Str 144
color	X	X	X		X	X	X	X
fabric texture	X	X	X	X	X		X	X
surface texture	X	X	X	X		X	X	X
core		X	X	X	X		X	
firing cloud		X	X	X	X	X		
knife-trimming			X	X	X	X	X	X
mold scar presence	X	X	X	X	X	X		X
mold made vs. handmade	X							
lip shaping	X			X	X			X
bowl forming		X			X	X		X
mouth-piece finishing	X				X			
pinching		X	X	X		X		X
multiple bores	X		X				X	
bowl form	X						X	
bowl base	X	X	X		X	X		X
striation type	X	X	X	X	X	X	X	X
decoration presence	X	X					X	
dentate tool	X	X	X	X	X	X	X	X
paint/slip				X			X	

What is most telling is that pairs of neighboring antagonists share almost as many traits as neighboring friends, and *more* than distant friends. As with the friendly neighbors described above, enemy pairs have more similarities having to do with pipe-forming techniques than with pipe materials or decoration. But overall, physical distance seems to have more of an effect than social distance when we are looking for similarities between site pairs.

Among pairs of distant friends, materials and evidence of firing conditions show more differences than do tools used. For example, Page and Structure 100, Rich Neck and Structure 144, pairs that were owned by the same individual, or allied individuals, do not seem to necessarily have drawn on pipemakers using identical firing technologies as determined from fabric color, texture, or the presence of firing clouds. These attributes are among the least susceptible to conscious manipulation or control by the pipe maker; that is to say, deliberate standardization. Despite the strong, close social ties among elite owners, these sites yielded pipes with significant differences in manufacturing routines, processes, and facilities.

The impression of distinctiveness is reinforced by the evidence for decoration, form, and surface treatments. For example, most pairs differed significantly in the proportion of the various kinds of bases a pipe can have (heelless, round heel, square heel, and so forth). When examining other attributes that also could be considered decorative style, distinctions appear most notably among distant friends. Bowl profile and the more general comparison between molded shapes and handmade shapes are two examples of attributes that show differences principally between pairs of sites separated by a considerable distance. This means that between pairs of distant friends, distinct sets of makers were represented at each site, and these makers seem not to have been looking at (or at least imitating) each other's work. For example, using these criteria, the pipes from Page and Structure 100 likely came from different workshops. This finding is all the more remarkable given the evidence that Page's *bricks* have been found on a nearby tract at Jamestown (Metz et al. 1998:50).

Table 5.2 Pairs of structures characterized by different degrees of social and spatial distance can be compared, noting statistically significant differences between them, here marked with an "X." Attributes are grouped according to whether they represent decorative or technological style, materials, firing conditions, or evidence of skill. The calculations used the chi-square test and Fisher's exact, as appropriate.

Even more interesting is the fact that although differences in surface decoration (burnishing versus smoothing, form of dentate tool, presence of white slip or paint) showed a slightly greater rate of significant differences between distant friends than between antagonistic pairs, there were even more differences between pairs of close friends. The close friends are the very pairs where one would expect to have the *greatest* overlap of decorative style, and especially if elite social networks had anything to do with pipe circulation networks.

Some decorative attributes showed sharp differences between both pairs of close friends *and* pairs of distant friends. Curiously, these are attributes which generally did not distinguish sites from one another in the group comparisons of Chapters 3 and 4. As we have already seen, the presence of paint or slip on the surface of a pipe seldom varied significantly from site to site. All the more surprising, then, that it did differ between pairs of "friendly" sites—Page and Green Spring, Rich Neck and Port Anne. Similarly, the proportion of decorated pipe fragments was not a good way to distinguish among sites overall, but *did* mark differences between three pairs of friends. Such differences speak to ideas that pipemakers (and possibly pipe smokers) had about how pipes should look. The people making the pipes found at these pairs of sites were not operating with the same ideals in mind.

Nor were the pipemakers whose work appeared at friendly sites necessarily using the same techniques to achieve these decorative ideals. The dominant surface treatment techniques varied between many pairs. Rich Neck and Structure 100 had disproportionately more burnishing than their opposite numbers, sites like Page and Structure 144. Though dentate decoration appeared at all sites, as noted previously, the tools used to create the decoration came in different sizes. The pipemakers whose products appeared at Green Spring relied more on tool 4, while tool 1 was more dominant in the assemblages from Drummond, Page, and Port Anne.

What all of these observations show is that the attributes that can differ without affecting the functionality of a pipe, do. And if anything, similarities link sites that are near to each other geographically, rather than those connected by elite alliances. The patterns of decorative style (the attributes traditionally examined for locally made pipes) suggest the existence of micro-regional styles, styles that are not overridden by relationships among elite labor owners.

A simple comparison of the numbers of similarities and differences for "friends" versus "foes" or "near" sites versus "far" sites yields no clear distinctions statistically.[19] Neither dichotomy does a particularly good job of separating "similar" pairs from "different" pairs, but the near/far distinction is, at least, less bad. The distinction between near and far sites is slightly less likely to be due to the effects of random variation. So now is the time to turn to the effects of physical, as opposed to social, distance as a factor in structuring the circulation of pipes in and around Jamestown.

Testing Proximity

The analysis in Chapter 4 showed that most of the pipes from the Jamestown structures exhibit attributes associated with mass production and specialized tool kits. These artifacts share many characteristics with the pipes from Green Spring. The pipemakers had smoothed them while they were still slightly plastic, rather than waiting until they reached the leather-hard stage to burnish them. These pipes have significant numbers of round heels (almost exclusively associated with pipes made in molds) rather than square heels (associated with pipes shaped individually by carving or modeling—see Figure 5.2). The bowl-forming techniques imply specialized equipment, rather than the use of generalized tools such as knives. These pipemakers did more than simply leave the lip rough after cutting or wipe it quickly (see Figure 5.3); pipe bowl lips show use of a finishing tool for the task, and a significant number of pipe fragments have clearly visible mold scars. The plantation sites more distant from the capital—Port Anne, Rich Neck, and, to a lesser extent, Page—do not share in this constellation of traits. If we were relying on attributes like decorative motifs, we might again group Port Anne and Rich Neck, based on the occurrence of "bow-tie" designs at both. So there are several reasons to suspect that some of the variation seen among the different sites can be explained by proximity to each other.

Figure 5.2 These pipes with square heels all came from Jamestown Structure 100.

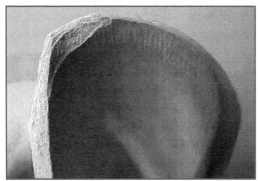

Figure 5.3 The bowl fragment from Rich Neck (*top*) shows that the lip was formed by cutting straight across the unfinished bowl. The fragment from Green Spring (*bottom*) has a finely shaped lip. The tool for creating that clean line left chattering marks all around the interior of the bowl, which the trimmer ignored in finishing the pipe.

A systematic way of further testing this observation is to group the sites by proximity and mutual accessibility to see if such "neighborhood" groups are as good as, or better than, simple site attribution at distinguishing among assemblages of pipes. The first level of aggregation ("Neighborhood I" in Table 5.3) includes four sets that encompass sites within one-and-one-half miles of each other, and are for the most part connected by known seventeenth-century roads or waterways. The second set ("Neighborhood II") combines sites within three-and-one-half miles of each other, essentially dividing "west" from "east." If location were the primary factor influencing who got what pipes, then statistical comparisons should show more significant differences among these neighborhoods than among the sites generally. Such a pattern would indicate that the neighborhoods are more meaningful units of analysis than individual sites. As before, these comparisons use both metric and nominal attributes, especially the latter: sorting and re-sorting the pipes to test how well different grouping strategies bring together similar modes.

Neighborhood I			
Jamestown	*Pasbehegh*	*Archer's Hope Creek*	*Page*
Jamestown	Drummond	Port Anne	Page
	Green Spring	Rich Neck	

Neighborhood II	
West	*East*
Jamestown	Port Anne
Drummond	Rich Neck
Green Spring	Page

Table 5.3 Grouping the sites into neighborhoods further tests the idea that proximity was a factor in how people moved pipes around.

Nominal Differences

Combining pipe fragments into the neighborhoods described was seldom more effective at discriminating among pipe fragments, at explaining pipe variability, than the sites. All attributes but one—the presence of paint or slip—made for statistically significant differences among the six sites (the five plantations plus Jamestown). The groups that make up Neighborhood I, however, are distinguished from one another by fewer attributes than are the sites. The number of attributes without significant differences rises from one to three (compare column "SITE <0.05?" with column "N I <0.05?" in Table 5.4). The breakdown into the two sets represented by Neighborhood II fares even worse; seven attributes fail to distinguish between east and west (column "N II <0.05?"). So sorting pipe fragments according to whether they were from Green Spring, Page, Rich Neck, and so forth yielded more distinctive groups than when the fragments were designated as being from Pasbehegh, Archers Hope Creek, and so forth.

Furthermore, if the neighborhoods—groups larger than sites and organized by proximity—represented zones within which pipemakers circulated their wares, then sorting pipe fragments into those neighborhoods should show *stronger* distinctions than the sites do (here, indicated by a

	Str. <0.05?	Str. V	Site <0.05?	Site V	N I <0.05?	N I V	N II <0.05?	N II V
mold-made vs. handmade	n/a	—	Y	0.41	Y	0.39	Y	0.38
bowl base	N	—	Y	0.39	Y	0.37	Y	0.35
mold scar presence	Y	0.18	Y	0.29	Y	0.24	Y	0.23
heel shape	Y	0.58	Y	0.28	Y	0.27	N	—
surface texture	Y	0.16	Y	0.27	Y	0.12	Y	0.06
mouthpiece finishing	n/a	—	Y	0.24	Y	0.21	Y	0.30
lip shaping	Y	0.42	Y	0.22	Y	0.11	N	—
striation type	Y	0.18	Y	0.20	Y	0.19	Y	0.14
bowl forming	n/a	—	Y	0.19	Y	0.09	N	—
multiple bores	Y	0.15	Y	0.19	N	—	N	—
inclusions	Y	0.34	Y	0.15	Y	0.07	Y	0.07
decoration presence	N	—	Y	0.14	Y	0.06	Y	0.06
firing cloud	Y	0.13	Y	0.13	Y	0.12	Y	0.11
scraping/ cutting	Y	0.12	Y	0.12	Y	0.10	Y	0.04
core	Y	0.16	Y	0.09	Y	0.05	N	—
fabric texture	Y	0.24	Y	0.09	N	—	N	—
pinching	Y	0.11	Y	0.05	Y	0.04	Y	0.03
paint/slip	Y	0.13	N	—	N	—	N	—

Table 5.4 At a glance, it is possible to see that the sites are more easily distinguished according to the various modes than are either the smaller (N1) or larger (N2) neighborhood groupings. The sites are more likely to differ significantly from one another (Y). For modes that show significant variation at each level of aggregation (site, N1 and N2), the strength of association is generally higher for the sites. The Jamestown Structures (leftmost two columns) offer an interesting comparison. The modes are organized in order of descending strength of explanation (for sites).

higher Cramer's V, which measures strength of association between a category and its characteristics). As can be seen in Table 5.4, V values nearly always decline (slightly or notably) as one moves from lower to higher levels of aggregation. In most cases the same attributes showed significant variation, whether among sites or among neighborhoods, but the percentage of variability explained by the scale of the group (site, Neighborhood I, or Neighborhood II) was almost always less for neighborhoods than for sites—sometimes by a considerable amount.

The neighborhood groups showed a slightly better ability to discriminate among pipe fragments than site assemblages in only a few instances. For example, the differences in mouthpiece forming techniques (see Figure 5.4) contrasted between east and west more starkly than among the six sites. However, this is the only attribute related to technological style that does so. The other attributes that work better for neighborhoods than sites have to do with the *appearance* of the pipe—specifically surface texture, surface treatment, and the use of painted or slipped decoration. This finding offers further support to the idea that pipemakers adhered to micro-regional decorative styles, but that these decorative similarities do *not* signify distinct pipemaking operations.

Further evidence to support the idea of shared aesthetics *across* multiple makers comes from the fact that attributes which could be influenced by geographically localized conditions (fabric texture, surface texture, and inclusions) show sites as markedly better than neighborhoods at grouping like with like. The patterns in decoration are not congruent with those in materials. Support also comes from the data from the Jamestown structures—including the fact that assemblages from those structures, despite

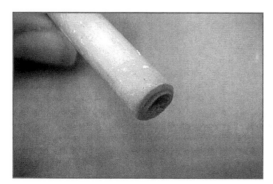

Figure 5.4 Most mouthpieces were cut and then either left untreated or additionally smoothed. On this pipe stem from Green Spring, however, the pipe maker did not take either of these extra steps.

the structures' being within earshot of each other, are even more distinct from one another with respect to inclusions and fabric texture than those from the plantation sites are. The pipes smoked in the town came from makers who not only used different manufacturing techniques, but different materials, perhaps even distinct sources of clay. High variation among assemblages from structures, sometimes higher than among assemblages from sites, is another good indicator that while proximity mattered, it was not the sole factor determining the source of one's pipes.

All of these individual arguments converge on a single conclusion. Neighborhoods are seldom better than sites at capturing significant differences among pipes. Also, neighborhoods are usually worse than sites at explaining the significant differences that do exist among pipes. Instead of seeing one or more regional traditions split randomly among several sites, we seem to have sites that share some easily imitated pipe characteristics with their neighbors while still having distinctive and heterogeneous technological characteristics.

Measured Differences

As with the nominal attributes, measurements of pipe fragments show that site designation is more effective for discriminating among pipe fragments than either of the neighborhood designations (see Table 5.5). The comparison of the neighborhoods Jamestown, Pasbehegh, Archer's Hope Creek, and Page yields results very similar to the site-by-site comparison. In all cases the significance value is the same, but the percentage of variability "explained" by the groupings is somewhat less for neighborhoods. The larger scale neighborhoods of "east" and "west" show fewer significant differences between them than either the smaller neighborhoods or the sites did. And for all the measures, the percent explained is notably lower than for the smaller neighborhoods or the sites.

Stem bore diameter is an exception in that the difference in bore size is more effectively explained by the divisions among Neighborhood I groups than among sites. As this measurement appears to be sensitive to time for local as well as imported pipes (Monroe and Mallios 2004), the difference suggests that the assemblages of Page and Pasbehegh (both averaging 7.4/64ths of an inch) are slightly more recent than Jamestown (8.1/64ths average), and the Archer's Hope Creek sites are the earliest (8.8/64ths average). Because the settlement of these areas within the colony occurred in a different order, we may be seeing the development

	Site < 0.05?	Site % explained	N I < 0.05?	N I % explained	N II < 0.05?	N II % explained
volume	Y	31.92	Y	25.42	N	—
bowl diameter (interior)	Y	31.48	Y	26.65	Y	11.01
heel length	Y	22.68	Y	22.51	Y	17.30
bore diameter	Y	18.30	Y	21.12	Y	8.46
mouthpiece diameter	Y	15.20	Y	14.70	Y	7.53
stem diameter (indeterminate location)	Y	13.06	Y	12.61	Y	6.42
bowl diameter (juncture)	Y	11.78	Y	10.87	Y	10.36
bowl diameter (exterior)	Y	8.85	Y	8.07	N	—
stem height	Y	6.09	Y	4.38	Y	1.50
angle	N	—	N	—	N	—
thickness	N	—	N	—	N	—

Table 5.5 The metric data show similar results to the nominal data in Table 5.4. Grouping the pipe fragments by site shows more significant differences and/or better explains the differences than grouping them by neighborhood. The measurements are organized in order of descending strength of explanation.

of the industry—starting on far-flung plantations with hand-building techniques and only later being taken up by households, including ones in town, with established ceramic manufactures. As with the nominal attributes, the neighborhood groupings do even less to explain the variability in the overall assemblage than the site attributions. Proximity was not the sole guiding principle that structured pipe distribution networks.

Conclusion

We have seen how difficult it is to learn much about craft production in early Virginia from the archival record. Likewise, we view the colony's large laboring class through a glass, darkly. Though the elites are slightly better represented, the sharp distinction between factions that we might expect considering the documentary record is not evident among the pipes. If anything, proximity corresponds—somewhat weakly when comparing aggregations of sites to the sites themselves—with similarity of styles of pipe manufacture. Elite social relationships may have played a minor role, all else being equal, but when all factors are taken into account, it is the sites that are nearest to each other that share the most attributes, including attributes that indicate that the similarity is due to more than imitation of popular decorations. However, the fact that proximity alone doesn't *fully* explain the distribution of variables across the assemblages argues for there still being an x-factor—the pipemakers themselves.

The preceding chapters have shown that in some places specialists were the engines driving the pipemaking industry. These individuals sometimes used specialized tools, such as vertical-half molds, but even in the absence of such tools skilled pipemakers managed to produce relatively standardized products. Their distribution networks seem to have been affected by a variety of factors, but placement in the physical landscape had an impact as important as, perhaps even greater than, the social networks of the elites who dominated the regional economy. While someone may have been using Page's kiln to fire pipes, it seems that person would have done so on his or her own terms. This revelation places ideas about the demise of the local pipe tradition in a new light.

Archaeologists who favor the attribution of local pipes to Afro-Virginian makers have suggested that beginning in the early eighteenth century, locally made pipes became anathema to elite planters, who recognized (at some level) their symbolic import for an increasingly African workforce. This argument implies that as the planters' legal and social web tightened around these men and women, it eliminated opportunities for distinctive artistic expression (Emerson1988; Monroe 2002). But perhaps the issue is wider than that: the "English"-looking locally made pipes disappear, too. Perhaps the end of the tradition is symptomatic of a general social reorganization following the tumultuous events of the later seventeenth century that occurred in both the colony and in the metropole. It was not only a question of what message the pipes' symbols might convey, it was *the very fact of their production* that made them a threat—the independence that they indexed. On this view the tradition may have died out *because* of the lack of elite involvement—either their deliberate stifling of trades they could not control, or simply by neglect and redirection of the labor that they could control. The scanty references to pipemaking in the documentary record support the latter explanation, as does the spatial association of these pipes with site loci used by laborers rather than owners of labor. The evidence related to manufacture leaves intact the picture developed from spatial analyses of pipe disposal on plantations (Neiman and King 1999). I have not attempted to divine whether the makers of these pipes were free or bound, or from what continent their ancestors may have come, but the foregoing analyses certainly lend support to the argument that the trade was *theirs*, which is saying something given the time and place in which they were living.

To give a sense of their world, I point to two proclamations by governors of Virginia with specific reference to bondage and the right to move about. Bonded laborers were indeed on the move in seventeenth-century Virginia, and this was a matter of no small concern for provincial authorities. In 1687/8 Francis, Lord Howard of Effingham, expressed dismay that so many "Negroe slaves" had taken to "walking and rambling on broad on Satterdayes and Sundayes." He associated the practice with an increased risk of "plotts and designes to exempt and free themselves from their present slavery." To forestall such plots, he banned all such movement: "for the future noe Negroes slaves [shall] bee suffered to carry or arme himselfe… *nor presume to depart from off his Master or Mistress ground* without the permission of his Master, Mistress or overseer and that to bee made manifest by certificate under Master, Mistress or overseer hand" (York DOW 1687/8:8:99–100, emphasis added).

Proclamations, however, do not necessarily change behavior, and in fact, Effingham's was simply restating a law that had been passed eight years before—to little effect, apparently. In 1690, Francis Nicholson found it necessary to again proclaim the importance of "prevent[ing] the rambling about of Negroes (which must frequently happen on the Sabbath day) *& against Masters of families & overseers that shall entertain or suffer them to be in their plantacons*" (York DOW 1690:498–499, emphasis added). To this end, the act of 1680 was to be read in all county courts and churches every six months as originally stipulated (Hening 1823 II:481–482). The deck was stacked pretty clearly against bonded laborers in early Virginia, but apparently enough people found ways to subvert the system that authorities felt the need to constantly reiterate what they no doubt saw as the natural order of things: the hierarchy that extended from God to King to governor to masters and mistresses to the men, women, and children whose time and bodies they owned.

To return to the pipes, though, it may or may not be a coincidence that the technique that permits this view on the limits of social hierarchy is itself *non*-hierarchical. One might think of modal analysis as something like the analytical equivalent of Crumley's concept of heterarchy—social power distributed along multiple, non-congruent axes (Crumley 1995). The seventeenth-century colony was nothing if not hierarchical; forms and sources of power aligned rather neatly, in fact. But my method runs counter to the situation on the ground in Virginia. The analysis also resonates with biological anthropology's idea of clines, where the unit of analysis is the population, rather than the "type." If nothing else, this chapter shows that variation is best understood across entities, whether those are artifacts or sites. In any event, this is where the technique has brought us: a view of a society in flux, where elite authority has limits. The pipes, artifacts of colonialism and imperial domination, are revealed to play a role in resistance as well. Such findings force us to consider more seriously the proposition that the local pipe tradition is not a unitary phenomenon, and to appreciate techniques that allow us to examine the distribution of these varieties in greater detail.

Classification matters. Thinking about pipes in a new way in the twenty-first century allows a new view on social and economic power in the early Virginia colony. So, too, in the seventeenth century thinking about people in a new way opened up new strategies for social organization and domination. I turn, finally, to the words of seventeenth-century Virginians to examine how they saw themselves in relation to their fellows, and the ramifications of their new classificatory system in the lives of the men and women who made and smoked these pipes.

Little Tubes of Mighty Power, or, Doing Things with Words

Chapter 6

Little Tube of mighty Pow'r
Charmer of an idle Hour,
Object of my warm Desire,
Lip of Wax, and Eye of Fire....

Pleasure for a Nose divine,
Incense of the God of Wine.
Happy thrice, and thrice agen,
Happiest he of happy Men.

Isaac Hawkins Browne,
"A Pipe of Tobacco: Imitation II"

In Browne's poem of the 1740s, we see none of the associations between pipes and radicalism cited by Johnson (1996), nor the struggle entailed in delivering the pleasure of a smoke to the fireside of an English wit and bon vivant (Scott 2004). Unlike the pipe with the "snowy taper Waist" in Browne's poem, the pipes made in colonial Virginia a generation earlier resonated with power, and in fact continue to do so. Previous research has emphasized the symbolic power of the pipes' decorations. I have argued for harnessing the wider explanatory power of the pipes, using technological attributes and non-hierarchical classification methods. The result of this exercise was a new view on craft production and labor specialization in the Virginia colony's plantation economy.

Over the course of the "long" seventeenth century, Virginian elites tightened their hold on society—in part by relaxing it. The hostility between elite and non-elite free men was sublimated and redirected onto the growing enslaved population (Morgan 1975). The great planters built their new hegemony on a foundation of racial antagonism as well as raw power. In 1683, for example, one could still find examples of a nameless "Negro" running away along with "servants" John Hooker, Mary Ditton, and Mary Howlett (York DOW 1682/3:6:448), or of Elizabeth Bancks bearing a child whose father was an unnamed "Negroe slave" (York DOW 1683:6:498). The emerging racial regime would project the interests of labor-owners as aligning with those of all free people, while making race the criterion that determined one's freedom or enslavement.

Twenty-first-century Americans are still living with the legacy of the racial ideologies developed to support this new social structure. By way of conclusion, this chapter examines more closely the idea of social power, specifically its implication in creating new categories of person, which in turn reinforced existing power relations. I examine the growth and development of a racial ideology that enabled the enslavement of African Virginians, whose role in the production and consumption of pipes has been the object of such discussion.

Locally made pipes were products of the colony's large laboring class in a way that tobacco never was. So here I explore in more detail the manner in which that class was constituted and, furthermore, how its members were understood and defined by elite land- and labor-owners. Studies of the pipes and the development of categories-of-person are linked. They are both part of the modern scientific project that attempts to understand the world by classifying it. As I will argue at the end of this chapter, our attempts as archaeologists to identify the pipes with the ethnic and racial categories that we understand stems from our own colloquial (rather than scientific) interests and ideologies. These interests and ideologies we have inherited, in part, from colonial Virginia, and they underlie modern day efforts to understand the pipes specifically as signifiers of racial meanings. In the case of both the pipes and the people, patterns that we "know" to be real and meaningful, on closer examination, dissolve into air.

To review, race is a social classification. Phenotypic and genetic differences among groups of people are real, but they do not correspond to the neat "racial" categories of the modern imagination (American Anthropological Association 1998; Baker 2010; Keita and Kittles 1997; Montagu 1997; Mukhopadhyay and Moses 1997; Visweswaran 1998). A long line of scholars attempted, and failed, to perfect the categories proposed in Linnaeus's taxonomy (see Chapter 2). Biological anthropologists in recent generations have moved away from the concept of "races" to embrace the idea of clines, examining the frequency of individual attributes in populations rather than attempting to use clusters of traits to define and characterize groups (Brace 2005; Livingstone 1962). I have alluded to an analogy to be made between clines and modes, but my concern *here* is with the social aspects of race and racial categories. The structuralist approach to this problem would be to ask about the relationships (differences) among concepts. How did "slaves" differ from "servants"? I am concerned also with the relationship between the concept and its referent. By what process did "Negro" come to signify a type and a legal status? A semiotic and pragmatic approach also examines these relationships in their discursive contexts, as they are used, and watches what they do (Preucel 2006; Preucel and Bauer 2001). Like other projects animated by the concerns of critical race theory, this chapter examines the way that racial categories are created and their implication in the exercise of power.

I begin with seventeenth-century texts that explicitly addressed the problem of defining Virginia's people. I review several key laws pertaining to race and slavery, as categories-of-person became increasingly conflated with rights and roles within the social structure of the plantation economy. I then turn to other documents to see how these legal categories were operationalized in day-to-day social interactions—in other words, the pragmatic consequences of these ideas. These county records offer an opportunity to examine what Virginians "said" about race and bondage when they weren't explicitly talking about it. Land certificates and wills from York County were written by a limited number of people, from a very particular set of perspectives, but nevertheless offer a wider window on the language of racialization and what it signified. Their words were written, in part, to regulate social relationships. My analysis explores how language was implicated in the dynamics of social power.

Power in the Early Virginia Colony

To say that power was unevenly distributed in the seventeenth-century colony is an understatement. Power, understood here as the ability to act according to one's own will (Wolf 2001:384), shaped relations at the family and household levels, as described in Chapter 5. Labor relations, too, structured seventeenth-century Chesapeake society. Irrespective of wealth, a planter was head of a household that probably included his[1] spouse, dependent children, perhaps wards or siblings, and bound laborers. On the smaller plantations, planters and their families were likely to work alongside, live in the same house as, and lead lives *materially* little different from, their bondsmen and bondswomen. This is not to say that their relations were in any way equitable. Ownership of another person, or another person's indenture, conferred almost absolute authority. Bonded laborers performed desperately difficult work, for which they were meant to receive food and shelter. If a planter neglected these bare minimum obligations, or was abusive, a bondsperson's only recourse was to a court composed of other planters, who were unlikely to be sympathetic. Indeed, the case could very well be tried before the offending planter, or at least his close relatives and dear friends. McCartney and Walsh cite the case of Robin Santy, an indentured servant—a black man—who sued Philip Ludwell for freedom, after his term ended. The James City County court ruled against him, so he appealed to the General Court, on which, incidentally, Ludwell served. The higher court found for Ludwell (McCartney and Walsh 2000:71). The laws pertaining to bonded laborers were concerned with terms of contract and regulating their behavior, not protecting their rights.

So, it was not self-evident to seventeenth-century Virginians that all men were created equal. Bonded laborers were severely constrained by the laws of the colony. The few regulations designed to protect them were, court records suggest, regularly violated. "Freemen," a term applied to people who successfully completed their terms of indenture, were somewhat better off since they owned their own labor. However, political power was predicated on property ownership—especially land, as only landowners could vote.[2] An established position within the community social network was also critical. Of course, property and status accrued to those with power, leading to a vicious circle in which power, wealth, and high status were increasingly concentrated in a few well connected hands.

The strong correlation between power and wealth has long been obvious to historians of the Virginia colony. Systematic study shows that wealth (as measured by the cash value of one's estate and the maximum number of acres and bound laborers controlled over a lifetime) was strongly correlated with the highest social honorific conferred (for example, Mister, Gentleman, or Esquire) and the highest county office achieved (for example, juror, bailiff, court clerk, sheriff, councilor, and so forth). There was also a link between wealth and the highest military office achieved (D. Rutman and A. Rutman 1984a:133–140). Wealthy men made and enforced community rules, and profited handsomely from their offices. They expected deference from those whom they outranked socially. This congruity of legal and traditional authority (for these terms, see Weber 1978) was clear to their contemporaries, and very difficult for subordinates to challenge.

Following the rapid expansion of the colony and proliferation of counties in the first half of the seventeenth century, many of the duties that had been administered at the provincial level were turned over to the county courts. A landowning man of good character, or at least good connections, might serve his neighbors as a constable, surveyor of the highways, or tithe-taker. A man in a better position might hope to become a justice of the peace, sheriff, or clerk. County courts were responsible for collecting taxes as mandated by the provincial government, maintaining public facilities (roads, ferries, ecclesiastical property), holding elections, and presiding over non-capital criminal trials. Counties identified and punished thieves, runaways, slanderers, adulterers, fornicators, drunks, assailants, and blasphemers. They kept important records such as patents, deeds, wills, and polls.[3] Local officials who met with the approval of their constituents—that is to say, landowning men like themselves—might have been sent to Jamestown as burgesses. The House of Burgesses formed the lower house of the colonial legislature, the General Assembly. The upper house was the Governor's Council, an appointed body that drafted most of the laws, and on which men served for life or until removed by the governor. Such was the cream of the Virginia colony. The Acts (I capitalize

"Act" where it denotes a law) they passed bear testament to their efforts to shape a society very unlike the one that produced metropolitan laws and institutions. They were the persons whose words, along with those of their fellow land- and labor-owners, are recorded in the York County records— words by which they acted on the world.

Acts as acts

The General Assembly of Virginia turned its attention to establishing standards for bound labor around mid-century. In 1662, for example, they determined that a person over the age of sixteen could legally be bound for five years. Anyone younger would serve until age twenty-four (Hening 1823 II:113). In that same year, the Assembly affirmed that any person born to a woman who was herself enslaved would consequently be a slave as well:

> WHEREAS some doubts have arrisen whether children got by any Englishman upon a negro woman should be slave or ffree, *Be it therefore enacted and declared by this present grand assembly*, that all children borne in this country shalbe held bond or free only according to the condition of the mother. (Hening 1823 II:170)[4]

The Assemblies of 1670 and 1682 codified the status of "slaves," who were, for all practical purposes, servants-for-life. The earlier Act "declareing who shall be slaves" states simply that "all servants not being christians imported into this colony by shipping shalbe slaves for their lives; but what shall come by land shall serve, if boyes or girles, until thirty yeares of age, if men or women twelve years and no longer" (Hening 1823 II:283). The 1682 Act clarified the intent of the Assembly by repealing the earlier Act and further specifying that conversion to Christianity could not free the convert:

> all servants except Turkes and Moores, whilest in amity with his majesty which from and after publication of this [Act] shall be brought or imported into this country, either by sea or land, whether Negroes, Moors, Mollattoes or Indians, who and whose parentage and native country are not christian at the time of their first purchase of such servant by some christian, although afterwards, and before such their importation and bringing into this country, they shall be converted to the christian faith; and all Indians which shall hereafter be sold by our neighbouring Indians, or any other trafiqueing with us as for slaves are hereby adjudged, deemed and taken, and shall be adjudged, deemed

and taken to be slaves to all intents and purposes, any law, usage or custome to the contrary notwithstanding. (Hening 1823 II:491–492)

The only people eligible for enslavement were people brought into the colony from non-Christian nations. In practice this translated into Native American prisoners-of-war and Africans.

Africans had been living in the colony since at least 1619. While many of them lived their entire tenures in bondage, freedom was not an impossibility. Early on, loopholes in the colony's laws meant that some people of African descent successfully sued for their freedom, claiming that conversion to Christianity or non-African parentage made their enslavement illegal, hence Acts like those above, which attempted to foreclose such options (Billings 1991:56–57; Haney López 1995). The 1667 Assembly also addressed the first argument:

> WHEREAS some doubts have risen whether children that are slaves by birth, and by the charity and piety of their owners made pertakers of the blessed sacrament of baptisme, should by vertue of their baptisme be made ffree; *It is enacted and declared by this grand assembly, and the authority thereof,* that the conferring of baptisme doth not alter the condition of the person as to his bondage or ffreedome; that diverse masters, ffreed from this doubt, may more carefully endeavour the propagation of christianity by permitting children, though slaves, or those of greater growth if capable to be admitted to that sacrament. (Hening 1823 II:260)

The second strategy was, for some, undercut by the abovementioned Act of 1662.

A few of the arrivals of African descent appear to have been bound only for a period of indenture, and were freed at its end, just like their counterparts from "christian" nations. Others were manumitted in an owner's will, or somehow managed to earn enough money to buy their freedom (Breen and Innes 1980). However, as the seventeenth century progressed, opportunities to escape enslavement diminished, particularly because planters like the men in the Assembly realized that their future economic success depended upon African, rather than European, labor (Parent 2003).

In 1671, Governor William Berkeley, responded to a questionnaire from the metropole:

We suppose, and I am very sure we do not much miscount, that there
is in Virginia above forty thousand persons, men, women, and children, and of which there are two thousand *black slaves*, six thousand
christian servants, for a short time, the rest are born in the country or
have come in to settle and seat, in bettering their condition in a growing country... Yearly, we suppose there comes in, of servants, about
fifteen hundred, of which most are English, few Scotch, and fewer
Irish, and not above two or three ships of Negroes in seven years.
(Hening 1823 II:515, emphasis in the original)

But the tide was in the process of turning. European servant immigration
to the Chesapeake began to decline in the 1660s and 1670s, but until the
1680s indentured servants outnumbered slaves in the colony (Tomlins
2001:13). Possible causes for the decrease in servant migration include
improved political and economic conditions in England (the main source
of Virginia's European immigrants), a greater range of destinations for
potential migrants, and the gradual realization among potential migrants
that Virginia was not a particularly good poor man's country anymore.
Planters did not turn to African labor until it was clear that Europe was no
longer meeting their demands (Menard 1977).

So in the last quarter of the century, unprecedented numbers of
Africans were brought into the colony. Kulikoff estimates that the black
population of the Chesapeake (combining Virginia and Maryland) was
probably 1,700 in 1660. Another 3,000 arrived between 1674 and 1695,
a twenty-year period. The next 3,000 people arrived in only five years,
1695–1700. These transformations occurred earliest in the oldest and
wealthiest portions of the colony, particularly the peninsulas bordering
the James and York Rivers (Kulikoff 1986:40).

Ethnohistoric accounts suggest that the *apparatus* of rural farming life
in seventeenth-century Virginia would have represented only a minor shift
to many of the Africans who came into this new world. They were familiar
with hoe agriculture, had an appreciation for tobacco, and perhaps had even
used the former to fulfill the latter (Walsh 1999:68–69). However, the *social
organization* that they encountered on Virginia plantations was another
matter entirely. The institution of bound labor in the African context bore
little resemblance to the system developing in the Americas (Kopytoff and
Miers 1977; Thornton and Heywood 2007; Tibbles 2005).

Throughout the seventeenth century, bound laborers generally com-
prised 25 to 35 percent of the labor force in the Chesapeake (Tomlins

2001:14), with the enslaved coming to outnumber the indentured only towards the end of the century. The transition to slavery was more rapid in the areas where "sweet scented" tobacco was grown, particularly in the areas with suitable soil and a longer history of settlement, between the James and Rappahannock Rivers. For example, in York County in the 1670s one-third of the bound population was of African descent. By the 1680s, black people were four-fifths of all bound laborers; by the 1690s, they were nineteen-twentieths of that group (Kulikoff 1986:41).

In addition to the colony-wide perspective, it is also important to understand how these ethnic and occupational groups constituted themselves at the household level. A review of York County probate inventories reveals the shift from indentured to enslaved labor (Menard 1977). Until 1685, the ratio of servants to slaves hovered at slightly less than 2:1. In each of the five year periods from that date onward, the ratio ranged from about 1:4 to 1:50. The rising reliance on slave labor also meant that smaller planters—who could not amass the higher initial outlay for the right to exploit someone for a lifetime instead of only five years—were priced out of the labor market. Thus, they lost even more ground to elite planters who had money or connections or owned enough women of childbearing age to meet their labor needs for generations to come.

How to Do Things with Words/How to Thing People with Words

The intentions of the General Assembly were relatively clear: to create a class of person, members of which may be permanently bound to others and whose bondage would pass to their children in perpetuity. We can reflect on what the laws say, but were they prescriptive or reactive, or something in between? The Acts could be either a leading or a lagging indicator of how power-full Virginians thought about categories-of-person and how these categories fit into the colony's social and economic structure. I am interested in specific acts generated by the Acts—in the mechanics of implementation. The laws were, in a sense, a grammar for the production of social meanings. And as pragmatic analysis would have it, words can "do things," but this feat is accomplished in the context of interactions (Austin 1975). The title of this section plays on Austin's *How to Do Things with Words*, which concerns "pragmatics" in spoken language. I have altered it to indicate that this chapter is also about how people can and (as in seventeenth century Virginia) do use words to make people into things. The documents considered next reveal what land- and labor-owners *did* with the ideas in circulation about human difference and power, how they transformed persons into property.

This analysis of how categories-for-people developed examines the language of bondage and race in seventeenth-century county records from York County, Virginia. It has been customary to infer ideas about race from didactic statements written at the time, or from period legislation, such as the Acts cited earlier in this chapter (for example, Billings 1991; Morgan 1975; Parent 2003). Meanwhile, the county records are mined for quantitative information about the institution of slavery and its development (for example, Coombs 2011; Menard 1977; Tomlins 2001). Here I tap the very *language* of the county records, utterances that are not ostensibly "about" race but which nevertheless reveal the underlying organizational structures. This indirect approach is useful for examining explicit as well as covert meanings in texts (Bernard and Ryan 2010), in this case revealing the ways that colonial elites established categories-of-person and used these categories to make and organize their society.

Berlin (2010:55) cites a writer who in 1680 opined, "these two words, Negro and Slave [have] by custom grown Homogeneous and convertible," yet an examination of contemporaneous written records from the Virginia colony suggest that this synonymy was a work in progress. Rather, in Virginia "Negro" was *becoming* a word about status, about essence, but showed traces of its origins as a simple descriptive term. The distinction is analogous to developing pipe typologies based on descriptions of attributes. Like archaeologists, seventeenth-century Virginians were learning to think categorically.

Seventeenth-century Virginians referred to a range of ideas using words like "servant," "slave," "Negro," or "English." It is in the contexts of their use that we begin to understand how these ideas shaped society in the colony. The pragmatist approach to these utterances, these acts, certainly attends to the semantic meanings of the developing terminology of race and slavery. It also is concerned with the effect that these terms have on the world—what happens next. Here I focus on several specific aspects of these new social identities. First, I consider the words used to specify what a twenty-first-century Virginian might recognize as "ethnic group" and/or "race" (Agbe-Davies 1999b). Next comes a consideration of naming and personhood. I then turn to the nascent idea of "slavery" in relation to the older, more established concept of servitude. This analysis leads to a reflection on the consequences of these distinctions—the lived outcomes for people of various kinds. Finally, I address these concepts as *words*: how they fit into specific utterances and what that reveals about the underlying ideology. How do you speak about a person as if he or she were property and not a fellow member of society? As it turns out, it takes practice.

Terminology

Being official governmental records, the York County texts are limited in their scope and stylized in their format. Still, they reveal variation and change through time that suggests a gradual and halting adoption of the concepts already inscribed into law. The terms that appear in these texts are "shifters"—their meanings vary according to context. That context may be temporal. It may also have to do with the purpose of the text. Here I focus on land certificates and wills.

The two kinds of documents used here have different interpretive strengths due to their characteristics. Land certificates are a product of provincial policy that allotted fifty acres of land to anyone credited with the entry of a person into the colony.[5] A head of household could claim land for bringing in himself or family members. Those who held indentures, or purchased slaves, could claim land in the names of those whose time or persons they owned (Morgan 1972). This was the procedure followed by Menefie and Kemp as they created Rich Neck (as described in Chapter 3). The texts are short, but encompass considerable variety and contain a wealth of information about social roles and statuses. Part of their utility is in the ways in which slight variations emerge in what are otherwise very standardized documents. Wills, though they follow conventional forms and often use stylized turns of phrase, have much more room for variation—sometimes to the point of idiosyncrasy. Even if they do not represent the actual language of the testator, a greater number of people contributed to the production of wills, and the assertion *of* will marks out the contours of society the testators wished to create.

With the exception of "Negro," terms that reference ethnicity—including names for what a twenty-first-century Virginian might designate as "races"—are rare. The wills refer to "Indian field[s]" and "Indian corn" fairly regularly; the only person, though, was an "Indyan boy by the name of Ben".[6] Englishness was normative and generally unmarked. When it or other indicators of European origin appear in the land certificates, they are attached to people, like "James an Irishman"; William a frenchman"; "[faded], an English wench"; and "Scotch Andrew"— individuals with no recorded surname, or perhaps in the case of the "English wench," any name at all.[7] These are the only instances where people the Acts call "christians" have any labels. Several other people appear without full names. "Ralph a man," "David a boy," and "Joseph a man" are all listed in the same certificate as "William a Frenchman" (York DOW 1662:3:*f*169), but even so their origins go, literally, without saying.

In general, writers of the land certificates seldom saw the need to specify that a person was "English." Ralph's Englishness[8] is *unmarked*. The state of Englishness was the norm. William's Frenchness, on the other hand, was specifically commented upon and is *marked*, just as we might mark Sarah Drummond as a "female head of household," but not be compelled by language or custom to call Philip Ludwell a "male head of household." The "persons" listed in the land certificates were by definition English, just as heads of household were by definition men. It is only when things are not what they "should" be that one feels the need to comment upon it (Waugh 1982).

The few instances of "English servants" in wills are contained in lists: "my whole Estate of lands, Mill, Negroes, English servants, horses, Mares...." One idiosyncratic will pairs the unusual constructions "English servant" and "Negro servant." That text, though an outlier in some respects, nevertheless honors the rule that documents in which "English" people appear always also include one "Negro" or more. Without the presence of the "Negroes" there would be no need to point out the other servants' "Englishness." In the wills, too, terms other than "Negro" are rare, and occur mostly with individuals who have only a given name.[9] These are the people who "need" description. In instances where terms do appear, including "English," they compensate for the lack of specificity when no surname exists or is acknowledged. However, as we shall see, the omission of a family name is also an important marker of difference.

Naming and Personhood

Students of the origins of slavery in the American colonies often point to evidence of increased separation between Virginians of African and European descent. This division existed not only between owner and owned, but among bonded laborers as well. A foreign observer who visited the colony during 1686 or 1687 reflected on the physical landscape of plantations:

> Whatever their rank, & I know not why, they build only two rooms...
> but they build several like this, according to their means. They build
> also a separate kitchen, a separate house for the Christian slaves,
> one for the negro slaves, & several to dry the tobacco. (Chinard
> 1934:119–120)

But even if his observation reflected the norm, this clear separation is not
as clearly borne out in the lists of individuals coming into the colony, nor
the documents created when people were accounted as property—either
in their person or in their time.

A land certificate is at its most basic a list of people. An early example
(York DOW 1648:2:412) reads simply:

> Certificate granted to Row Burnham for 400 acres of land for transport-
> ing Katherine Burnham, Mary Richford, Aron Elcocke and 5 negroes.

Another, dated 1660, states:

> Certificate is granted to Roger Malory to the use of Phillip Malory
> for 750 acres of land for the Importation of 15 persons into Virginia,
> vizt: John Penne, Elizabeth Mallard, Winifree a Negro woman,
> Anthony a Negro boy, Sarah Pope, William Birch, William Coldwell,
> Thomas Brown, John Hill, Francis Hill, Dr. Francis Haddon, Thomas
> Brown[sto]re, John Phillipps, Roger Lambert, Ann Yeo. (York DOW
> 1660:3:*f*85)

The documents differ in several notable features. In Burnham's list,
the "negroes" are segregated from the other people and are not named
individually. Malory's list, on the other hand, intersperses Winifree and
Anthony among the other persons, and names them. Their difference is
still clearly marked, however. As is usual, only given names are listed for
them. They are also the only two people further described by age or sex.
What is interesting about the comparison between the two texts is that the
earlier document more clearly approximates the approach of a society that
treats something we might call "race" as a significant difference among
people. It declines to name the "5 negroes." It lists them separately from
the other people mentioned. And these characteristics are in fact more
common among the earlier texts of the over 170 land certificates examined.[10] The segregated lists (twenty-two in all) have average and median
dates that are *earlier* than lists in which the people labeled "Negroes" are
interspersed among the others. How should we understand this tendency?

In a few cases it is possible to consider change over time by examining successive lists for the same landowner, but the results do not show a clear pattern or trend. In one instance the later list is segregated, but the earlier is not; in another case the pattern is reversed. For the remaining two cases there is no change in organization. The certificates reflect neither a steadily growing, nor a sudden and revelatory, sense of categorical difference. This does not mean that the later listmakers did not *perceive* difference, only that their sense of difference and what it meant seems to have undergone little directional change. In fact, the majority of lists that contain both black and white people are segregated. One important difference is the fact that of the twenty-two segregated lists, people of African descent appear at the end of twenty-one of them. People with surnames that match the certificate holders' tend to appear at the beginning of lists. The consistent pattern of end placement, then, could reflect ideas about social distance of list-makers from the list-enders. The aforementioned lack of surnames is another indicator that people described as "Negroes" were not considered to be the same as other "persons."

The certificates may have been transcribed verbatim from lists provided by the seekers of land patents, but they may also reflect the conventions of a limited number of clerks or scribes. Wills can speak to the ideas held by a broader swath of society. Here again, there is no clear trend in the placement of "Negroes" among other forms of heritable wealth, including the "time to serve" of indentured laborers. Of course, wills are usually organized by legatee rather than category of good, so that the general effect is one of interspersal, but in some cases testators referred to categories in lists, which allows us to compare placement. Where servants were the only human property mentioned, they tended to be first in the list (sometimes last, seldom in the middle). In the few wills that include both "servants" and "Negroes" as general categories, there is no pattern to their order relative to each other. Based on the clarity in the Acts, one might expect testators to situate owned persons midway between, on the one hand, persons who would eventually join free society and, on the other hand, forms of living property (such as livestock) that can also be given using the term "with their issue." No such tendency exists, nor is it introduced over time.

The surprising (to twenty-first-century eyes) tendency towards greater segregation *early* in the seventeenth century—at least in the land certificates—appears to be explained by an early willingness to lump people without naming them individually. It was exceedingly rare to omit the name of an "[English]" headright. And as we have seen, only very seldom do English headrights appear without surnames. In fact, in one certificate which lists people with only given names, the scribe dutifully drew a blank line next to each one, acknowledging the rule even as he violated it (York DOW 1658:3:*f*57). But nine of thirty-six land certificates mentioning people of African descent refer to them only en masse. It seems unlikely that unfamiliar names were what prompted listmakers to combine a group of "Negroes" into a single entry; Chop Chop, Cuffey, and Sassaw all appear by name (York DOW 1695:10:188–189). The significant difference is that the certificate that names them was entered into the record towards the end of the century, when the number of African Virginians was increasing rapidly. It was no longer sufficient to refer generically to a handful of people who would be easily identifiable—marked even—by their appearance. As the number of African Virginians increased, given the purpose of the documents, the greater specificity provided by names became essential.

Whether people called "Negro" were named or not had no correlation with whether the lists were interspersed or segregated. And although the un-naming of "Negroes" was more frequent in the early texts, there was no identifiable temporal trend; in fact, a notable cluster of texts omitting people's names appeared in the turbulent 1670s. Even so, both placement and naming were still quite significant (in the non-statistical sense). The namelessness of these people at once denied them full personhood and compelled the use of ethnic and racial terminology. It allowed listmakers to group them and more conveniently set them apart at the beginning or end of a list. So, what's in a name?

In some cases, names themselves were markers of difference and status. It is not difficult to see the assertion of power in the decision to call two men "old Negroe Peter & Negroe Tom," even in the act of giving them "their true and perfect liberty & freedom" (York DOW 1699:11:248–249). Whether these men actually answered to such names, and what names they used with their families, peers, and associates, we cannot know from Richard Trotter's will.

The power to name was also abundantly clear in the cases of three individual women all called some variation of "Black Betty." It is perhaps not a coincidence that each of these women was represented in the will of another woman, two of whom were themselves named "Elizabeth" (York DOW 1675:5; 1686/7:7:257–259). Unlike "Molatto Kate," discussed later in the chapter, none of these women was a beneficiary. Each will furthermore pointedly underscored the woman's powerlessness to control the fate of her own children, living and yet-to-be-born. In 1674 "Blacke Betty" went to a different owner than "the first child male or female the said Betty shall bring" (York DOW 1674:5) The same fate befell her name-mate a year later. At least the woman called "bla[?] Betty" in Elizabeth Read's will went to the same owner as her child, but this was probably because Read owned so many people that by her will each one of *her* five children became the owner of between two and seven people, while her three grandchildren each received a "girl" (they were named Kate, Murriah, and Hanah), "with her increase" (York DOW 1686/7:7:257–259).

The "Bettys" were more typical than young "Elizabeth," a "Negroe Girle…Christened in Charles Parish Church." Just as records omit family names of African Virginians, their given names—when of European origin—were frequently diminutives. Elizabeth was clearly special; no one else's christening was mentioned in this way. Still, in accordance with the Act of 1682, the ceremony did nothing to prevent her from becoming the property of Richard Dixon "and his heirs for ever" (York DOW 1700:11:401–402). Likewise, the surname of "a molatto man called Thomas Eyers" did not mark a distinction between his fate and that of his peers. What is interesting about such exceptional cases is that the texts that contain them were written when racial slavery had been the law of the land for a generation. People like Elizabeth and Eyres were not a social novelty, with will-writers being forced to make it up as they went along.

"Slavery"

So even though the laws of the colony clearly stipulated several varieties of bound labor, and used the term "slave" fairly consistently from around 1660 onward (Hening 1819–1823 I:540), the owners of labor had not yet developed a uniform vocabulary for discussing these differences. The word "slave"—which is the term we are accustomed to using when referring to people whose bondage was permanent and heritable—appears very seldom, and even then, quite late in the "long" seventeenth century. Thirty years after the General Assembly had begun to link permanent bondage to "not being [a] christian" and furthermore to having been "imported into this colony by shipping," labor owners used the language of *race,* rather than status, to refer to people so bound. Mostly.

"Slaves" never appeared in the land certificates. The authors of wills used related terms only four times in the transcripts available for study. In one instance, a testator manumitted a man named Tony, freeing him from "all maner of Slavery" (York DOW 1703:12:151). The other three instances of the term "slave" appear in lists of generic heritable goods, such as those described earlier in the chapter. Note that these are all at the later end of the time frame studied and two in fact date to 1700 and later. John Page's will, written in 1686/7 and probated in 1691/2, shows how labor owners were still experimenting with this new terminology. The text refers to "Such Negroes or slaves" that he may die possessed of (York DOW 1691/2:9:107). Another testator refered to "all the rest of my estate Negroes Slaves Servants Cattle Hoggs…" (York DOW 1703:12:152).

Like "slave" in both kinds of texts, "servant" is seldom used in the land certificates—only four times total. In the wills, however, "servant" appears somewhat more often (n=64) and spans the full temporal range of the available texts. What is interesting about the construction "English servant" in the wills, and the relatively few instances of "servant" in the land certificates, is that both cluster in the socially disruptive years surrounding Bacon's Rebellion.

The only mentions of "English servant" in wills occurred between 1668 and 1677. Again, it is significant that these "English servants" occur only in documents that also contain "Negroes." It seems that testators felt the need to distinguish an "English servant" only in the presence of individuals who might also be thought of as (confused for?) a "servant."[11] Only between 1680 and 1686 did anyone think to label immigrants to the colony as "servants" when they were being counted for headrights. This group of only four examples includes one in which members of the Read family claimed land "for the importation of 21 servants into this colony [?] 4 Negroes." This certificate was issued two years before the General Assembly revised its definition of who should be considered a slave, and perhaps is an example of the kind of messiness the Act was intended to eliminate. It is clear that these four people were different from the others. For one thing, they were identified with a distinguishing term. However, the framing statement is followed by a list of only seventeen names; the four nameless "Negroes" had been included in the total "21 servants" (York DOW 1679/80:6:177).

Which begs the question: What then is servitude? The just mentioned list and the Huguenot exile's anecdote about "Christian slaves" (Chinard 1934) notwithstanding, slavery was not servitude; servants were not slaves. What is interesting is the process of bringing language into conformity with these two mutually exclusive concepts. Berkeley, in his report of 1671 quoted earlier in this chapter, made clear the correlation of essential qualities and status in his distinction between "*black slaves*" and "*christian servants*, for a time." From the county records examined here, it seems that the key in the minds of his contemporaries was that clause, "for a time." A "servant" eventually came to refer exclusively to a person whose labor was owned only temporarily.[12] But this linkage developed haltingly and the term was used inconsistently. Contextual cues are a better indicator of a differential status than the labels themselves. For example, as stated earlier, "servant" rarely appears in the land certificates (four instances during a very limited period), even as planters were increasingly replacing indentured servitude with slavery as an economic strategy. In each instance, the concept of "servant" is invoked, and then in most cases, is followed by a list of names; for example:

> It is ordered that Mr Thomas Harwood have A Certificate for one hundred and fifty Acres of Land he having taken the oath according to Law for the Importation of three Servants Imported into this Collony vizt. Francis Ludley, John Ferment, & Mary Clarke according to Act. (York DOW [illegible date between 1683 and 1686]:7:236)

Writers also used this format ([category]: [list of names]) with African arrivals, but had been doing so since 1659. These later "servants" seem to be drawing closer to the concept of "Negro [slave]" and, in fact, as we have seen, in one instance the list of "servants" included "4 Negroes" (unnamed). I maintain that the texts that mark a person's servitude, and treat it grammatically in the same way that one treats a concept that applies to people who were unlikely to ever be free, are idiosyncratic manifestations reflecting a deeper shift in thinking about status as being bound up with the essential qualities of a person.

There were plenty of other cases where the rules were inconsistently applied. Armiger Wade gave to his servant Thomas a young heifer and a young sow "if he serves out his time of servitude" (York DOW 1677:6:6). Here we note that while Thomas's term was clearly limited, his name is given treatment that is much more typical for people who were either bound for life, or non-English. His example shows, again, that in the tumultuous years surrounding Bacon's Rebellion the theoretically neat and consistent associations between race, religion, personhood, and status broke down.

Also, in the wills many people clearly had terms to serve but were not called "servant." For example, Thomas Curson stated that "Elizabeth

Millington that now lives with me [is] to be paid upon Demand at the Expiration of her time Six hundred pound of good sweet scented Tobacco & cask to contein it besides what her Indenture specifies." Nowhere is she identified as a "servant" (York DOW 1704:12:211–212). The Acts made an association between "servants" and time, but wills give us the best evidence for how that link was really applied—not in the semantic content of words, but in acts, when the beneficiaries, like Thomas and Millington were the bound men and women themselves.

Consequences

If we think in terms of consequences, the real impact that words had on people's lives—on a daily basis, or in terms of a long term trajectory—we can see the difference between "servitude" and "slavery." In the wills, it is revealed particularly clearly by what people of each status received from the people who held their bonds. Servants generally received two kinds of bequests: livestock and time off their terms. Stock was more common and would have been a considerable upgrade from the customary "corn and clothes" that were frequently the only possessions with which a former servant might expect to start a free life. What is interesting is the fact that the early bequests consist solely of stock; only later do we see planters stipulating, for example, that "at the finish of the Cropp all my Servants bee sett free" (York DOW 1673:5). Before 1671, all of the bequests to servants were for livestock; after that date, a bequest was just as likely to be a reduced term or outright freedom as stock or other material goods. A few lucky individuals got both.

"Negroes" and other people of African descent, on the other hand, always received freedom.[13] In nearly every case, however, there were strings attached. Phill and Nicholas each received from Nicholas Martin clothing, barrels of corn, "nayles to build them a house," and "land sufficient for themselves to plant…for their lives." But if they left the land, or hired themselves out, they were to be re-bound (York DOW 1656/7:1:232). Joseph was to serve his owner's heirs for eleven more years before becoming free. "Old Negro Peter" and "Negro Tom," like Tony and William, had to leave the colony—in accordance with an Act of 1691 designed to "suppress outlying Slaves" (Hening 1823 III:87–88). Only "Molatto Kate," freed by the will of Nathaniel Bacon the elder, got her freedom unconditionally (1692), seemingly in spite of the recent Act, which required all manumitted persons to leave the colony.

So this is the state of conversation about race and slavery in early colonial Virginia. Effectively, the only ethnic or racial category used with any frequency was "Negro," a term on its way to becoming synonymous with a new term/idea: "slave." Officially, a servant was a person whose labor was owned only temporarily, but individuals continued to conflate different kinds of bondage, in part because the laborers performed similar tasks within the economy. Far from being a linear or progressive (or regressive as the case may be) process, the redefinition of persons as things occurred in fits and starts. The changes in provincial law also signal this moment of flux, in part by trying to rein it in—to make clear the waters muddied by clerks and testators in the process of doing things with words. The documents they left behind show how partial and halting these changes were. The neat categories of the lawmakers' Acts dissolved into the mess of daily acts.

Words

One category-confounding social fact was the existence of people with both African and European ancestry. The conundrum eventually required the adoption of a new word. The term, "mulatto" and its variants, first appeared in the York wills in 1687, well after the Act which specified that a child inherited his or her mother's "condition." There does not appear to have been any pragmatic difference between their experiences and those of "Negroes." As mentioned earlier in this chapter, the surname of Thomas Eyres survives in the record—very rare for a person of African descent,[14] but even so he was bequeathed to Elizabeth Diggs, along with Jeffrey, Pegg, Bess, and a number of other people, including "one Molatto woman called Nanny & her child." Across the wills, people called "mulatto" all appear to have been enslaved, including a boy named William, who, by his owner's will, was to be free at twenty-one years of age. John Hayley's plans for William were by no means typical; people described as "mulatto" were not significantly more likely to be manumitted than people described as, or called, "Negro." Other evidence of the connection between these two categories includes the fact that "Mollatos" Nanny and Thomas Eyers were included in a list of "Negroes brought...with me of Virgr," demonstrating that the latter term encompassed the former (York DOW 1698:11:51–53).

"Negroes," on the other hand, appeared in the earliest surviving land certificates. Early on, all such people were either nameless or named as part of a list in which the category was made specific by the list of names: "4 negroes sufficiently proved vizt Peeter John Grace & Kathren" (York

DOW 1646:2:146). After 1659 the function of the racial term shifted—a person's identity was made more specific by a descriptor, for example, "Dicke a Negro and Hagar a Negro" (York DOW 1659:3:*f*58). For African Virginians there continue to be instances of

[number] + "Negro" + [optional name(s)]

but they are outnumbered by the *new* style of reference:

[name] + "a Negro"

The change is not simply a general grammatical shift in sentence structure because servants continue to be

"servant(s)" + [name(s)]

never

[name] + "a servant."

The shift occurred at approximately the same time as a flurry of adjectival uses appeared: "Winfree a Negro woman, Anthony a Negro boy" (1660). Throughout the seventeenth century one might refer to a person as "a Negro" or refer to a group of "Negroes," but between 1660 and 1662, we start to see this new adjectival form of the word. It is used only with named persons and in particular, women and boys—people who differ from the norm, an adult man. This new adjectival usage is another instance in which authors of these texts named marked categories, and ignored the rest.

In the wills, "Negro" is the only ethnic or racial term that appears as a noun—a *type* of person. Even so, in wills the adjectival instances far outnumber the nominal uses, unlike the land certificates, where the noun form of "Negro" is more common. Yet it is not possible to argue simply that "Negro"-as-noun projected the thing-ness of these people vis-à-vis "servants." In fact, the distinctive construction from the land certificates—"Maria a Negro"—is entirely missing from the wills. So when nominal forms were used, will writers would mention a "Negro called by the name of Moll," for example, but out of nearly 100 cases, nobody was described as "Moll, a Negro." "Servants," on the other hand, were equally likely to be described as an individual first, and a servant second, as to be introduced as a servant first, and which servant second. The forms varied according to type of text and part of speech. What remains constant is the *difference* between these two groups.

In fact, the explanation for the different usage in the two types of texts seems to lie in the contexts of their usage. Land certificates, by their nature, are supposed to name individual persons very specifically, so that a headright would be used only once to claim land. A person's individuality was the primary concern of the document. Wills have room to refer vaguely to "my Estate which God hath been pleased to Indow me with of Negroes, Cattell, Hogges, horses...." Wills also address the characteristics of a person-as-property that are a part of his or her value. Hence, the utility and greater prevalence of the adjectival form, which allows the introduction of age and gender, which also help to answer the implicit question: *Which* "Negro"? The fact that the two kinds of documents encourage different constructions is less important than the fact that both kinds of texts found a way to mark the difference of African Virginians.

That being said, the fact that "Negro" appears in the wills as a noun, when other terms don't, also speaks to the increasingly embodied qualities of racial terminology. Even though both forms of "Negro" can be used either generically or specifically, nouns were used significantly more often than adjectives to refer to generic persons. So it was more typical to bequeath "a Negro" than the "value of an able Negro man in money" (York DOW 1689:8:259). Adjectives were more frequently employed than nouns to describe specific persons—"one Negro man called Silver"— though one sees an occasional specific nominal form: "my Negro Jacke."

While it is interesting that the same string ("Negro") has both adjectival and nominal uses (unlike, say, "Irish," which must be transformed into "Irishman"), the important thing is that, although how the nouns and adjectives were deployed changed according to (con)text, they always managed to reinforce the difference of people marked "Negro." It is true that nominal forms other than "Negro" are rare, but the noun form itself was not necessarily how the difference was made. Marking individual people called out their difference and named their inequality. Syntax, too, could be used to reinforce the idea that some persons are talked about differently than others. What all of these words and structures may have been doing was making it possible to refer to persons without acknowledging their personhood.

Where we really see a significant shift in the wills is in the use of generic terminology. The generic uses, of either the adjectival or noun form, occur later in time. After one early example, all of the others appear after 1689. Documents using "Negro" + [name] date to, on average, 1680. Documents including "Negroes" in a list of generic property average 1686. The average date for the use of "Negro" as a standard unit of (monetary) value is later still, 1689. Slowly, literate people found ways to talk about other people that —without necessarily adopting new words or making semantic changes to familiar ones—erased their individuality and their humanity.

❖

Thus, Virginians "did things with words," frightful things that are so sad to recount. And these words did things in (con)texts. Shape-shifting words made new pragmatic meanings, like the arrow of a compass always pointing towards the idea of essential inequality. A close reading of the county records shows that the social tumult of the third quarter of the seventeenth century—the circumstances out of which Bacon's Rebellion emerged—is reflected (if imperfectly) in the language with which people tried to make their world. These were not the words of people fully accli-mated to the ideas expressed in the law of the land. Nor did they represent the gradual, incremental development of a system that equated ancestry with perpetual bondage. Just as the structures of racial slavery developed in fits and starts, the means of expressing these structures verbally was chaotic and lagged even further behind. The written record shows labor-owners actively working out the contours of their peculiar institution. The fluctuations in the ways that the colony's powerful defined, categorized, and conceived of their ownership of other Virginians demonstrate the principle that, as with language, a category or concept has meaning *in rela-tion to* others.

The county records reveal the truth articulated by Barth, that eth-nic groups are defined not by their origins—though that is an important part of their rhetoric—but in their opposition to an other (Barth 1969). The logic of slavery could not be imposed effectively on "all servants not being christians imported into this colony by shipping," as was shown by the Act's repeal and rewording in 1682. Though the appeal to origins remained, the terrible breakthrough came in defining "slave," "Negro," *in opposition to* the unspoken (the unspeakable?) [English].

Coda

The task of a racial ideology is to cement, to naturalize such oppositions. The scribes and testators of seventeenth-century York County were on their way to thinking categorically about people—a difficult habit to break. The concepts developed during this colonial encounter went on to inform metropolitan Enlightenment ideas about human difference and influenced such scientific endeavors as natural history and, in time, archaeology's sister discipline, anthropology. Whether this inheritance is a product of being partakers of modernity in addition to being scientists, or of the relationship between science and modernity itself, is perhaps moot. We are conditioned to seek answers in origins, traditions, and continuity, when in fact the explanatory power of our objects is in their iterative comparison with others.

Pipes, human bodies, and social identities can be put into typological boxes, but we mustn't believe the story the boxes tell us, especially if we want to know what these phenomena mean or what they did, and do. The key is to disentangle the elements of the essential "type" package and examine attributes one by one. In this chapter the individual texts could not be neatly categorized as, for example, conforming or not conforming to an incipient racial ideology. Rather, each text was sorted and resorted, according to various criteria: Was "Negro" used as a noun or an adjective? What kinds of bequests did "servants" receive? And so forth. Understanding only emerged when the characteristics of the documents were disentangled from one another and the various themes addressed in turn. Difference along multiple variables was key to understanding the documents no less than understanding the pipes.

This book is in part an argument that identifying the origins of the decorative attributes of pipes is only one of many keys to their meaning. But old habits die hard. Having *un*marked the pipes as "African" or "Indian," I am often understood to be assigning their production to unmarked, that is to say [English], hands. Nothing could be further from the truth. A similar phenomenon is described by Matthews and Phillippi in their analysis of the timeless dominance of the dominant, by which post-contact archaeological sites in the Americas belong in the unmarked [white] column until proven otherwise (Matthews and Phillippi 2013). Following the logic that they critique, that a person, that a pipe, is [English] goes without saying. Literally. The power latent in not/naming is itself notable. How many times in writing this book did I refrain from writing "European pipes" to refer to ball clay pipes made in Europe, because of the meanings that emerge when invoking the unspoken? Conversely, how many times did I pause before typing N-e-g-r-o for fear of what the word might do, unleashed on these pages? All of which brings us back to the conversation that opened this book.

David and I wanted to know "who" made the little pipe from Pope's Fort, not for its own sake, but so that we could begin to work out what it meant. Without a method for thinking beyond the categories embedded in our discipline and in our society, without a critical systematics, we seized upon the one method that most effectively obscured the very answers we sought. The pipes can tell us a story about essential qualities and their replication, or they can tell a story about the exercise of power from above and below. For my money, the latter is more useful and has more significant consequences (Agbe-Davies under review b).[15]

This book is not really about pipes, nor about race, as such, but about the structures that we use to make meaning and create order out of the chaos of lived experience. So, in addition to discovering how pipes were made and exchanged in and around Virginia's seventeenth-century capital, this book has simultaneously been an opportunity to explore the complexity of (material) culture and an attempt to critically examine classificatory practice. As a text, it has been meant to do three things. First, it attempts to *center* the analysis of material culture in a work of historical archaeology. The challenge throughout has been to wrap the written record around the analysis of the pipes, and not vice versa.

Second, it demonstrates how non-typological, non-hierarchical thinking can be applied to our various datasets, whether they be artifacts or texts. The examples show that the ideal of unitary classes based on conventionally chosen characteristics fails to harness the full explanatory power of our materials, in the same way that it mystifies parallel efforts to understand variety within our own species. However, by critically examining the *consequences* of our practice, we situate it in the larger social setting in which we participate and thus are better equipped to proceed.

Finally, I have tried to show that our categorical understandings of things and people have a history. Archaeologists, like pipemakers, like lawmakers, learn our craft socially—our ideas come from something we might call tradition. The way that we as analysts think about archaeological materials is, at least in part, a legacy of the ideas used by seventeenth-century Virginians to develop a system of human bondage.

Decorative motifs offer a fascinating window into the worlds within which people made, shared, smoked, and discarded pipes. The archaeological debates of the last six decades have shown that, try as we might, neither typological thinking nor tracing the origins of decorative styles can settle the question of who made pipes in early colonial Virginia (or Maryland). This is particularly so if we understand "who" in terms of essential identities (cultural, ethnic, racial) produced the artistic traditions to which pipe makers adhered. It's an interesting question, but one that I have ultimately decided not to answer.

However, we can bend that "who" a little bit and consider the problem of race in the early colony, taking the opportunity to think about the history of our own (intellectual and popular) fascination with race, why we might be so predisposed to use it as an explanation for what we see in the pipes. I have argued that the [unmarked: racial] "who" of the pipemakers has become our problem in part because of the imperatives that enabled, among other things, the settlement and domination of colonial Virginia.

Though elite land- and labor-owners held all the cards, they still feared for their security and jealously guarded their position at the top of the colonial hierarchy. Even a relatively conservative challenge from Nathaniel Bacon—one of their own—provoked a reaction that showed how precarious they felt their situation to be. The pipes, too, challenged the established social order—certainly not as directly, but they gave lie to the prevailing ideology that credited the wealth of colonial Virginia primarily to the people who stole the lives and labor of others.

If we think around the human categories that our long-gone predecessors tell us mean so much—mean everything in fact—the pipes allow us to see a bit of life that wasn't dominated by the ones who lived in the brick houses, whose names fill the written record, to whose hand we tend to attribute every archaeological trace, however small. While Berkeley and his associates fantasized about a Virginia that produced more than tobacco, the men and women who built the colony seem to have actually done something about it.

It is by thinking around artifact categories that we arrived at this insight. Categorical thinking can obscure our understanding of both individual entities and broader scale phenomena. Just as biological anthropologists have decomposed the idea of a race to better make meaning from human variation, I have found that decomposing the idea of a type permits a new focus on the variables themselves and, thus, new meanings for the pipes.

The indexical meanings of the individual modes (signs of specific pipe making routines) allowed us to connect pipemaking traditions across settlements, unimpeded by the distractions of easily imitated decorative style, or the vagaries of fragmentation. The indexical meanings of the pipes themselves (signs of production and exchange relationships that extended beyond individual plantations and owed little, if anything, to elite interest) may hold the clue to the demise of the tradition. It's hard to tell what would have mattered more: whether the outlandish decorations (Emerson 1999; Mouer et al. 1999); the solidarity that they signaled (Monroe 2002; Sikes 2008); or the very fact of the pipes' existence (Luckenbach and Cox 2002; Luckenbach and Kiser 2006; Neiman and King 1999) most troubled the delicate balance of Virginia's hierarchy. Simply knowing of the challenge raised by the colony's laboring men and women adds a new dimension to our understanding of their lives and gives me hope.

That last bit is important, because I wish this matter of smoking, exchange, capital, race, and power were just a subject of scientific and historical interest, but it's not.[16] Essentialist ideas about types inform access to, and adequacy of, medical care. They determine access to employment, professional development, and educational opportunities. They determine whether one is seen as a real human being or an existential threat. The consequences are insidious and devastating. Brew's pragmatic exhortation, that we need more classifications, for new ends, is good advice, and not just for archaeologists. It is time for us to consider what our categories are *for* that we may appreciate the full extent of their power.

Notes

Chapter 1: Introduction

1 The most reliable clue that a pipe is "local" rather than "imported" is the clay, which seldom fires to a bright white and is coarser in texture than the tight-grained ball clays used across the Atlantic.

2 These egalitarian attitudes toward smoking shifted in later years and were after a time found only among the working classes (Bell 1995:26).

3 This "sameness" is non-specific and multiscalar (the same individual; the same polity; the same racial or ethnic group; the same residential unit; and so forth).

4 Analogies are incomplete when they, like an argument analyzed by Wylie (2002a:151), "trade on an intimation rather than a demonstration of relevance." She continues, "Establishing principles of connection based on careful analysis of prospective sources—as important as this is for both the selection and for the evaluation of analogs—is not enough. In addition to determining what kinds of determining structure may link particular material and cultural or behavioral variables, it is crucial to determine whether it is likely that this structure could have held (or did hold) in a specific past cultural context."

5 Archaeologists have had similar debates about the origins of "colonoware," a covering term for hand-built earthenwares produced in the Americas after colonization (see, for example, Cobb and DePratter 2012; Ferguson 1992; Hauser and DeCorse 2003; Mouer et al. 1999).

6 For its application in archaeology see, for example, Agbe-Davies and Martin (2013) and Epperson (2004).

7 No pipes from Jamestown were included in Stewart's study. His argument is notable because, unlike many later researchers, he emphasized the tools used to decorate the pipes rather than the content of the decoration (anticipating many of the issues raised in Chapter 2).

8 For more on the classification of these pipes, collected sometime between 1928 and 1935, see Chapter 2.

9 Recent excavations of the very earliest settlement at Jamestown may call Emerson's hypothesis into question, as there are locally made pipes in the

earliest contexts (Deetz and Straube 2008) that precede the arrival of significant numbers of Africans into the colony by a decade.

10 Harrington's technique is discussed in detail in Chapter 2.

11 "Fallibilism" means accepting certain premises as "given" for the purposes of
the inquiry at hand, with the full knowledge that they may prove to be false at
a later date. One moves ahead anyway, with the idea that one has to start *somewhere* (Peirce 1994b). "Foundationalism," on the other hand, means insisting
that no steps toward new knowledge can be taken until we are certain that the
investigation rests on an infallible foundation: "the view that there are firm,
unchangeable foundations to knowledge" (Baert 2005a:147).

12 I have found discussions about the "darker brothers" of pragmatism (W. E. B.
DuBois, Alain Locke, and Ralph Ellison) to be especially interesting (Agbe-
Davies in prep; Harris 1999; Magee 2004; Muller 1992; West 1989).

13 "Our idea of anything *is* our idea of its sensible effects.... Consider what
effects, that might conceivably have practical bearings, we conceive the
object of our conception to have. Then, our conception of these effects is the
whole of our conception of the object" (Peirce 1994c:401).

14 All of the pipes came from previously excavated collections. While I have had
the privilege of working at some of the sites—Jamestown, Rich Neck, and
Page—only in the last instance did I participate during the field seasons that
yielded the pipes I analyzed.

15 At the sites for which detailed contextual information is available, the pipe
fragments come from more tightly dated sealed contexts.

16 James's (1907) take on the pragmatic method was thoroughly inductive, as in
"producing knowledge from experience, based on a system of handling sense
data" (Samuels 2000:214).

Chapter 2: Classification, or, This Is Not a Pipe

1 Although there is some precedence for using "classification" as a verb form
(Hill and Evans 1972:232; Read 1989:158), to avoid confusion, here the process will be called "classifying" (Adams 1988:44).

2 Deetz has argued that the span of a site's occupation is more valuable to the
archaeologist than a single date within that range (Deetz 1987). Both methods are widely used in North American historical archaeology, although
they are less generally accepted among archaeologists in Europe (Crossley
1990:275; Walker 1977:9–11).

3 Using the mean bore diameter for the entire assemblage (8.017), and the subset consisting of decorated pipes (7.846) as "population" and "sample" means,
the standardized normal deviate shows that the probability of obtaining the
mean of the decorated pipes as a random sample from the population of pipes
at large is between 0.02 and 0.03 ($p = 0.0287$). In other words, the decorated
pipes have significantly smaller bore diameters.

4 I used the chi-square statistic to assess the probability that decorated pipe
fragments were representative of all pipe fragments in terms of bowl forming

technique (p = 0.099), presence of multiple bores (p = 0.828), core configuration (p = 0.001), and surface treatment (p < 0.001).

5 From 60 to 65 percent.

6 The results included low "expected" values for some of the bowl shapes. Nevertheless the chi-square results are x^2 = 122.230, df = 13, p < 0.001, V = 0.774. When the bowl shapes are combined into larger generic groups of "mold-made" and "handmade," following Henry's identification of forms, the results are x^2 = 106.793, df = 1, p < 0.001, V = 0.711. The correlation is not perfect, which probably has mainly to do with the fact that scar presence is a conservative measure for mold manufacture.

7 The chi-square results are x^2 = 119, df = 3, p< 0.001.

8 The chi-square results are x^2 = 257, df = 3, p< 0.001.

9 The results for the test may be problematic due to the low "expected" values, nevertheless the chi-square results are x^2 = 51.222, df = 16, p < 0.001, V = 0.531. When the bowl shapes are combined into larger generic groups of "mold-made" and "free-form," the results are less convincing x^2 = 0.047, df = 1, p > 0.25, V = 0.016.

10 The chi-square results are x^2 = 86.0, df = 6, p < 0.001.

11 The chi-square results are x^2 = 54.582, df = 9, p < 0.001, V = 0.398.

12 These eight colors included over two thirds of all non-agatized fragments.

13 The chi-square results are x^2 = 114.93, df = 7, p < 0.0001. The comparison of mold-made and handmade bowl shapes also finds a significant association, but is not statistically sound.

14 Compared with the general population, the association of x&grid motifs with agatized clays is represented by the statistic x^2 = 1021.151, df = 1, p < 0.001. This unusual style of pipe is found throughout the Chesapeake (for example, Henry 1979; Luckenbach and Cox 2002; Luckenbach and Kiser 2006; I. Noël Hume and A. Noël Hume 2001).

15 For more on cultural production and reproduction, see Urban 2001; 2010.

16 Each pipe fragment was recorded separately, rather than batching like with like. Likewise, each decorative element was recorded separately, with each of the different components of a decorative element—organization, mode of execution, and location—being contained within its own field. This system allows one to select, for example, all pipes with a starburst motif, and furthermore allows one to search for that attribute independently of other attributes (like the "banded" lip, with which the starburst motif sometimes—but not always—occurred). Such a system also makes it easy to sort for, for example, how often a starburst motif occurs, whether it appears on the back of a bowl, on the front of a bowl, wrapped around a bowl, and whether rendered in dentate lines or with incised lines.

17 Postmanufacturing modifications are not used to identify manufacturing groups, but to identify pipes which clearly were *used* and therefore likely to reflect consumers' actions.

18 European pipe clay is often, inaccurately, called "kaolin," which properly refers to the clay used in the manufacture of porcelain (Walker 1977:223–229).

19 This mode excludes decorative motifs, such as facets, that are created using blades, as well as the use of blades to remove mold scars.

20 Walker (1977:166–167) notes that other materials, particularly wood, were feasible, but no such molds had ever been reliably identified for English makers. Clay and wooden molds have been reported for seventeenth-century Poland.

21 Latex impressions of the interior of English pipe bowls (ca. 1600–1850) found only asymmetrical interiors, indicating the use of a device like the one Holme described, shown in Figure 2.9. Mid-eighteenth-century Dutch bowls were symmetrical, with fine striations encircling the interior, indicating the use of a tool like that shown in Figure 2.10 that was twisted inside the bowl, not fixed to the mold (Walker 1977:197).

22 Surface texture is distinguished from striation type. One refers to the "feel" of the surface; the other describes evidence for actions on the part of the pipe-maker creating the surface (Shepard 1956:187–191).

23 In general, an oxidizing atmosphere leads to clear colors, whereas poor oxidation leads to grayish colors.

24 Muffles are quite large and are fixed in place, whereas saggars are designed to be taken in and out of the kiln.

25 Physical tests of locally made pipes suggest a firing temperature between 550 and 950 degrees Celsius (Key and Jones 2000:90).

26 Only pipe bowls complete enough to see all elements in profile were used to record this variable.

27 Livingstone remarked, "There are no races, there are only clines" (1962:279).

Chapter 3: "The Subberbs of James Cittie"

1 Vaulx was the widow of James Vaulx, an associate of John Page (whom we'll meet in more detail later in this chapter). For example, the two men served together as justices for York County in 1677, immediately after Bacon's Rebellion (York DOW 1677:6:9).

2 James City, York, and Williamsburg share many historical developments and even share a history in a very tangible sense—the records of Williamsburg were divided between the courts at York and James City. York is frequently used as a proxy for the whole James-York Penninsula.

3 Part of the dispute stemmed from Wells's objection to Macarty calling him by the name "Taylor" (as Burley and several other witnesses did in their testimony).

4 Here I follow the conventions of the day and use the term "household" to designate all persons under the authority of a head-of-household—offspring, siblings, bound laborers, etc.—regardless of the nature of their relationship to that head, or their actual dwelling place. Those seeking more information on the changing composition of plantation households and the social structure of the colony can peek ahead to Chapters 5 and 6.

5 This theme is taken up at greater length in Chapter 5, but suffice to say that there were forces pulling people out from the plantations that, to a certain extent, structured their identities.

6 He received the 984-acre parcel by "headright" (Carson 1954:9), which would typically indicate that he had brought twenty people into the colony. Headrights are discussed in greater detail in Chapters 5 and 6.

7 When Bacon took over the colony, he made the plantation one of his headquarters. After the Rebellion was squashed, and Berkeley returned triumphant, Green Spring was the site of the imprisonment, trials, and executions of many former rebels. For more on the Green Spring faction, see Chapter 5.

8 Dimmick removed the contents of three of the five cellars associated with the principal structures. He published a two-page report and map of his findings, but the National Park Service—which now owns Green Spring and its collection—does not possess documentation or artifacts from that excavation (William Cahoon 2000, personal communication).

9 Open-topped kilns also require upside down stacking of ceramic vessels, as seems to have been the case at Green Spring (Caywood 1955:13).

10 Smith suggests that the pottery kiln may have begun life as a tile kiln for the production of roofing tiles for the main dwelling, but was later converted to the production of pottery, with spare or waster tiles serving as kiln furniture and to cover the kiln while firing. Interestingly, *all* of the tiles recovered from the kiln had lugs for attachment, rather than peg holes, whereas the tiles from the dwelling house had lugs *and* peg holes (Smith 1981:93). Smith identified eight different vessel forms in the Green Spring collection. The minimum number of vessels by the Green Spring potter recovered from Green Spring itself is 193 (Smith 1981:92). According to Smith's calculations, 400 vessels could have been produced in a kiln the size of the one at Green Spring with between two and six firings (Smith 1981:96). From this, and the generally short use-lives of similar kilns in Europe, he concludes that the output of the kiln was minimal, and the venture probably of short duration—maybe a year or less. However, this interpretation does not take into account the presence of Green Spring pottery at other sites in the region (for example, Straube 1995).

11 Information regarding the excavation and its findings comes from manuscript field and lab records in the possession of Alain C. Outlaw and Merry A. Outlaw (Outlaw and Outlaw n.d.) as well as personal communication.

12 The brick floored cellar is designated Feature 224. The pit in the craft area is Feature 332. Feature 442 is the sawpit, and the possible privy is Feature 255.

13 The settlement he established was sometimes known as Argall's Gift, Argall's Town, or Paspaheigh. Pasbehegh (also Pasbyhaye or Paspaheigh) was the name of a Virginia Indian town that had preceded the English settlement. The idea of a "governor's land" leasehold persisted until the American Revolution, over 160 years after the initial English settlement at Argall's Gift (Forman 1940:476; Outlaw 1990).

14 Drummond may have arrived in the colony as early as 1637, when a William Drummond was listed as a headright for Theodore Moyses's 2,000 acres in James City County "Upon Tanks Pasbye hayes Cr.[eek],...butting on Chichahominy Riv.," not far from where Drummond ended up settling. A William Drummond also appears in the headright list for Stephen Webb's 500 acres patented in 1639 in "James City County"—in the Southside portion soon to become Surry County (Nugent 1934:58,124).

In Drummond's next lease, he took on 200 acres in the governor's land. The full text reads, "Mr. Wm. Drummond one of ye tenants of ye Governrs Land peticoning to this court that leases for 99 yeares might be granted, and the court considering what great damage many of ye tenants have been in building and other Improvemts doth thinke fitt and accordingly grant and Order all the Tenants inhabiting upon the said Passbehayes have their leases renewed 99 years paying ye accustomed Rents to ye Governr and his successrs" (Nugent 1977:103).

15 Sometime after April 1656, he came into possession of a half-acre lot at the eastern end of New Towne, which he sold sometime prior to December 1664. Sarah Drummond also owned a half-acre lot, to the west of the church-yard (the William and Mary Quarterly 1903:22). According to McCartney (2000b:108), the Drummonds' brick house—reputed to be the best in town—was located on the lot belonging to Sarah. It was this town house, rather than his own dwelling, that Drummond personally burned when Bacon's army set fire to Jamestown in 1676. He patented 4,750 acres in Westmoreland County (Nugent 1934:403–404). These acres were "deserted" by Drummond (that is, not improved in the required time) and repatented in 1667 by other men. Note that this lapse coincided with Drummond's governorship of the Albemarle, in what is now North Carolina (1664–1667). He also owned 1,200 acres on the James City County side of the Chickahominy River, which he enlarged and repatented at 1,442 acres in 167[–] (Nugent 1934:400; 1977:103; the William and Mary Quarterly 1903:23). He had 960 acres in Lower Norfolk County (Nugent 1977:123). This patent notes twenty persons by name, including three "Negroes." This acreage was eventually declared abandoned. But Samuel Swan was the man who took up the patent (Nugent 1977:303), and he was married to Drummond's daughter Sarah at the time (1686). It is unclear what is meant by the patent: "Mr. Wm. Drommond, 461 A., 1 R. 4 P.,. James City County., N. side James Riv., 19 Oct. 1674, p. 495. Bet. The Orphant of Edloe, & 700 acs., 'belonging to the Orphant purchased of Young'." From the description of the bounds, and the fact that it is credited to the transportation of ten persons (by name, including one "Negroe"). McCartney (2000b:107) has interpreted the passage to mean that the patent was for 1,161 acres, 461 for persons transported and 700 purchased from the property owned by the orphan Edloe, which was managed by Young.

16 The depth of animosity between Berkeley and Drummond is given fuller treatment in Chapter 5.

17 The site is located on a broad terrace roughly 2 1/2 miles from the James River, but only 3/4 of a mile from a major tributary now called College Creek.

Currently, the site is surrounded by a suburban housing development, the construction of which prompted the archaeological surveys that identified the seventeenth-century manor complex as well as the eighteenth- and nineteenth-century features related to its later role as an outlying plantation, inhabited primarily by the Ludwells' enslaved workforce. (For a discussion of the later occupation of Rich Neck, see Agbe-Davies 1999a; Franklin 2004; Samford 1991.)

18 Archaeologists from Colonial Williamsburg's Department of Archaeological Research undertook excavations at Rich Neck—as well as much of the historical background—are from the technical report by Muraca, Philip Levy, and Leslie McFaden (2003), unless otherwise noted. Compass directions are given with reference to magnetic north, rather than grid "north," so as to be comparable with Muraca et al. (2003).

19 The main house was altered, including the replacement of the central hearth with two end chimneys, one of which was ornamented with tin-glazed fireplace tiles bearing whimsical scenes. Two rooms were added to the rear of the dwelling, and the entire structure was re-roofed with curved pan tiles, rather than flat tiles. The kitchen/quarter was also expanded with the addition of flanking rooms, each with a full paved cellar. The entire structure received a new pan tile roof as well. Five of the post buildings at Rich Neck also date to Thomas Ludwell's tenure.

20 Another room was added to the dwelling. Muraca et al. (2003) date the demolition of two post buildings (Structures F and H) to the Philip Ludwell/Philip Ludwell II period at Rich Neck. The remaining post structures were apparently demolished at the same time as the brick structures, which nevertheless may have persisted after the Ludwell family left Rich Neck in favor of their property at Green Spring.

21 The site is located on a high terrace above a ravine leading to Queens Creek about one mile away. The Page site—on a tract of land now called Bruton Heights, and part of the research campus of the Colonial Williamsburg Foundation—was excavated between 1992 and 1995 by archaeologists from Colonial Williamsburg. Project archaeologists John Metz and Dwayne Pickett led the excavation teams. The description of the Page site is drawn from Metz et al. (1998) unless otherwise noted.

22 Although they are marked 1669, a time lag of five to seven years is common, putting the window installation between ca. 1669 and ca. 1676 (Metz et al. 1998:71).

23 The seventeenth-century site at Port Anne was discovered in 1986 in the course of constructing a suburban housing development. The Phase III excavation was carried out by archaeologists with the Colonial Williamsburg Office of Archaeological Excavation under the supervision of Andrew Edwards and principal investigator Marley Brown. Information on the archaeological findings at Port Anne is taken from the site report (Edwards 1987) unless stated otherwise.

24 Among the features identified and excavated by the archaeologists were the graves of seven adults and one child.

25 A hearth was all that remained of the dwelling house (Edwards 1987:39).

26 A preliminary study of the local pipes Port Anne (Lester and Hendricks 1987) found that when the pipe bowls were ordered stratigraphically, they appeared to follow the developmental sequence identified by Henry (1979). However, the authors noted that the rapid filling of the borrow pit undermined any discussion of real stylistic change over time.

27 In the Jamestown assemblages studied here, the proportion of local pipes ranged from 61 percent to 13 percent. On the other hand, one of the Port Anne *trash pits* had 134 imported pipe fragments and only one fragment of a locally made pipe (Lester and Hendricks 1987:i).

28 A Richard Brewster of Archer's Hope appears in the records as a petitioner for tax relief after suffering losses during the 1622 Powhatan uprising. He also appeared before the Assembly in 1630, representing a community of settlers at the Neck O' Land in Archer's Hope (McCartney 2000b:54).

29 A man named William Davis appears in the records in 1642 as leasing 50 acres in Middle Plantation from Richard Kemp. He was a member of the Assembly in 1643 and 1647, representing James City County. Documents also testify to his being the husband of Bridget Buck Burrows and, therefore, the likely owner of the land her father had owned at Jamestown. He died sometime before 1652. Another William Davis appears in the record as a servant of Thomas Swan in 1658, and a litigant against a Jamestown resident in 1674 (McCartney 2000b:101).

30 Rice (1996:179) advocates using the term "standardization" to refer to the process, and "uniformity" to refer to the resultant characteristics.

31 In this case, the Student's T test. For an explanation, see Drennan 1996; Thomas 1986.

32 All of the measurements were in millimeters, with one exception. The 64ths of an inch scale was used for stem bore diameter because of the vast existing literature on pipe stem bores using that mode of measurement (for example, Binford 1961; Deetz 1987; Harrington 1954). Here, the primary purpose is to record the range of sizes and identify standardization within the assemblages, not to establish dates, though recent work on local pipe stem bores suggests that the bore sizes can be used for dating pipe assemblages using techniques patterned on those employed for imported pipes (Monroe and Mallios 2004).

33 The bowl angle measurement approaches the level of completely random variability (roughly 57 percent, according to Eerkens and Bettinger 2001). Even if we exclude one pipe with a backward-tilting bowl, the overall angle CV is still 37.2 percent.

34 For the first iteration of this test, Jamestown was treated as a single "site."

35 What follows is not, strictly speaking, "modal analysis," as it is not comparative, unlike the work done in Chapters 4 and 5.

36 This dominance of simple linear motifs is, incidentally, typical of all the plantations, though the incidence of *juncture* decorated fragments is exaggerated at Green Spring, as it is at Jamestown.

37 Of course, multiple molds do not necessarily mean multiple makers. Alvey and Laxton (1974; 1977) have demonstrated that Nottingham pipemakers routinely used more than one mold at a time.

38 An ANOVA (analysis of variance) test performed on the CV values themselves shows that any differences in degree of variability among the sites have little significance. $F = 0.235$, $df = 26.319$, 112.057, $p > 0.05$.

39 When all of the CV values are ranked in one batch, and the six sites are compared, a Kruskal-Wallis test can be used to determine whether there is a significant difference in the ranking of the different sites. $H = 1.011$, $df = 5$, $p > 0.95$. The chances are better than 95 percent that the relative ranking of the CV values of the different sites is due to chance. By that measure, the sites are not significantly different from one another in terms of standardization.

Chapter 4: Jamestown, Cities, and Crafts

1 While Jamestown may not have been a real town in the eyes of its contemporary critics (see discussion in Horning 1995) or some modern-day historians, others have argued that the *functions* of an urban area are as important to the definition of a town as population density or architectural complexity (Ernst and Merrins 1973; Samford 1996:68).

2 He was assisted at Jamestown, and surrounding properties (including Green Spring), by Edward Jelks, B. Bruce Powell, Joel Shiner, Louis Caywood, and J. Paul Hudson.

3 All of the archaeological information for the various structures is from Cotter (1958) unless otherwise noted. All of the information regarding property boundaries and ownership history is likewise from McCartney and Kiddle (2000), unless otherwise noted.

4 This association is based primarily on the idea of its having been a warehouse, the location of the Bland's warehouse being unclear from the records available.

5 For a discussion of the evolution of the English wine bottle, see Noël Hume (1969:60–71).

6 The proportions reported in the most recent and most complete artifact catalogue (rather than the version published in 1958) suggest a date range of 1620–1680.

7 A chi-square comparison of Structure 127 to the population of pipe fragments yields $x^2 = 27.4$, $df=1$, $p <0.001$. A chi-square comparison of Structure 127, Rich Neck, and Structure 144 yields $x^2 = 31.9$, $df = 2$, $p <0.001$.

8 Other records confirm that Hunt was actually a resident of Jamestown, and that therefore in this case, "house" may actually refer to his primary dwelling.

9 See the brief discussion of "country houses" earlier in the chapter, with greater detail in Horning (1995).

10 Thomas Hill, a gentleman, merchant, and sometime James City burgess, owned one of the lots, patenting it in 1638. Richard Kemp, briefly also the owner of Rich Neck, patented the neighboring lot on the same day and built a

brick house on it. Barely three years later, their new owner, Governor Francis Wyatt, merged the two lots. Sometime between 1641 and 1644, when he died, Wyatt sold his Jamestown lot to his successor, Sir William Berkeley. Berkeley, in turn, sold it to Walter Chiles in 1649. Chiles was a merchant, and apparently lived in the house—which cannot be said definitively for the previous owners of Kemp's brick house—reputedly "the fairest ever known in this country for substance and uniformity" (McCartney and Kiddle 2000:85). Chiles served as a burgess for Charles City and James City, successively. His son, also named Walter Chiles, continued to reside at Jamestown and served as a James City burgess, as well as a justice of the peace, and vestryman. For some period during Walter II's ownership, he leased a house on the lot to Theophilus Hone (sometimes transcribed as "Stone"). In 1673, after Walter II had died, his widow Susanna and her new husband sold the lot to Colonel John Page (incidentally, the father of Walter II's first wife). Sometime between 1676 and 1682, Page sold to William Sherwood. In 1696, Sherwood sold a half-acre portion of the three-and-one-half acre lot, noting that it had been recently occupied by Secretary Ralph Wormley. The purchaser was John Harris, who only held it for five years before selling to William Drummond II. This ownership history in particular highlights the deep and extensive entanglements among elite families.

11 The researchers cited as evidence: 1) the finishing on the "interior" (south) face of the brickwork, and lack thereof on the "exterior" (north) face; 2) the closers on each end of the wall; 3) the lack of bricks in the east and west trenches; and 4) the size of the wall, which was too high and narrow to adequately support even a frame superstructure. They further argue that the projected size of the building is "the wrong shape and size for a seventeenth-century building without evidence of internal divisions" (Bragdon et al. 1992:n.p.). They also point to the feature's alignment with the structure labeled 44-53-138 and suggest that the two are therefore related, with Structure 44-53-138 being the principal dwelling and Structure 100 being ancillary to it.

12 Based on the mid-century dates of the artifacts and assuming that the artifacts accumulated after the structure fell into disuse, Cotter concluded that the occupation of the structure dated to the first quarter of the seventeenth century. Later interpretations, because they consider non-structural functions, tend to hew more closely to the dates of the artifacts themselves, and place the feature in the mid to late seventeenth century (Bragdon et al. 1992; Horning and Edwards 2000).

13 In reality, there are not so many more pipes here than from the structures interpreted as private houses.

14 Architectural historians with the Colonial Williamsburg Foundation have summarized the decades of archaeological, architectural, and documentary research at Structure 144 (Carson et al. 2002). The discussion of Structure 144's history and architectural development is drawn from this most recent and comprehensive report, unless otherwise noted.

15 This mid-century work, supervised by Louis Caywood and Joel Shiner, produced little information to support or refute Yonge's ideas, as much of their energy focused instead on a group of burials that predated the construction of the brick buildings (May 2003). The pipes for the present study were excavated in the 1950s by the NPS/APVA crew directed by Caywood, and in 2000–2001 by the APVA crew directed by May. The more recent excavation consisted of a series of small, strategically located test units, as well as re-excavation of areas already disturbed by previous digging. Most of the pipes examined here came from backfill contexts that APVA excavators removed from House 2. Datable material from House 2 included two coins (1660–85 and 1702) and a window lead, dated 1671. The other artifacts are more generally fourth-quarter seventeenth century, with a few intrusive objects of much later date (May 2003; B. Straube, personal communication).

16 The interpretation is based on a 1694 land grant to Philip Ludwell that can be linked to the contemporary landscape and describes "the Ruins of his three Brick houses between the State house and Country house" (Carson et al. 2002:3-B-2).

17 The structure uncovered by Yonge consisted of brick foundations for four similar units, each approximately twenty by forty feet, placed end to end, with later additions to the rear that nearly doubled their size (incidentally, this renovation resembles what the Ludwells did to the main house at Rich Neck). Attached to the eastern end of the row was a much larger unit, originally seventy-four by twenty feet, with additions to the center of the north and south walls. The foundations for Houses 1 and 2 (numbered from west to east) are continuous, but the brickwork for House 3 abuts that of House 2, and House 3 uses House 2's existing east wall to form its own west wall. So it appears that Houses 1 and 2 represented a single separate construction phase and that they were the first of the group to be built. Other differences between the two pairs of houses include slight variations in the layout, different roofing materials, and variable mortar composition (May 2003). As between House 2 and House 3, there is a straight joint between House 4 and House 5; House 5 was built with only three walls of its own, using the east wall of House 4 for its west wall. For additional information on dating and the construction sequence, see Agbe-Davies 2004b.

18 Philip Ludwell owned the lot for at least ten years and is the only individual who can be irrefutably linked to Structure 144.

19 The chi-square tests used to establish the comparison between Jamestown as a whole and the individual structures produced such low "expected" values (less than 5), that the calculated probability may not be very accurate.

20 Strength of association is measured by a statistic called Cramer's V—in some cases, the results are statistically significant, but the actual association between attributes and sites/structures is not particularly strong (that is, <0.1). The weak association may be due to the actual association of a variate with more than one site, or the association of a site with more than one variate.

21 This test is called an "analysis of variance," or ANOVA.

22 For this work, the structures at Jamestown were grouped as a single site.

23 Angle is a poor measure for distinguishing among sites because the sites themselves are more variable than the combined assemblage (see Table 4.4).

Chapter 5: Moving Pipes through Social and Physical Space

1 Even the values given for pipemaking apprentices were less than those for apprentices in other trades (Arnold 1977:315).

2 Walker does note that other sources suggest a journeyman:master ratio as high as 5:1 (Walker 1977:134,174).

3 Du Monceau's account is the basis of the information about pipe making in Diderot's *Encyclopedie* (see Walker 1977:80–121 for a summary).

4 Remarriage was also a significant means of wealth accumulation. Even a woman who did not inherit her dead husband's property outright, and may not have owned anything independently of him, might have control of his estate while their children were minors, making her doubly attractive to potential partners.

5 In *Tobacco Culture*, T. H. Breen dramatically evokes the frustration of eighteenth-century planters, who saw themselves as masters of their own fate—dependent on no one—who nevertheless were so universally encumbered by debt and powerless before their "friends" the tobacco merchants that they eventually rose up to throw off the colonial yoke (Breen 2001). The economic system that so frustrated these eighteenth-century planters was organized along what we recognize today as classic mercantilist principles. But the golden age of mercantilism in the eighteenth and nineteenth centuries rested on a foundation laid in the seventeenth century (Wallerstein 1980:236–241).

6 While the Virginia elite dominated the political scene at the county and colony level, they, in turn, were subject to the authority that emanated from London. It is important to note that the mercantilist principles on which the colonial relationship was based did not evolve "naturally." It was a conscious policy that began to take explicit shape early in the reign of Charles II. Two early actions of his, the passage of the Navigation Acts and the organization of two new councils for Trade and Plantations, revealed an increased royal interest in the administration of England's colonies (Rainbolt 1967) and reflected a new concept of royal authority over Virginia and Virginians.

7 From a letter by William Berkeley, describing the events of Bacon's Rebellion, reproduced in Washburn (1957).

8 There had been hints prior to Bacon's Rebellion—early in Berkeley's second term—that England was rethinking its relationship with its colonies. The Navigation Acts restricted trade with important foreign partners, most notably the Dutch, and seemed to herald a new era of increased metropolitan meddling in colonial affairs. But these interferences paled in comparison with post-Rebellion occupation by British troops, the ouster of the governor, and the reorganization of the political structure of the colony that followed (Billings 1996:446, 452).

9 Rich Neck and Port Anne are certainly connected by proximity, and our best estimation of the ownership and occupation of the latter suggests that the social ties between them would have been largely positive. This pattern stretches back to the earliest years of English settlement of Middle Plantation, with Richard Kemp, and persists at least through the secretarial tenures of the two Ludwells. The connection between the long-time governor of the colony (at Green Spring) and its "Statehouse" (Structure 144) should be obvious, but we can also add the decades-long friendship and patronage relationships between Berkeley and the Ludwells to that equation. Green Spring and Structure 144 are not as close together as Rich Neck and Port Anne, but they were certainly within walking distance along a relatively well-established thoroughfare.

10 The respective owners of Rich Neck and Green Spring had extraordinarily close ties throughout the seventeenth century, from the initial settlement of each, and one might say culminating in the marriage between Philip Ludwell and Frances Berkeley, which brought the two plantations into the same family. A portion of Structure 144 was owned by—and likely built at the initiative of—the Ludwells, and there is still some discussion as to how involved William Berkeley was in the development of Jamestown seventeenth-century statehouses, so both Green Spring and Rich Neck have connections to this Structure. John Page had periodic, relatively positive, interactions with William Berkeley, and in any event they clearly had political and business dealings. Page also owned the Structure 100 lot, and had familial and financial ties to many of the individuals whose ownership or tenancy preceded and followed his ownership.

11 The antagonism that characterized relations between William Berkeley and William Drummond was multi-layered in the sense that they clashed over land transactions and political administration in both North Carolina and Virginia, and seemed to develop a personal antipathy to one another. The bad blood even persisted after both their deaths—through the actions of their widows, Frances Berkeley and Sarah Drummond. The Drummond site and Green Spring are geographically close, yet their owners were worlds apart. As close allies of Berkeley, the Ludwells of Rich Neck also participated in this animus, as is seen in their complicity in Drummond's execution, and by Thomas Ludwell's treatment of Sarah Drummond's petition, among other actions.

12 John Page had numerous dealings with his fellow elites in his capacity as a merchant. He also acted as a local agent for merchants Jeffrey Jeffries and John Jeffries. For example, he petitioned for reimbursement on Jeffries's behalf when Berkeley seized part of a large stock of wine during the siege of Jamestown, the remainder of which was destroyed when the town burned. Page also reported having delivered "4 men, Negroes," to William Berkeley on behalf of Jeffries, but claimed that he had not been paid the £100 he was owed (McCartney 2000b:260–262; McCartney and Kiddle 2000:95). Other interactions between Berkeley and Page suggest a more cooperative, if perhaps one-sided relationship. In a letter dated 21 January 1676/7, Berkeley

wrote that he had had Drummond executed the day before, and continued, "I am now at Mr. Brayes, *just going to Major Page's, where I shall rest this night, and to-morrow intend to Green Spring*" (Hening 1823 III:569, emphasis added). Page and Berkeley had probably made the arrangements the day before, because despite having signed Bacon's loyalty oath, Page served on the court-martial panel that condemned Drummond to death by hanging (Hening 1823 II:546). Page's seeming change of heart may be explained by intimidation by either the ascendant rebel, or by the later restored governor. It may also indicate his disenchantment with a movement that would resort to kidnapping his wife and forcing her, along with other women, to stand as a human shield for Bacon's army during their siege of Jamestown (Anonymous 1915 [n.d.]:68–69).

13 John Page was at one point Walter Chiles II's father-in-law. Later on, Chiles's widow (not Mary Page Chiles, but a later wife) sold the Structure 100 lot to Page. Even while it was still in Chiles's hands, he had rented a house on the lot to Theophilus Hone, another member of the Pages' orbit. Hone, Drummond, and John Page's brother Matthew accepted a contract from the provincial government to put up a set of gun carriages and a 250-foot-long brick fort at Jamestown, paid in advance. After Matthew Page died in 1673, Drummond and Hone were called before the court and instructed to complete the job and replace the defective brick (McCartney 2000b:108; Washburn 1956:368–369). Although not mentioned in the suit, it seems that John Page took on the obligation of his late brother (the William and Mary Quarterly 1898a). A separate suit, also in 1673, has a bricklayer named John Bird suing John Page specifically as executor of his brother's estate (McCartney and Kiddle 2000:93). Bird was probably the man responsible for actually *executing* the work for which Matthew Page, Drummond, and Hone were contracted. It is noteworthy that Matthew Page chose to get involved in the construction of a brick fort (an unusual kind of structure, by the way) at the same time that his brother John owned a fairly elaborate brick and tile operation.

14 The documentary record associated with Port Anne being so sparse, only the faintest of traces situate it within the colony's alliance matrix. The hints that do exist point to parallels with Rich Neck. Early in the century, Secretary of the Colony Richard Kemp had custody of a property somewhere on Archer's Hope Creek, at the same time that he owned Rich Neck (in a play on the name of his own plantation, Kemp called the tract associated with his office as secretary, "Barren Neck"). And William Davis, one of the individuals who might have been resident at Port Anne, has been documented as a tenant of Kemp's (Edwards 1987; McCartney 2000b; McCartney and Kiddle 2000:85–87).

15 Kemp, even while living at Rich Neck, nevertheless maintained close connections with the capital. In the disputes that had characterized the first half of the seventeenth century, Kemp had been a staunch ally of Governor Harvey. In addition to the men named above, Kemp also had an important relationship with Thomas Hill. Hill had been another member of Harvey's faction. In 1643, Hill purchased a 600-acre portion of Kemp's original Rich

Neck tract (McCartney and Kiddle 2000:86, 83). Earlier, in 1641, Kemp and Hill had joined forces to sell their adjoining Jamestown lots—the location of Structure 100—to Governor Francis Wyatt. Kemp's dealings with Wyatt were not always mutually satisfying. Wyatt's Council forced Kemp from his office as secretary of the colony. Kemp complained that it was because he had been loyal to Governor Harvey that he had been ousted. Interestingly enough, Kemp was restored to his post after he made a trip to England to plead on Harvey's behalf, and ended up attaching himself to the new governor, William Berkeley (Muraca et al. 2003:16). So great was Kemp's influence, that when Berkeley had to leave the colony just after the second Powhatan uprising in 1644, Kemp was appointed acting governor.

Later, Kemp was closely allied with Berkeley and other members of his Green Spring faction. So the patterns noted for the first half of the century persisted into the second. The next known owner of Rich Neck, Thomas Lunsford, a royalist refugee of the English Civil War, had married Kemp's widow and was welcomed into the colony by Berkeley, who appointed him to the Council and made him lieutenant-general of the militia (Muraca et al. 2003:39). The next resident owner of consequence was Thomas Ludwell, who had come to Virginia as a headright of his cousin, Governor Berkeley. That close relationship eased his passage into the ranks of the elite. Like Richard Kemp, Thomas Ludwell served as secretary of state for the colony, and so may have had rights to "Barren Neck" (Port Anne?) as well as his own Rich Neck.

16 Although he had a permanent home at Rich Neck, Thomas Ludwell also participated in the land buying and selling that went on at Jamestown. In 1667, he and Thomas Stegg patented "1/2 acre. In James City, on the river side, and adjoining to the westernmost of those three houses, all which jointly were formerly called by the name of the Old State house" (William and Mary Quarterly 1903:23). To purchase a lot with a partner in that fashion suggests an uncommon degree of cooperation. Philip Ludwell's ownership of one of the tracts associated with Structure 144 is one of the few verifiable pieces of evidence linking that structure to the documentary record (Carson et al. 2002:iv).

17 One key relationship, that began as a tenancy, blossomed into patronage, but eventually went sour, was between Drummond and Berkeley, the occupants of the eponymous Drummond site and Green Spring. Drummond became a tenant of Berkeley's in 1648, with the lease of twenty-five acres in the governor's land. Years later, when Berkeley was among the proprietors of the newly formed colony of Carolina, they selected Drummond to be the first governor of Albemarle—now eastern North Carolina. His three-year term began in the fall of 1664 and was renewable, but he was succeeded by Samuel Stephens (incidentally, the first husband of Frances Culpepper Stephens, later Berkeley, then Ludwell) in October 1667. (In yet another twist, Philip Ludwell also became governor of the Albemarle in 1689, some years after his marriage to Frances [Weeks 1892].) In 1666, Drummond had written a letter critical of Berkeley's administration of Virginia and management of North Carolina, remarking, "here are an abundance of people that are weary of Sir

Williams Government. More I could Say as to his obstructing all things of Carolina; but I conceive it not safe in regard I live soe neare him." Apparently, his self-censorship was not thorough enough because the criticism infuriated his neighbor and landlord, who somehow got a copy of the letter and had it entered into the public record of the Virginia colony (Washburn 1956:368).

Berkeley and Drummond next butted heads about leaseholds in the governor's land. The trouble started as early as 1666, in which year a petition of Drummond's appeared several times before the Assembly. Each time, the Assembly refused to rule on the matter referring it back to the governor and his council (Hening 1823 II:253). The exact nature of Drummond's petition is not clear from the available records, but it may have been connected with his crusade for longer leases. William Drummond played an instrumental role in extending the lease length within the governor's land for himself and his neighbors. Whereas lease terms had been only twenty-five years, he got them extended to ninety-nine years. After this triumph, he took on 200 acres in the governor's land. The patent, which is dated "167—" notes that it was in "Pasbehayes," and that it adjoined the land of William Drewet, John White, Daniel Liell, and Sir Francis Wyatt.

One of the explanations historians give for Drummond's harsh treatment for his role in the Rebellion is the preexisting animosity between him and Berkeley that continued to be expressed, even after both of their deaths, by their widows. Yet Drummond's actions during the Rebellion were also a contributing factor. Drummond was, and is, widely regarded as the legal and strategic mind behind much of Bacon's agenda (Washburn 1956:365; Webb 1995; Wertenbaker 1959). Berkeley was evidently aware of this threat to his authority, warning the Assembly, according to one witness, to "beware of Two Rogues amongst us, naming Laurence and Drummond, both dwelling at James Town" (Mathews 1915 [1705]:23–24), and asserting in a private letter written in early 1677 that "I soe much hate Drummond and Lawrence, that though they could put The Country in peace into my hands, I would not Accept it from Such Villaines as Both those are in Their Nature" (cited in Washburn 1956:367–368).

18 Drummond's appreciation for the finer legal points can be observed in his behavior when Bacon's army burned Jamestown. He is credited with saving the colony's records so that they would not burn along with the statehouse (His Majesties Commissioners 1915 [1677]:135–136). This action resembles that of Philip Ludwell, who did his part to preserve the colony's documents by taking them to Rich Neck for safekeeping in February 1677 (Hening 1823 II:404). And yet, Berkeley's animosity towards Drummond was paralleled in his associates, Thomas and Philip Ludwell, the likely owners of at least a portion of Structure 144.

Thomas Ludwell was widely regarded as a partisan who used his authority to perpetuate the domination of the Green Spring faction. For instance, he presided over the hearing given to Sarah Drummond in which she attempted to regain property seized from her dead husband's estate and in the possession of Frances Berkeley. Thomas Ludwell threw out the case, saying it was "all lies." He was given this opportunity to be useful to the widow of his cousin and patron (a woman who was soon to become his sister-in-law) by the fact that the new governor, who should have been presiding, had been "seized a short time before the Court was appointed, with a most violent fitt of sickness" (Washburn 1956:361).

19 In other words, neither chi-square test meets the typical p < 0.05 threshold.

Chapter 6: Little Tubes of Mighty Power, or, Doing Things with Words

1 A widow like Elisheba Vaulx or Sarah Drummond could act as a head of household in many respects, a married woman could not.

2 The property requirement was occasionally relaxed, most notably by Governor Berkeley in an attempt to appease the free populace immediately before Bacon's Rebellion.

3 Taxes were assessed by the size of one's household rather than income.

4 The Act continues, "*And* that if any christian shall committ ffornication with a negro man or woman, hee or shee soe offending shall pay double the ffines imposed by the former act."

5 As Morgan (1972) makes clear, these headrights circulated on an open market and so the person who eventually claimed the land may not have been directly responsible for the immigrant's transport.

6 All selections from the York County Records are from transcriptions created by the York Records Project, housed in the Colonial Williamsburg Foundation's Department of Historical Research (York DOW 1634 et al.). For the remainder of the chapter, when I provide a date alone in parentheses, these records are being cited.

7 She was the only specific person described as "English" (1673).

8 We know that Ralph, David, and Joseph are not "Negroe's," despite their lack of surnames, because the latter appear separately at the end of the same list.

9 An exception is found in the wills: "a French boy, Nickolice Morrele" (1687).

10 The close analysis focused on the certificates that included reference to people of African descent. The others I read for context. Among the wills, it was rare to find a mention of "servants" without a mention of "Negroes."

11 One of the few examples of "English servants" occurs in the only document to use the construction "Negro servant," which appears repeatedly: "my young Negro servant called Jacke...my negro Servt. called Franke" and so forth. Interestingly, the English servants are in a completely different part of the will from these bondsmen and bondswomen (York DOW 1668:4).

12 Usage changed again in the antebellum era, when the term "servant" was often applied to enslaved persons engaged in household or personal service. One still finds residues of this usage today when some people discuss bound labor in the pre-Emancipation era.

13 In 1658 Richard Barkeshyre gave to "my man Robert" his freedom, along with a hat. This case would be unusual for a servant in several respects; the

lack of a surname for Robert, the use of the construction "my man," and the fact that he was given freedom suggest that he may have been enslaved.

14 Nanne Mo[g]a is listed in a land certificate from 1662.

15 Of course, these stories are not mutually exclusive and in fact are found interwoven in the best of new research on pipes made in the Virginia colony (Bollwerk 2012; Monroe 2002; Sikes 2008).

16 I'm writing these words in the last few days of summer, 2014. Fresh in my mind, research showing that: black children admitted to emergency rooms are less likely to receive adequate pain management than other children (Johnson et al. 2013); children of color attend poorer quality schools and are disciplined at rates far exceeding those of white children (Goff et al. 2014; Rich 2014); and professors—my peers—respond differentially to requests for advice about their programs depending on the perceived racial or ethnic background and gender of the letter writer (Milkman et al. 2014). The deepest sadness is inspired by recent funerals in New York and Missouri where one black man was choked to death by police (he was selling cigarettes illegally) (Goodman and Goldstein 2014) and the effort to explain away the police shooting of a black teenager included the assertion that he stole (cigars) from a convenience store (Robles and Schmidt 2014). It remains to be seen whether the incident in Missouri has sparked a movement.

References

Adams, William Y.
  1988   Archaeological Classification: Theory Versus Practice. Antiquity 61:40–56.
Adams, William Y., and Ernest W. Adams
  1991   Archaeological typology and practical reality: a dialectical approach to artifact classification. Cambridge, UK: Cambridge University Press.
Agbe-Davies, Anna S.
  1999a Archaeological Excavation of a Small Cellar on Rich Neck Plantation. Williamsburg, Virginia. research.history.org/Archaeological_Research/ Technical_Reports/ DownloadPDF.cfm?ReportID=Archaeo1012: The Colonial Williamsburg Foundation, Department of Archaeological Research
  1999b The Legacy of "Race" in African-American Archaeology: A Silk Purse from the Wolf's Ears? World Archaeology Congress 4, Cape Town, 1999. www.wac.uct. ac.za/wac4/symposia/papers/S074gbd1.pdf
  2000   Phase II Archaeological Assessment of the Jamestown Shoreline, James City County, Virginia. Yorktown, Virginia: The Colonial Williamsburg Foundation, Department of Archaeological Research.
  2001   The Production and Consumption of Local Pipes along the Tobacco Coast. Paper presented at the annual meeting of the Society for American Archaeology, New Orleans, Louisiana, 2001.
  2004a The Production and Consumption of Smoking Pipes along the Tobacco Coast. In Smoking and Culture: Recent Developments in the Archaeology of Smoking Pipes in Eastern North America. S. Rafferty and R. Mann, eds. Pp. 273–304. Knoxville: University of Tennessee Press.
  2004b Up in Smoke: Pipe Production, Smoking, and Bacon's Rebellion. Ph.D. dissertation, Anthropology, University of Pennsylvania.
  2006   Alternatives to Traditional Models for the Classification and Analysis of Pipes of the Early Colonial Chesapeake. In Dirt and Discussion: Methods, Methodology, and Interpretation in Historical Archaeology. S. Archer and K. Bartoy, eds. Pp. 115–140. New York: Springer.
  2010   Social Aspects of the Tobacco Pipe Trade in Early Colonial Virginia. In Social Archaeologies of Trade and Exchange: Exploring Relationships among People, Places, and Things. A. A. Bauer and A. S. Agbe-Davies, eds. Pp. 69–98. Walnut Creek, CA: Left Coast Press, Inc.
  2011   Reaching for Freedom, Seizing Responsibility: Archaeology at the Phyllis Wheatley Home for Girls, Chicago. In The Materiality of Freedom:

217

    Archaeologies of Postemancipation Life. J. A. Barnes, ed. Pp. 69–86. Columbia: University of South Carolina Press.

in prep Laboring Under an Illusion: Steps to Align Method with Theory in the Archaeology of American Slavery. Historical Archaeology.

under review a How to Do Things with Things, or, Are Blue Beads Good to Think? Semiotic Review.

under review b Where Tradition and Pragmatism Meet: African Diaspora Archaeology at the Crossroads. Historical Archaeology.

Agbe-Davies, Anna S., and Claire Fuller Martin

2013 "Demanding a Share of Public Regard:" African American Education at New Philadelphia, Illinois. Tranforming Anthropology 21(2):103–121.

Alcock, N. W., and Nancy Cox

2000 Living and Working in Seventeenth Century England: Descriptions and Drawings from Randale Holme's Academy of Armory: The British Library, CD-ROM.

Alden, John R.

1982 Marketplace Exchange as Indirect Distribution: An Iranian Example. In Contexts for Prehistoric Exchange. J. E. Ericson and T. K. Earle, eds. Pp. 83–101. New York: Academic Press.

Alvey, R. C., and R. R. Laxton

1974 Analysis of Some Nottingham Clay Pipes. Science and Archaeology 13:3–12.

1977 Further Analysis of Some Nottingham Clay Tobacco Pipes. Science and Archaeology 19:20–29.

Alvey, R. C., R. R. Laxton, and G. F. Paechter

1985 Statistical Analysis of Some Nottingham Clay Tobacco Pipes. In The Archaeology of the Clay Tobacco Pipe. P. Davey, ed. Pp. 229–252. Oxford: British Archaeological Reports, British Series No. 63.

American Anthropological Association

1998 AAA Statement on "Race." Anthropology Newsletter 39(6):3.

2011 Race: Are We So Different? www.understandingrace.org/home.html, accessed 10 July 2014.

Anonymous

1846 A Narrative of the Indian and Civil Wars in Virginia, in the Years 1675 and 1676. In Tracts and Other Papers Relating Principally to the Origin, Settlement, and Progress of the Colonies in North America, from the Discovery of the Country to the Year 1776. P. Force, ed. Pp. 1–47. Washington, D.C.: P. Force.

1915 [n.d.] The History of Bacon's and Ingram's Rebellion. In Narratives of the Insurrections, 1675–1690. C. M. Andrews, ed. Pp. 47–98. New York: Scribner's Sons.

Arnold, C. J.

1977 The Clay Tobacco-Pipe Industry: An Economic Study. In Pottery and Commerce: Characterization and Trade in Roman and Later Ceramics. D. P. S. Peacock, ed. Pp. 313–336. London: Academic Press.

Atkinson, David, and Adrian Oswald

1969 London Clay Tobacco Pipes. Oxford: Oxford University Press.

Austin, J. L.

1975 How to Do Things with Words. Oxford: Clarendon.

Bacon, Nathaniel
  1893 [1676] Nathaniel Bacon, Esq'r, His Manifesto Concerning the Present Troubles in Virginia. Virginia Historical Magazine (The Virginia Magazine of History and Biography), 1(1):55–58.
Baert, Patrick
  2005a Philosophy of the Social Sciences: Towards Pragmatism. Cambridge, UK: Polity Press.
  2005b Towards a Pragmatist-Inspired Philosphy of Social Science. Acta Sociologica 48(3):191–203.
Baker, Lee D.
  2010 Anthropology and the Racial Politics of Culture. Durham, NC: Duke University Press.
Baram, Uzi
  1999 Clay Tobacco Pipes and Coffee Cup Sherds in the Archaeology of the Middle East: Artifacts of Social Tensions from the Ottoman Past. The International Journal of Historical Archaeology 3(3):137–151.
Barth, Fredrik
  1969 Introduction. In Ethnic Groups and Boundaries: The Social Organization of Cultural Differences. F. Barth, ed. Pp. 9–38. London: Allen & Unwin.
Battle-Baptiste, Whitney L.
  2011 Black Feminist Archaeology. Walnut Creek, CA: Left Coast Press, Inc.
Bauer, Alexander A., and Anna S. Agbe-Davies, eds.
  2010 Social Archaeologies of Trade and Exchange: Exploring Relationships among People, Places, and Things. Walnut Creek, CA: Left Coast Press, Inc.
Bell, Alison
  1995 Widows, "Free Sisters," and "Independent Girls": Historic Models and An Archaeology of Post-Medieval English Gender Systems. Kroeber Anthropological Society Papers 78:17–32.
Bell, Derek
  1987 And We Are Not Saved: The Elusive Quest for Racial Justice. New York: Basic Books.
Berlin, Ira
  2010 The Making of African America: The Four Great Migrations. New York: Viking.
Bernard, H. Russell, and Gery W. Ryan
  2010 Analyzing Qualitative Data: Systematic Approaches. Thousand Oaks, CA: Sage.
Billings, Warren M.
  1970 The Causes of Bacon's Rebellion. Virginia Magazine of History and Biography 78(4):409–435.
  1975 The Old Dominion in the Seventeenth Century: A Documentary History of Virginia, 1606–1689. Chapel Hill: University of North Carolina Press.
  1976 A Quaker in Seventeenth-Century Virginia: Four Remonstrances by George Wilson. William and Mary Quarterly 3rd series 33(1):127–140.
  1991 The Law of Servants and Slaves in Seventeenth-Century Virginia. Virginia Magazine of History and Biography 99(1):45–62.
  1996 Sir William Berkeley and the Diversification of the Virginia Economy. Virginia Magazine of History and Biography 104(4):433-454.

Binford, Lewis R.
  1961   A New Method of Calculating Dates from Kaolin Pipe Stem Samples. Southeastern Archaeological Conference Newsletter 9(1):19–21.
Blackman, M. James, Gil J. Stein, and Pamela B. Vandiver
  1993   The Standardization Hypothesis and Ceramic Mass Production: Technological, Compositional, and Metric Indexes of Craft Specialization at Tell Leilan, Syria. American Antiquity 58(1):60–80.
Boas, Franz
  1912   Changes in the Bodily Form of Descendants of Immigrants. American Anthropologist 14(3):530–562.
  1963   The Instability of Human Types. In The Mind of Primitive Man. Pp. 78–98. New York: Collier.
Bollwerk, Elizabeth Anne
  2012   Seeing What Smoking Pipes Signal(ed): An Examination of Late Woodland and Early Contact Period (A.D. 900–1665) Native Social Dynamics in the Middle Atlantic. Ph.D. dissertation, Anthropology, University of Virginia.
Brace, C. Loring
  2005   "Race" is a Four-Letter Word: The Genesis of the Concept. New York: Oxford University Press.
Bragdon, Kathleen, Cary Carson, Edward A. Chappell, and Willie Graham
  1992   Report on Jamestown Archaeological Survey. Williamsburg, Virginia: The Colonial Williamsburg Foundation.
Breen, T. H.
  2001   Tobacco Culture: The Mentality of the Great Tidewater Planters on the Eve of Revolution. Princeton, NJ: Princeton University Press.
Breen, T. H., and Stephen Innes
  1980   "Myne Owne Ground": Race and Freedom on Virginia's Eastern Shore, 1640–1676. New York: Oxford University Press.
Brew, John O.
  1971 [1946] The Use and Abuse of Taxonomy. In Man's Imprint from the Past: Readings in the Methods of Archaeology. J. Deetz, ed. Pp. 73–107. Boston: Little, Brown.
Brown, Gregory J.
  1986   Phase I and II Archaeological Investigations of the Port Anne Development. The Colonial Williamsburg Foundation, Department of Archaeological Research.
Brown, Marley R., III, and Patricia Samford
  1994   Current Archaeological Perspectives on the Growth and Development of Williamsburg. In Historical Archaeology of the Chesapeake. P. A. Shackel and B. J. Little, eds. Pp. 231–245. Washington, D. C.: Smithsonian Institution Press.
Browne, Isaac Hawkins
  1744   "Imitation II." In A Pipe of Tobacco: In Imitation of Six Several Authors. Pp. 9–10. London: W. Bickerton.
Brumfiel, Elizabeth M., and Timothy K. Earle
  1987   Specialization, Exchange, and Complex Societies: An Introduction. In Specialization, Exchange and Complex Societies. E. M. Brumfiel and T. K. Earle, eds. Pp. 1–9. Cambridge, UK: Cambridge University Press.

Capone, Patricia, and Elinor Downs
2004 Red Clay Tobacco Pipes: A Petrographic Window into Seventeenth-Century Economics at Jamestown, Virginia and New England. In Smoking and Culture: Recent Developments in the Archaeology of Smoking Pipes in Eastern North America. S. Rafferty and R. Mann, eds. Pp. 305–316. Knoxville: University of Tennesee Press.

Carr, Lois Green, and Russell R. Menard
1979 Immigration and Opportunity: The Freedman in Early Colonial Maryland. In The Chesapeake in the Seventeenth Century: Essays on Anglo-American Society. T. W. Tate and D. L. Ammerman, eds. Pp. 206–242. New York: W. W. Norton.

Carr, Lois Green, and Lorena S. Walsh
1988 Economic Diversification and Labor Organization in the Chesapeake 1650–1820. In Work and Labor in Early America. S. Innes, ed. Pp. 144–188. Chapel Hill: University of North Carolina Press.

Carson, Cary, Norman F. Barka, William M. Kelso, Garry Wheeler Stone, and Dell Upton
1981 Impermanent Architecture in the Southern American Colonies. Winterthur Portfolio 16(2/3):131–196.

Carson, Cary, Willie Graham, Carl Lounsbury, and Martha McCartney
2002 Description and Analysis of Structure 144, Jamestown, Virginia. Williamsburg, VA: APVA Jamestown Rediscovery.

Carson, Jane
1954 Green Spring Plantation in the 17th Century: House Report. The Colonial Williamsburg Foundation, John D. Rockefeller Library.

Caywood, Louis R.
1955 Green Spring Plantation: Archeological Report. Yorktown, VA: Colonial National Historical Park, NPS.
1957 Green Spring Plantation. Virginia Magazine of History and Biography 65:67–83.

Chilton, Elizabeth S.
1999 One Size Fits All: Typology and Alternatives for Ceramic Research. In Material Meanings: Critical Approaches to the Interpretation of Material Culture. E. S. Chilton, ed. Pp. 44–60. Salt Lake City: University of Utah Press.

Chinard, Gilbert, ed.
1934 A Huguenot Exile in Virginia; or Voyages of a Frenchman Exiled for His Religion, with a Description of Virginia and Maryland. New York: The Press of the Pioneers.

Clark, John E.
1995 Craft Specialization as an Archaeological Category. Research in Economic History 16:267–294.

Cobb, Charles R., and Chester B. DePratter
2012 Multisited Research on Colonowares and the Paradox of Globalization. American Anthropologist 114(3):446–461.

Conkey, Margaret W.
1990 Experimenting with Style in Archaeology: Some Historical and Theoretical Issues. In The Uses of Style in Archaeology. M. W. Conkey and C. A. Hastorf, eds. Pp. 5–17. Cambridge, UK: Cambridge University Press.

Coombs, John C.
2011   Beyond the "Origins Debate": Rethinking the Rise of Virginia Slavery. In Early Modern Virginia: Reconsidering the Old Dominion. D. Bradburn and J. C. Coombs, eds. Pp. 239–278. Charlottesville: University of Virginia Press.

Costin, Cathy Lynne
1991   Craft Specialization: Issues in Defining, Documenting, and Explaining the Organization of Production. Archaeological Method and Theory 3:1–56.
1998   Introduction: Craft and Social Identity. In Craft and Social Identity. C. L. Costin and R. P. Wright, eds. Pp. 3–16. Arlington, VA: Archeological Papers of the American Anthropological Association Number 8.

Cotter, John L.
1958   Archeological Excavations at Jamestown, Virginia. Washington, D. C.: The National Park Service, U. S. Department of the Interior.
1994   Archeological Excavations at Jamestown, Virginia. Richmond: The Archeological Society of Virginia.

Courtwright, David
2001   Forces of Habit: Drugs in the Making of the Modern World. Cambridge, MA: Harvard University Press.

Crass, David Colin
1981   A Formal Analysis of the Clay Pipes from Green Spring. M. A., Anthropology, College of William and Mary.
1988   The Clay Pipes from Green Spring Plantation (44 JC 9), Virginia. Historical Archaeology 22(1):83–97.

Crenshaw, Kimberlé, Neil Gotanda, Gary Peller, and Thomas Kendall, eds.
1995   Critical Race Theory: The Key Writings That Formed the Movement. New York: The New Press.

Crossley, David
1990   Post-medieval Archaeology in Britain. London: Leicester University Press.

Crumley, Carole
1995   Heterarchy and the Analysis of Complex Societies. In Heterarchy and the Analysis of Complex Societies. R. M. Ehrenreich, C. L. Crumley, and J. E. Levy, eds. Pp. 1–5. Archeological Papers of the American Anthropological Association. Washington, D. C.: American Anthropological Association.

DAACS   (The Digital Archaeological Archive for Comparative Slavery)
2014   DAACS Cataloging Manual: Tobacco Pipes, www.daacs.org/wp-content/uploads/2013/04/tobacco-pipes.pdf

Deetz, J. Eric, and Bly Straube
2008   Pit 5 (JR731). In 2000–2006 Interim Report on the APVA Excavations at Jamestown, Virginia. W. M. Kelso and B. Straube, eds. Pp. 17–19: Association for the Preservation of Virginia Antiquities.

Deetz, James
1965   The Dynamics of Stylistic Change in Arikara Ceramics. Urbana: University of Illinois Press.
1987   Harrington Histograms Versus Binford Mean Dates as a Technique for Establishing the Occupational Sequences of Sites at Flowerdew Hundred, Virginia. American Archaeology 6(1):62–67.

Deetz, James F., and Edwin S. Dethlefsen
1972   Death's Head, Cherub, Urn and Willow. In Contemporary Archaeology: A Guide to Theory and Contributions. M. Leone, ed. Pp. 402–410. Carbondale: Southern Illinois University Press.

Deetz, John Eric
2002   Architecture of Early Virginia: An Analysis of the Origins of the Earth-fast Tradition. M.A. thesis, Archaeology, University of Leicester.

Delgado, Richard, ed.
1995   Critical Race Theory: The Cutting Edge. Philadelphia: Temple University Press.

Diderot, Denis, and Jean le Rond d'Alembert
1777   Suite du Recueil de planches, sur les sciences libéraux et les arts méchaniques. Paris: Panckouke.

Dietler, Michael, and Ingrid Herbich
1998   Habitus, Techniques, Style: An Integrated Approach to the Social Understanding of Material Culture and Boundaries. In The Archaeology of Social Boundaries. M. T. Stark, ed. Pp. 233–263. Washington, D. C.: Smithsonian Institution Press.

Dimmick, Jesse
1929   Green Spring. William and Mary Quarterly second series, 9(2):129–130.

Drennan, Robert D.
1996   Statistics for Archaeologists: A Commonsense Approach. New York: Plenum Press.

Dunnell, Robert C.
1971a   Sabloff and Smith's "The Importance of Both Analytical and Taxonomic Classification in the Type-Variety System." American Antiquity 36(1):115–118.
1971b   Systematics in Prehistory. New York: The Free Press.
1978   Style and Function: A Fundamental Dichotomy. American Antiquity 43(2):192–202.
1986   Methodological Issues in Americanist Artifact Classification. Advances in Archaeological Method and Theory 9:149–207.

Earle, Carville V.
1979   Environment, Disease, and Mortality in Early Virginia. In The Chesapeake in the Seventeenth Century: Essays on Anglo-American Society. T. W. Tate and D. L. Ammerman, eds. Pp. 96–125. New York: W. W. Norton.

Earle, Timothy K.
1982   Prehistoric Economics and the Archaeology of Exchange. In Contexts for Prehistoric Exchange. J. E. Ericson and T. K. Earle, eds. Pp. 1–12. New York: Academic Press.

Edwards, Andrew C.
1987   Archaeology at Port Anne: A Report on Site CL7, An Early 17th Century Colonial Site. The Colonial Williamsburg Foundation, Office of Archaeological Excavation.

Eerkens, Jelmer W.
2000   Practice Makes within 5% of Perfect: Visual Perception, Motor Skills, and Memory in Artifact Variation. Current Anthropology 41(4):663–668.

Eerkens, Jelmer W., and Robert L. Bettinger
    2001   Techniques for Assessing Standardization in Artifact Assemblages: Can We Scale Material Variability? American Antiquity 66(3):493–504.

Emerson, Matthew C.
    1988   Decorated Clay Tobacco Pipes from the Chesapeake. Unpublished Ph.D. dissertation, Anthropology, University of California at Berkeley.
    1994   Decorated Clay Tobacco Pipes from the Chesapeake. In Historical Archaeology of the Chesapeake. P. A. Shackel and B. J. Little, eds. Pp. 35–49. Washington, D. C.: Smithsonian Institution Press.
    1999   African Inspirations in a New World Art and Artifact: Decorated Tobacco Pipes from the Chesapeake. In I, too, Am America: Studies in African-American Archaeology. T. A. Singleton, ed. Pp. 47–74. Charlottesville: University Press of Virginia.

Epperson, Terrence W.
    2001   "A Separate House for the Christian Slaves, One for the Negro Slaves:" The Archaeology of Race and Identity in Late Seventeenth-Century Virginia. In Race and the Archaeology of Identity. C. E. Orser, Jr., ed. Pp. 54–70. Salt Lake City: University of Utah Press.
    2004   Critical Race Theory and the Archaeology of the African Diaspora. Historical Archaeology 38(1):101–108.

Ernst, J. A., and H. R. Merrins
    1973   "Camden's turrets pierce the skies!": The Urban Process in the Southern Colonies during the Eighteenth Century. William and Mary Quarterly 30(4):549–574.

Espenshade, Christopher T.
    2001   Two Native Potters "Speak" about Punctates: Harding Flats Data and the Clemsons Island Concept. Journal of Middle Atlantic Archaeology 17:59–84.

Fausz, J. Frederick
    1985   Patterns of Anglo-Indian Aggression and Accommodation along the Mid-Atlantic Coast. In Cultures in Contact: The Impact of European Contacts on Native American Cultural Institutions A.D. 1000–1800. W. W. Fitzhugh, ed. Pp. 225–268. Washington, D. C.: Smithsonian Institution Press.

Fennell, Christopher C.
    2007   Crossroads and Cosmologies: Diasporas and Ethnogenesis in the New World. Gainesville: University Press of Florida.

Ferguson, Leland G.
    1992   Uncommon Ground: Archaeology and Early African America, 1650–1800. Washington, D. C.: Smithsonian Institution Press.

Ford, James A.
    1954   On the Concept of Types. American Anthropologist 56:42–54.

Forman, Henry Chandlee
    1940   The Bygone "Subberbs of James Cittie." William and Mary Quarterly 2nd series 20(4):475–486.

Franklin, Maria
    2004   An Archaeological Study of the Rich Neck Slave Quarter and Enslaved Domestic Life. Richmond, VA: Dietz Press. research.history.org/Archaeological_Research/Technical_Reports/DownloadPDF.cfm?ReportID=Archaeo0005

Galucci, Elizabeth Andersen, David Muraca, and Pegeen McLaughlin
 1994 Identifying Producer-Client Relationships at the Bruton Heights Tile Kiln. Paper presented at the annual meeting of the Society for Historical Archaeology, Vancouver, BC, 1994.

Gifford, James
 1960 The Type Variety Method of Ceramic Classification as an Indicator of Cultural Phenomena. American Antiquity 25:341–347.

Gleach, Frederic W.
 1997 Powhatan's World and Colonial Virginia: A Conflict of Cultures. Lincoln: University of Nebraska Press.

Goff, Phillip Atiba, Matthew Christian Jackson, Brooke Allison Lewis DiLeone, Carmen Marie Culotta, and Natalie Ann DiTomasso
 2014 The Essence of Innocence: Consequences of Dehumanizing Black Children. Journal of Personality and Social Psychology 106(4):526–545.

Goodman, J. David, and Joseph Goldstein
 2014 Grand Jury to Take Up Death Linked to Chokehold. New York Times 20 August 2014:A18.

Goodman, Jordan
 1993 Tobacco in History: the Cultures of Dependence. London: Routledge.
 1995 Excitantia: Or, How Enlightenment Europe Took to Soft Drugs. In Consumng Habits: Drugs in History and Anthropology. J. Goodman, P. E. Lovejoy, and A. Sherratt, eds. Pp. 126–147. London: Routledge.

Graham, Willie, Carter L. Hudgins, Carl R. Lounsbury, Fraser D. Neiman, and James P. Whittenburg
 2007 Adaptation and Innovation: Archaeological and Architectural Perspectives on the Seventeenth-Century Chesapeake. William and Mary Quarterly 64(3):451–522.

Hall, Robert L.
 1977 An Anthropocentric Perspective for Eastern United States Prehistory. American Antiquity 42(4):499–518.

Haney López, Ian F.
 1995 The Social Construction of Race. In Critical Race Theory: The Cutting Edge. R. Delgado, ed. Pp. 191–203. Philadelphia: Temple University Press.

Hantman, Jeffrey L., and Stephen Plog
 1982 The Relationship of Stylistic Similarity to Patterns of Material Exchange. In Contexts for Prehistoric Exchange. J. E. Ericson and T. K. Earle, eds. Pp. 237–263. New York: Academic Press.

Harrington, J. C.
 1951 Tobacco Pipes From Jamestown. Quarterly Bulletin of the Archaeological Society of Virginia 5(4).
 1954 Dating Stem Fragments of Seventeenth and Eighteenth Century Clay Tobacco Pipes. Quarterly Bulletin of the Archaeological Society of Virginia 9(1):9–13.

Harris, Leonard, ed.
 1999 The Critical Pragmatism of Alain Locke. Lanham, MD: Rowman & Littlefield.

Hauser, Mark W., and Christopher R. DeCorse
 2003 Low-Fired Earthenwares in the African Diaspora: Problems and Prospects. International Journal of Historical Archaeology 7(1):67–98.

Hayden, Brian
    1984   Are Emic Types Relevant to Archaeology? Ethnohistory 31(2):79–92.
Hegmon, Michelle
    1992   Archaeological Research on Style. Annual Review of Anthropology 21:517–536.
Heite, Edward F.
    1972   American-Made Pipes from the Camden Site. Quarterly Bulletin of the Arche-
            ological Society of Virginia 27:94–99.
Hendon, Julia A.
    1996   Archaeological Approaches to the Organization of Domestic Labor: House-
            hold Practice and Domestic Relations. Annual Review of Anthropology
            25:45–61.
Hening, W. W.
    1819–1823 I The Statutes at Large, Being a Collection of All the Laws of Virginia from
            the First Session of the Legislature, in the Year 1619. New York: R. & W. & G.
            Bartow.
    1823 II The Statutes at Large, Being a Collection of All the Laws of Virginia from
            the First Session of the Legislature, in the Year 1619. New York: R. & W. & G.
            Bartow.
    1823 III The Statutes at Large, Being a Collection of All the Laws of Virginia from
            the First Session of the Legislature, in the Year 1619. New York: R. & W. & G.
            Bartow.
Henry, Susan L.
    1976   Preliminary Investigation into the Phenomenon of the Terra Cotta Clay
            Tobacco Pipe. In manuscript on file at the Jefferson Patterson Park and
            Museum Library. Leonardtown, MD.
    1979   Terra-cotta Tobacco Pipes in 17th-Century Maryland and Virginia: A Prelimi-
            nary Study. Historical Archaeology 13:14–37.
Heslep, J. W.
    2001   The Development of Slave Participation in Bacon's Rebellion. B.A. honors the-
            sis, College of William and Mary.
Hill, J. N., and R. K. Evans
    1972   A model for classification and typology. In Models in Archaeology. D. L.
            Clarke, ed. Pp. 231–273. London: Methuen.
Hill, James N., and Joel Gunn, eds.
    1977   The Individual in Prehistory. New York: Academic Press.
His Majesties Commissioners
    1677   An Exact Repertory of the Generall and Personall Grievances Presented to Us
            (His Majesties Commissioners) by the People of Virginia. Manuscript in the
            J. D. Rockefeller Library, The Colonial Williamsburg Foundation. Williams-
            burg, VA.
    1915 [1677] A True Narrative of the Late Rebellion in Virginia, by the Royal Commis-
            sioners, 1677. In Narratives of the Insurrections, 1675–1690. C. M. Andrews,
            ed. Pp. 105–141. New York: Scribner's Sons.
Horning, Audrey J.
    1995   "A Verie Fit Place to Erect a Greate Cittie": Comparative Contextual Analysis
            of Archaeological Jamestown. Ph.D. dissertation, American Civilization, Uni-
            versity of Pennsylvania.

Horning, Audrey J., and Andrew C. Edwards
  2000   Archaeology in New Towne, 1993–1995. Colonial National Historical Park, NPS, The Colonial Williamsburg Foundation.
James, William
  1907   Pragmatism: A New Name for Some Old Ways of Thinking. Cambridge, MA: Harvard University Press.
Jeppson, Patrice L.
  2001   Pitfalls, Pratfalls, and Pragmatism in Public Archaeology. Paper presented at the annual meeting of the Society for Historical Archaeology. Long Beach, CA. www.p-j.net/pjeppson/SHA2001/Papers/Jeppson.htm
Johnson, Matthew
  1996   An Archaeology of Capitalism. Oxford: Blackwell.
Johnson, Tiffani J., Matthew D. Weaver, and Sonya Borrero, Esa M. Davis, Larissa Myaskovsky, Nole S. Zuckerman, and Kevin L. Kraemer
  2013   Association of Race and Ethnicity with Management of Abdominal Pain in the Emergency Department. Pediatrics 132(4), E851–E858. pediatrics.aap-publications.org/content/early/2013/09/18/peds.2012-3127.full.pdf+html, accessed 30 August 2014.
Keita, S. O. Y., and Rick A. Kittles
  1997   The Persistence of Racial Thinking and the Myth of Racial Divergence. American Anthropologist 99(3):534–544.
Kelly, Kenneth G.
  1997   The Archaeology of African-European Interaction: Investigating the Social Roles of Trade, Traders, and the Use of Space in the Seventeenth- and Eighteenth-century Hueda Kingdom, Republic of Benin. World Archaeology 28(3):351–369.
Kelso, William M.
  2006   Jamestown: The Buried Truth. Charlottesville: University of Virginia Press.
Kelso, William M., and Beverly A. Straube
  2004   Jamestown Rediscovery 1994–2004. Richmond: The Association for the Preservation of Virginia Antiquities.
Key, Marcus M., Jr., and Tara E. Jones
  2000   Geoarchaeology of Terra Cotta Tobacco Pipes from the Colonial Period Davis Site (44LA46), Lancaster County, Virginia. Quarterly Bulletin of the Archeological Society of Virginia 55(2):86–95.
Kopytoff, Igor, and Suzanne Miers
  1977   African 'Slavery' as an Institution of Marginality. In Slavery in Africa: Historical and Anthropological Perspectives. I. Kopytoff and S. Miers, eds. Pp. 3–81. Madison: University of Wisconsin Press.
Krieger, Alex D.
  1944   The Typological Concept. American Antiquity 9:271–288.
Kulikoff, Allan
  1986   Tobacco and Slaves: The Development of Southern Cultures in the Chesapeake, 1680–1800. Chapel Hill: University of North Carolina Press.
Lathrap, Donald W.
  1983   Recent Shipibo-Conibo Ceramics and their Implications for Archaeological Interpretation. In Structure and Cognition in Art. D. K. Washburn, ed. Pp. 25–39. Cambridge, UK: Cambridge University Press.

Lechtman, Heather
  1977   Style in Technology—Some Early Thoughts. In Material Culture: Styles,
         Organization, and Dynamics of Technology. H. Lechtman and R. S. Merrill,
         eds. Pp. 3–20. New York: West Press.
Lester, Dave, and Chris Hendricks
  1987   Tobacco Pipes from Site CL7—Port Anne. In Archaeology at Port Anne: A Report
         on Site CL7, An Early 17th Century Colonial Site. A. C. Edwards, ed. Pp. i–vi.
Linton, Ralph
  1924   Use of Tobacco among North American Indians. Chicago: Field Museum of
         Natural History.
Livingstone, Frank B.
  1962   On the Non-Existence of Human Races. Current Anthropology 3(3):279–281.
Longacre, William A.
  1999   Standardization and Specialization: What's the Link? In Pottery and People:
         A Dynamic Interaction. G. M. Feinman and J. M. Skibo, eds. Pp. 59–80. Salt
         Lake City: University of Utah Press.
Luckenbach, Al, and C. Jane Cox
  2002   Tobacco-Pipe Manufacturing in Early Maryland: The Swan Cove Site (ca.
         1660–1669). In The Clay Tobacco-Pipe in Anne Arundel County, Maryland
         (1650–1730). A. Luckenbach, C. J. Cox, and J. Kille, eds. Pp. 46–63. Annapo-
         lis, MD: Anne Arundel County's Lost Towns Project.
Luckenbach, Al, C. Jane Cox, and John Kille, eds.
  2002   The Clay Tobacco-Pipe in Anne Arundel County, Maryland (1650–1730).
         Annapolis, MD: Anne Arundel County's Lost Towns Project.
Luckenbach, Al, and Taft Kiser
  2006   Seventeenth-Century Tobacco Pipe Manufacturing in the Chesapeake
         Region: A Preliminary Delineation of Makers and Their Styles. In Ceramics in
         America 2006. R. Hunter, ed. Pp. 160–177. Hanover, NH: University Press of
         New England.
MacCord, Howard A., Sr.
  1969   Camden: A Postcontact Indian Site in Caroline County. Quarterly Bulletin of
         the Archeological Society of Virginia 24(1):1–55.
Magee, Michael
  2004   Emancipating Pragmatism: Emerson, Jazz, and Experimental Writing. Tusca-
         loosa: University of Alabama Press.
Magoon, Dane T.
  1999   "Chesapeake" Pipes and Uncritical Assumptions: A View from Northeastern
         North Carolina. North Carolina Archaeology 48:107–126.
Mann, Rob
  2004   Smokescreens: Tobacco, Pipes, and the Transformational Power of Fur Trade
         Rituals. In Smoking and Culture: The Archaeology of Tobacco Pipes in East-
         ern North America. S. M. Rafferty and R. Mann, eds. Pp. 165–183. Knoxville:
         University of Tennesee Press.
Marks, Jonathan
  2002   What It Means to be 98% Chimpanzee: Apes, People, and their Genes. Berke-
         ley: University of California Press.
Mathews, Thomas
  1915 [1705] The Beginning, Progress, and Conclusion of Bacon's Rebellion,

1675–1676. In Narratives of the Insurrections, 1675–1690. C. M. Andrews, ed. Pp. 15–41. New York: Scribner's Sons.

Matthews, Christopher N., and Bradley D. Phillippi
2013   White Until Proven Black. Paper presented at the annual meeting of the Theoretical Archaeology Group:TAG USA. Chicago.

May, Jamie E.
2003   100 Years of Archaeology at Jamestown's Colonial Statehouse. Paper presented at the annual meeting of the Society for Historical Archaeology, Providence, Rhode Island.

McCartney, Martha W.
2000a   Documentary History of Jamestown Island: Volume I Narrative History. Colonial National Historical Park, NPS, The Colonial Williamsburg Foundation.
2000b   Documentary History of Jamestown Island: Volume III Biographies of Owners and Residents. Colonial National Historical Park, NPS, The Colonial Williamsburg Foundation.

McCartney, Martha W., and Christina Adinolfi Kiddle
2000   Documentary History of Jamestown Island: Volume II: Land Ownership. Colonial National Historical Park, NPS, The Colonial Williamsburg Foundation.

McCartney, Martha W., and Lorena S. Walsh
2000   A Study of the Africans and African Americans on Jamestown Island and at Green Spring, 1619–1803. Williamsburg, VA: The Colonial Williamsburg Foundation.

McDavid, Carol
2002   Archaeologies That Hurt; Descendants That Matter: A Pragmatic Approach to Collaboration in the Public Interpretation of African-American Archaeology. World Archaeology 34(2):303–314.

Menard, Russell R.
1977   From Servants to Slaves: The Transformation of the Chesapeake Labor System. Southern Studies 16(4):355–390.

Metz, John
1999   Industrial Transition and the Rise of a "Creole" Society in the Chesapeake, 1660–1725. In Historical Archaeology, Identity Formation, and the Interpretation of Ethnicity. M. Franklin and G. Fesler, eds. Pp. 11–30. Richmond,VA: Dietz Press.

Metz, John, Jennifer Jones, Dwayne Pickett, and David Muraca
1998   "Upon the Palisado" and other Stories of Place from Bruton Heights. Richmond, VA: Dietz Press.

Milkman, Katherine L., Modupe Akinola, and Dolly Chugh
2014   What Happens Before? A Field Experiment Exploring How Pay and Representation Differentially Shape Bias on the Pathway into Organizations. Social Science Research Network. ssrn.com/abstract=2063742 or http://dx.doi.org/10.2139/ssrn.2063742, accessed 30 August 2014.

Miller, Henry M.
1991   Tobacco Pipes from Pope's Fort, St. Mary's City, Maryland: an English Civil War Site on the American Frontier. In The Archaeology of the Clay Tobacco Pipe: Chesapeake Bay. P. Davey and D. J. Pogue, eds. Pp. 73–88. Oxford: B. A. R. International Series 566.

Mintz, Sidney W.
  1985 Sweetness and Power: The Place of Sugar in Modern History. New York: Penguin Books.
Mitchell, Vivienne
  1976 Decorated Brown Clay Pipebowls from Nominy Plantation: A Progress Report. Quarterly Bulletin of the Archeological Society of Virginia 31:83–92.
  1983 The History of Nominy Plantation with Emphasis on the Clay Tobacco Pipes. Historic Clay Tobacco Pipes 2:3–38.
Monroe, J. Cameron
  2002 Negotiating African-American Ethnicity in the 17th-Century Chesapeake. Volume B. A. R. International Series 1042. Oxford: Archaeopress.
Monroe, J. Cameron, and Seth W. Mallios
  2004 A Seventeenth-Century Colonial Cottage Industry: New Evidence and a Dating Formula for Colono Tobacco Pipes in the Chesapeake. Historical Archaeology 38(2):68–82.
Montagu, Ashley
  1997 Man's Most Dangerous Myth: The Fallacy of Race. Walnut Creek, CA: AltaMira Press.
Moore, Kevin Thomas
  1996 The X-Ray Diffraction of Clay Tobacco Pipes from Flowerdew Hundred in Hopewell, Virginia. BA honors thesis, Environmental Sciences and Anthropology, University of Virginia.
Morgan, Edmund S.
  1972 Headrights and Head Counts: A Review Article. Virginia Magazine of History and Biography 80(3, Part One):361–371.
  1975 American Slavery, American Freedom: The Ordeal of Colonial Virginia. New York: W. W. Norton.
Mouer, L. Daniel
  1993 Chesapeake Creoles: The Creation of Folk Culture in Colonial Virginia. In The Archaeology of 17th-Century Virginia. T. R. Reinhart and D. J. Pogue, eds. Pp. 105–166. Richmond, VA: Deitz Press.
Mouer, L. Daniel, Mary Ellen N. Hodges, Stephen R. Potter, Susan L. Henry Renaud, Ivor Noël Hume, Dennis J. Pogue, Martha W. McCartney, and Thomas E. Davidson
  1999 Colonoware Pottery, Chesapeake Pipes, and "Uncritical Assumptions." In I, Too, Am America: Studies in African-American Archaeology. T. A. Singleton, ed. Pp. 75–115. Charlottesville: University Press of Virginia.
Mrozowski, Stephen A.
  2012 Pragmatism and the Relevancy of Archaeology for Contemporary Society. In Archaeology in Society: Its Relevance in the Modern World. M. Rockman and J. Flatman, eds. Pp. 239–243. New York: Springer.
Mukhopadhyay, Carol C., and Yolanda T. Moses
  1997 Reestablishing "Race" in Anthropological Discourse. American Anthropologist 99(3):517–533.
Muller, Nancy Ladd
  1992 DuBoisian Pragmatism and 'The Problem of the Twentieth Century.' Critique of Anthropology 12(3):319–337.
Mullins, Paul R.

1999   Race and affluence: An Archaeology of African America and Consumer Culture. New York: Kluwer Academic.

Munsell Color Company

1975   Munsell Soil Color Charts. Baltimore: Munsell Color.

Muraca, David F., Philip Levy, and Leslie McFaden

2003   The Archaeology of Rich Neck Plantation (44WB52): Description of the Features. The Colonial Williamsburg Foundation, Department of Archaeological Research.

Nassaney, Michael

2004   Men and Women, Pipes and Power in Native New England. In Smoking and Culture: The Archaeology of Tobacco Pipes in Eastern North America. S. M. Rafferty and R. Mann, eds. Pp. 125–141. Knoxville: University of Tennesee Press.

Neff, Hector

1993   Theory, Sampling, and Analytical Techniques in the Archaeological Study of Prehistoric Ceramics. American Antiquity 58(1):23–44.

Neiman, Fraser D.

1993   Temporal Patterning in House Plans from the 17th-Century Chesapeake. In The Archaeology of 17th-Century Virginia. T. R. Reinhart and D. J. Pogue, eds. Pp. 251–283. Richmond, VA: Deitz Press.

Neiman, Fraser D., and Julia A. King

1999   Who Smoked Chesapeake Pipes? Paper presented at the annual meeting of the Society for Historical Archaeology, Salt Lake City.

Noël Hume, Audrey

1979   Clay Tobacco Pipes Excavated at Martin's Hundred, Virginia, 1976–1978. In The Archaeology of the Clay Tobacco Pipe. P. Davey, ed. Pp. 3–36. Oxford: B. A. R. International Series.

Noël Hume, Ivor

1969   Historical Archaeology. New York: Alfred A. Knopf.

1991   A Guide to Artifacts of Colonial America. Reprint of 1969 edition. New York: Vintage Books.

1994   The Virginia Adventure, Roanoke to Jamestown: An Archaeological and Historical Odyssey. Charlottesville: University Press of Virginia.

Noël Hume, Ivor, and Audrey Noël Hume

2001   The Archaeology of Martin's Hundred. Philadelphia: University Museum of Pennsylvania Museum of Anthropology and Archaeology.

Nugent, Nell Marion

1934   Cavaliers and Pioneers: Abstracts of Virginia Land Patents and Grants 1623–1800. Richmond, VA: Dietz Press.

1977   Cavaliers and Pioneers: Abstracts of Virginia Land Patents and Grants 1666–1695. Richmond: Virginia State Library.

O'Brien, Michael J., and R. Lee Lyman

2003   Cladistics and Archaeology. Salt Lake City: University of Utah Press.

Orser, Charles E., Jr.

2004   Race and Practice in Archaeological Interpretation. Philadelphia: University of Pennsylvania Press.

Orton, Clive, Paul Tyers, and Alan Vince

1993   Pottery in Archaeology. Cambridge, UK: Cambridge University Press.

Oswald, Adrian
  1975   Clay Pipes for the Archaeologist. Volume 14. Oxford: British Archaeological
         Reports.
  1985   On the Life of Clay Pipe Moulds. In The Archaeology of the Clay Tobacco
         Pipe, IX More Pipes from the Midlands and Southern England. P. Davey, ed.
         Pp. 5–22. Oxford: B A R.
Outlaw, Alain Charles
  1990   Governor's Land: Archaeology of Early Seventeenth-Century Virginia Settle-
         ments. Charlottesville: Published for The Department of Historic Resources.
         University Press of Virginia.
Outlaw, Alain Charles, and Merry Abbitt Outlaw
  n.d.   Governor's Land Archaeological District Records. Williamsburg, Virginia.
Parent, Anthony S., Jr.
  2003   Foul Means: The Formation of a Slave Society in Virginia, 1660–1740. Chapel
         Hill: The Omohundro Institute of Early American History and Culture and
         the University of North Carolina Press.
Pawson, Michael
  1969   Clay Tobacco Pipes in the Knowles Collection. Quarterly Bulletin of the
         Archeological Society of Virginia 23(3):115–147.
Peacy, Allan
  1996   The Development of the Tobacco Pipe Kiln in the British Isles. Internet
         Archaeology 1: intarch.york.ac.uk/journal/issue1/peacy_toc.html
Peirce, Charles Sanders
  1994a Division of Signs. In The Collected Papers of Charles Sanders Peirce. Electronic
         edition, Volume 2, Book 2, Paper 2. pm.nlx.com/xtf/view?docId=peirce/
         peirce.02.xml;chunk.id=div.peirce.cp2.11;toc.depth=1;toc.id=div.peirce.
         cp2.11;brand=default
  1994b The Fixation of Belief. In The Collected Papers of Charles Sanders
         Peirce. Electronic edition, Volume 5, Book 2, Paper 4. pm.nlx.com/xtf/
         view?docId=peirce/peirce.05.xml;chunk.id=div.peirce.cp5.1049;toc.id=div.
         peirce.cp5.1049;brand=default#cp5.fn322t.tm
  1994c How to Make Our Ideas Clear. In The Collected Papers of Charles Sanders
         Peirce. Electronic edition, Volume 5, Book 2, Chapter 5. pm.nlx.com/xtf/
         view?docId=peirce/peirce.05.xml;chunk.id=div.peirce.cp5.1049;toc.id=di
         v.peirce.cp5.1049;brand=default#cp5.fn322t.tm
Pratt, Scott L.
  2002   Native Pragmatism: Rethinking the Roots of American Philosophy. Bloom-
         ington: Indiana University Press.
Preucel, Robert W.
  2006   Archaeological Semiotics. Malden, MA: Blackwell.
Preucel, Robert W., and Alexander A. Bauer
  2001   Archaeological Pragmatics. Norwegian Archaeological Review 34(2):85–96.
Preucel, Robert W., and Stephen A. Mrozowski
  2010   The New Pragmatism. In Contemporary Archaeology in Theory: The New
         Pragmatism. R. W. Preucel and S. A. Mrozowski, eds. Pp. 3–49. Chichester,
         UK: Wiley-Blackwell.

Price, Jacob M.
    1995   Tobacco in Atlantic Trade: The Chesapeake, London and Glasgow 1675–1775. Hampshire, UK: Valorium.
Rainbolt, John C.
    1967   A New Look at Stuart "Tyranny": The Crown's Attack on the Virginia Assembly, 1676–1689. Virginia Magazine of History and Biography 75(4):387–406.
Read, Dwight W.
    1989   Intuitive Typology and Automatic Classification: Divergance or Full Circle? Journal of Anthropological Archaeology 8:158–188.
    2007   Artifact Classification: A Conceptual and Methodological Approach. Walnut Creek, CA: Left Coast Press, Inc.
Read, Dwight, and Glenn Russell
    1996   A Method for Taxonomic Typology Construction and an Example: Utilized Flakes. American Antiquity 61(4):663–684.
Reid, J. Jefferson, and Stephanie M. Whittlesey
    1998   A Search for the Philosophical Julian: American Pragmatism and Southwestern Archaeology. Kiva 64(2):275–286.
Rice, Prudence M.
    1981   Evolution of Specialized Pottery Production: A Trial Model. Current Anthropology 22(3):219–240.
    1984   The Archaeological Study of Specialized Pottery Production: Some Aspects of Method and Theory. In Pots and Potters: Current Approaches in Ceramic Archaeology. P. M. Rice, ed. Pp. 45–54. Los Angeles: The Institute of Archaeology, The University of California at Los Angeles.
    1987   Pottery Analysis: A Source Book. Chicago: University of Chicago Press.
    1996   Recent Ceramic Analysis: 2. Composition, Production, and Theory. Journal of Archaeological Research 4(3):165–202.
Rich, Motoko
    2014   School Data Finds Pattern of Inequality Along Racial Lines. New York Times 21 March 2014(A18).
Robles, Frances, and Michael S. Schmidt
    2014   Shooting Accounts Differ as Holder Schedules Visit. New York Times 20 August 2014:A1.
Rountree, Helen C.
    1989   The Powhatan Indians of Virginia: Their Traditional Culture. Norman: University of Oklahoma Press.
Rountree, Helen C., and E. Randoph III Turner
    2002   Before and after Jamestown: Virginia's Powhatans and Their Predecessors. Gainesville: University Press of Florida.
Rouse, Irving
    1939   Prehistory in Haiti: A Study in Method. Volume 21. New Haven, CT: Yale University Press.
    1971 [1960]   The Classification of Artifacts in Archaeology. In Man's Imprint from the Past: Readings in the Methods of Archaeology. J. Deetz, ed. Pp. 108–125. Boston: Little, Brown.

Rutman, Darrett B., and Anita H. Rutman

1979 "Now-Wives and Sons-in-Law": Parental Death in a Seventeenth Century Virginia County. In The Chesapeake in the Seventeenth Century: Essays on Anglo-American Society. T. W. Tate and D. L. Ammerman, eds. Pp. 96–125. New York: W. W. Norton.

1984a A Place in Time: Explicatus. New York: W. W. Norton.

1984b A Place in Time: Middlesex County, Virginia 1650–1750. New York: W. W. Norton.

Rye, Owen

1981 Pottery Technology: Principles and Reconstruction. Washington, D. C.: Taraxacum.

Sabloff, Jeremy A.

1996 Postscript: The Continuing Interest in V. Gordon Childe. In Craft Specialization and Social Evolution: In Memory of V. Gordon Childe. B. Wailes, ed. Pp. 229–231. Philadelphia: University of Pennsylvania Museum Press.

Sabloff, Jeremy A., and Robert E. Smith

1969 The Importance of Both Analytic and Taxonomic Classification in the Type-Variety System. American Antiquity 34(3):278–285.

Sackett, James R.

1990 Style and Ethnicity in Archaeology: The Case for Isochrestism. In The Uses of Style in Archaeology. M. W. Conkey and C. A. Hastorf, eds. Pp. 32–43. Cambridge, UK: Cambridge University Press.

Saitta, Dean J.

2007 The Archaeology of Collective Action. Gainesville: University Press of Florida.

Samford, Patricia

1991 Archaeological Investigations of a Probable Slave Quarter at Rich Neck Plantation. The Colonial Williamsburg Foundation, Department of Archaeological Research.

1996 The Archaeology of Virginia's Urban Areas. In The Archaeology of 18th-Century Virginia. T. R. Reinhart, ed. Pp. 65–86. Richmond, VA: Spectrum Press.

Samuels, Warren J.

2000 Signs, Pragmatism, and Abduction: The Tragedy, Irony, and Promise of Charles Sanders Peirce. Journal of Economic Issues 34(1):207–217.

Schrire, Carmel, James Deetz, David Lubinsky, and Cedric Pogeenpoel

1990 The Chronology of Oudepost I, Cape, as Inferred from an Analysis of Clay Pipes. Journal of Archaeological Science 17:269–300.

Scott, J. M.

2004 Browne, Isaac Hawkins (1706–1760). In Oxford Dictionary of National Biography. www.oxforddnb.com/view/article/3677, accessed 8 July 2014.

Shaw, Thurstan

1960 Early Smoking Pipes: in Africa, Europe, and America. Journal of the Royal Anthropological Institute 90(2):272–305.

Shepard, Anna O.

1956 Ceramics for the Archaeologist. Washington, D. C.: Carnegie Institution of Washington.

Sherwood, William

1893 [1676] Two Letters to the Right Honorable Secretary Joseph Williamson. Virginia Historical Magazine (Virginia Magazine of History and Biography), 1(2):168–174.

Sikes, Kathryn
　2008　Stars as Social Space? Contextualising Chesapeake Star-motif pipes. Post-Medieval Archaeology 42(1):75–103.

Singleton, Theresa, and Mark D. Bograd
　1995　The Archaeology of the African Diaspora in the Americas. Ann Arbor, MI: Braun-Brumfield.

Sinopoli, Carla M.
　1998　Identity and Social Action among South Indian Craft Producers of the Vijayanagara Period. In Craft and Social Identity. C. L. Costin and R. P. Wright, eds. Pp. 161–172. Washington, D. C.: Archeological Papers of the American Anthropological Association.

Sluiter, Engel
　1997　New Light on the "20. and Odd Negroes" Arriving in Virginia, August 1619. William and Mary Quarterly 54(2):395–398.

Smedley, Audrey
　1993　Race in North America: Origin and Evolution of a Worldview. Boulder, CO: Westview Press.

Smith, Frederick H.
　1993　Eighteenth Century History of the Ludwell Family at Rich Neck Plantation in Williamsburg, Virginia. The Colonial Williamsburg Foundation, Department of Archaeological Research.

Smith, James M.
　1981　The Pottery and Kiln of Green Spring: A Study in 17th Century Material Culture. M. A., Anthropology, College of William and Mary.

Smith, John
　1986 [1629]　The True Travels, Adventures, and Observations of Captaine John Smith, in Europe, Asia, Afrike, and America: Beginning About theYeere 1593, and Continued to This Present 1629. In The Complete Works of Captain John Smith. P. L. Barbour, ed. Pp. 153–251. Chapel Hill: University of North Carolina Press.

Spaulding, Albert C.
　1953　Statistical Techniques for the Discovery of Artifact Types. American Antiquity 18(4):305–313.

Sprinkle, John
　1992　Loyalists and Baconians: The Participants in Bacon's Rebellion in Virginia 1676–1677. Ph. D. dissertation, History, College of William and Mary.

St. George, Robert Blair
　1996　Maintenance Relations and Material Culture. Lecture in the University of Pennsylvania, Department of Anthropology Colloquium Series, Philadelphia.

Stark, Miriam T.
　1999　Social Dimensions of Technological Choice in Kalinga Ceramics. In Material Meanings: Critical Approaches to the Interpretation of Material Culture. E. S. Chilton, ed. Pp. 24–43. Salt Lake City: University of Utah Press.

Stewart, T. Dale
　1954　A Method for Analyzing and Reproducing Pipe Decorations. Quarterly Bulletin of the Archeological Society of Virginia 9(1).

Straube, Beverly
　1995　The Colonial Potters of Tidewater Virginia. Journal of Early Southern Decorative Arts XXI(2):1–40.

Taylor, Walter W.
  1983 [1948] A Study of Archeology. Carbondale, IL: Center for Archaeological
    Investigations.
Thomas, David Hurst
  1986   Refiguring Anthropology. Prospect Heights, IL: Waveland Press.
Thorndale, William
  1995   The Virginia Census of 1619. Magazine of Virginia Genealogy 33(3):155–170.
Thornton, John K., and Linda M. Heywood
  2007   Central Africans, Atlantic Creoles, and the Foundation of the Americas, 1585–
    1660. New York: Cambridge University Press.
Tibbles, Anthony, ed.
  2005   Transatlantic Slavery: Against Human Dignity. Liverpool, UK: Liverpool
    University Press.
Tomlins, Christopher
  2001   Reconsidering Indentured Servitude: European Migration and the Early
    American Labor Force, 1600–1775. Labor History 42(1):5–33.
Turnbaugh, William A.
  1975   Tobacco, Pipes, Smoking and Rituals among the Indians of the Northeast.
    Quarterly Bulletin of the Archeological Society of Virginia 30(2):59–71.
Urban, Greg
  2001   Metaculture: How Culture Moves through the World. Minneapolis: Univer-
    sity of Minnesota Press.
  2010   Objects, Social Relations, and Cultural Motion. In Social Archaeologiest of
    Trade and Exchange. A. A. Bauer and A. S. Agbe-Davies, eds. Pp. 207–225.
    Walnut Creek, CA: Left Coast Press, Inc.
The Virginia Magazine of History and Biography
  1894a   Public Officers in Virginia, 1702, 1714. Virginia Magazine of History and
    Biography 1(4):361–377.
  1894b   Two Wills of the Seventeenth Century. Virginia Magazine of History and
    Biography 2(2):174–177.
  1895   Instructions to Berkeley, 1662. Virginia Magazine of History and Biography
    3(1):15–20.
  1900   Colonial Officers. Virginia Magazine of History and Biography
    VIII(2):107–108.
  1901   Notes from the Council and General Court Records, 1641–1682. Virginia
    Magazine of History and Biography IX(2):186–188.
Visweswaran, Kamala
  1998   Race and the Culture of Anthropology. American Anthropologist
    100(1):70–83.
von Gernet, Alexander
  1995   Nicotian Dreams: The Prehistory and Early History of Tobacco in Eastern
    North America. In Consuming Habits: Drugs in History and Anthropology. J.
    Goodman, P. E. Lovejoy, and A. Sherratt, eds. Pp. 67–87. London: Routledge.
Voss, Barbara L.
  2008   The Archaeology of Ethnogenesis: Race and Sexuality in Colonial San Fran-
    cisco. Berkeley: University of California Press.

Wailes, Bernard, ed.
1996   Craft Specialization and Social Evolution: In Memory of V. Gordon Childe. Philadelphia: University of Pennsylvania Museum Press.
Walker, Iain C.
1975   The Potential Use of European Clay Tobacco Pipes in West African Archaeological Research. West African Journal of Archaeology 5:165–193.
1977   Clay Tobacco Pipes, with Particular Reference to the Bristol Industry. Ottawa: Parks Canada.
Wallerstein, Immanuel
1980   The Modern World-System. Volume II: Mercantilism and the Consolidation of the European World-Economy, 1600–1750. New York: Academic Press.
Walsh, Lorena S.
1993   Slave Life, Slave Society, and Tobacco Production in the Tidewater Chesapeake, 1620–1820. In Cultivation and Culture: Labor and the Shaping of Slave Life in the Americas. I. Berlin and P. D. Morgan, eds. Pp. 170–199. Charlottesville: University Press of Virginia.
1997   From Calabar to Carter's Grove: The History of a Virginia Slave Community. Charlottesville: University Press of Virginia.
1999   Summing the Parts: Implications of Estimating Chesapeake Output and Income Subregionally. William and Mary Quarterly LVI(1):53–89.
Washburn, Wilcomb E.
1956   The Humble Petition of Sarah Drummond. William and Mary Quarterly 3rd series 13(3):354–375.
1957   Sir William Berkeley's "A History of Our Miseries." William and Mary Quarterly 3rd series 14(3):403–413.
Waugh, Linda R.
1982   Marked and Unmarked: A Choice Between Unequals in Semiotic Structure. Semiotica 38(3/4):299–318.
Webb, Stephen Saunders
1995   1676: The End of American Independence. Syracuse, NY: Syracuse University Press.
Weber, Max
1978   Types of Legitimate Domination. In Economy and Society. Pp. 212–245. Berkeley: University of California Press.
Weeks, Stephen B.
1892   William Drummond, First Governor of North Carolina, 1664–1667. National Magazine 15(6):616–628.
Wehner, Karen Bellinger
2006   Crafting Lives, Crafting Society in Seventeenth-Century Jamestown, Virginia. Ph.D. dissertation, Department of Anthropology, New York University.
Wertenbaker, Thomas Jefferson
1940   Torchbearer of the Revolution. Gloucester, MA: P. Smith.
1959   Richard Lawrence: A Sketch. William and Mary Quarterly 3rd series 16(2):244–248.
West, Cornel
1989   The American Evasion of Philosophy: A Genealogy of Pragmatism. Madison: University of Wisconsin Press.

Wilkie, Laurie A.
2000   Creating Freedom: Material Culture and African American Identity at Oakley Plantation, Louisiana, 1840–1950. Baton Rouge: Louisiana State University Press.
The William and Mary Quarterly
1898a   Berkeley Manuscripts. William and Mary College Quarterly Historical Magazine 1st series 6(3):135–152.
1898b   Historical and Genealogical Notes. William and Mary College Quarterly Historical Magazine 1st series 6(4):257–259.
1902   Proceedings in York County Court. William and Mary College Quarterly Historical Magazine 1st series 11(1):28–38.
1903   Patents Issued during the Regal Government. William and Mary College Quarterly Historical Magazine 1st series 12(1):18–24.
1905   Historical and Genealogical Notes. William and Mary College Quarterly Historical Magazine 1st series 14(2):139–140.
1906   Historical and Genealogical Notes. William and Mary College Quarterly Historical Magazine 1st series 14(4):287–288.
Winfree, R. Westwood
1969   Comparative Material: A Comment Upon Indian Brown Clay Pipes. Quarterly Bulletin of the Archaeological Society of Virginia 24:79.
Wobst, H. Martin
1977   Stylistic Behavior and Information Exchange. In For the Director: Research Essays in Honor of James B. Griffin. C. E. Cleland, ed. Pp. 317–342. Ann Arbor: Museum of Anthropology, University of Michigan.
Wolf, Eric R.
2001   Facing Power—Old Insights, New Questions. In Pathways of Power: Building an Anthropology of the Modern World. Pp. 383–397. Berkeley: University of California Press.
Wylie, Alison
2002a   The Reaction against Analogy. In Thinking from Things: Essays in the Philosophy of Archaeology. Pp. 136–153. Berkeley: University of California Press.
2002b   The Typology Debate. In Thinking from Things: Essays in the Philosophy of Archaeology. Pp. 42–56. Berkeley: University of California Press.
Yentsch, Anne
1991   The Symbolic Divisions of Pottery: Sex-Related Attributes of English and Anglo-American Household Pots. In The Archaeology of Inequality. R. H. McGuire and R. Paynter, eds. Pp. 192–230. Oxford: Basil Blackwell.
York DOW (York County Deeds, Orders, Wills)
1634 et al.   Deeds, Orders, Wills. In The York County Records Project, The Colonial Williamsburg Foundation. Williamsburg, Virginia.

Index

About the Author

Anna S. Agbe-Davies is an assistant professor in the Department of Anthropology at the University of North Carolina, at Chapel Hill, where she is also an adjunct assistant professor of Archaeology and of African and African-American Diaspora Studies. Several of the themes in her work can be traced to her time with the Department of Archaeological Research at the Colonial Williamsburg Foundation, which curates many of the pipes examined for this study. She counts among her research interests: classification; the archaeology of the African diaspora; museum and heritage studies; the relationship between archaeology, anthropology, and history; and the role of digital tools in archaeological practice.

Her current project has two components—reclassifying and digitizing archaeological collections from a slave quarter at Stagville State Historic Site (North Carolina) for inclusion in an online database, as well as digitizing plantation store records to analyze the antebellum economic relationships and purchasing patterns of the plantation's enslaved residents.

She is the co-editor with Alexander A. Bauer of *Social Archaeologies of Trade and Exchange: Exploring Relationships among People, Places, and Things* (Left Coast 2010).